Foreword

I could invent all sorts of excuses. I could say that my dogs, two of which were rescued, could never abide being shut up in kennels.

That Badger, a bundle of nerves and black and white fluff, feels abandoned even just being shut in the kitchen at night, and would go into terminal decline if we left him with strangers. Bella, a more robust character, would nonetheless be miserable too (unless, of course, she was slipped the odd Rich Tea biscuit, in which case she'd be fine) and Teg, my beautiful Welsh Sheepdog who needs more exercise than an Olympic athlete, would go crazy if cooped up and not allowed to run for hours at a time.

There is truth in all those excuses, but the real truth is – and I suspect this is the case with many of you dog owners – I just don't want to go away without them. And the thing about so many of the places listed in the Sawday's guides (I know, because I have stayed in quite a few of them) is that they will often be in beautiful parts of the country, with tantalising footpaths within easy reach that the oh-so-helpful owners will point you towards, while lending you the local Ordnance Survey map. What better way to discover your holiday surroundings than on foot? But without a dog at your heel? Unthinkable!

Now, with this latest *Dog-friendly Breaks in Britain*, you need never walk alone or leave your best friend behind again. I know, as fellow dog-owners, that you might be a little sceptical; that you too might have stayed in places that claim to be 'dog-friendly' and turn out to be one nasty, poky little bedroom at the back with lino on the floor. But don't worry… this is Sawday's, remember! Every single inn, B&B and self-catering cottage in this book has passed their rigorous checks to ensure that both you and your dog are made to feel equally welcome.

So pack up your walking boots and leads, the travel sweets and the Bonios, and set off for a break that will bring the wag back into your tails!

Kate Humble

Photo: Jake Eastman

Second edition
Copyright © 2014
Alastair Sawday Publishing Co. Ltd
Published in 2014
Reprinted November 2014
ISBN-13: 978-1-906136-67-3

Alastair Sawday Publishing Co. Ltd,
Merchant's House, Wapping Road,
Bristol BS1 4RW, UK
Tel: +44 (0)117 204 7810
Email: info@sawdays.co.uk
Web: www.sawdays.co.uk

The Globe Pequot Press,
P. O. Box 480, Guilford,
Connecticut 06437, USA
Tel: +1 203 458 4500
Email: info@globepequot.com
Web: www.globepequot.com

Series Editor Alastair Sawday
Content Manager Wendy Ogden
Editorial Assistance Stephanie Clement,
Jennie Coulson, Camilla Pease-Watkin,
Lianka Varga
Canopy & Stars Editorial
Rebecca Whewell, Andrea Savidge
Picture Editor Alec Studerus
Production Coordinators
Lianka Varga, Sarah Frost Mellor
Sales Angie Reid
Marketing & PR
Emily Enright, Lauren Amos
0117 204 7801
marketing@sawdays.co.uk

Production: Pagebypage Co. Ltd
Printing: Advent Print Group, Andover
Maps: Maidenhead Cartographic Services
UK distribution: The Travel Alliance, Bath
Diane@popoutmaps.com

Alastair Sawday's

Special Places to Stay

Dog-friendly Breaks in Britain

4 Contents

Front

	Page
A word from Alastair Sawday	6
Introduction	7
Inspections	7
What to expect	7
Map	8
Types of places to stay	8
Bedrooms	10
Bathrooms	10
Sitting rooms	10
Meals	10
Prices	10
Bookings and cancellations	11
Payment	11
Tipping	11
Arrivals and departures	11
Closed	11
Feedback	11
Complaints	12
Symbols	12
Quick reference indices	12
Treats	12
Subscriptions	12
Disclaimer	14
Cover Dog Competition	17–20
Days out with dogs	21–24
Maps	25–37

Guide entries

	Entry	Map
England		
Bath & N.E. Somerset	1, 2	2
Bristol	3, 4	2
Buckinghamshire	5-8	3
Cambridgeshire	9	3, 4
Cheshire	10-14	5, 6
Cornwall	15-35	1, 2
Cumbria	36-46	5, 6
Derbyshire	47-49	6
Devon	51-73	2
Dorset	74-84	2, 3
Essex	85, 86	4
Gloucestershire	87-97	2, 3
Hampshire	98-103	3
Herefordshire	104-109	2
Hertfordshir	110	3
Isle of Wight	111	2
Kent	112, 113	2
Lancashire	114	6
Leicestershire	115, 116	6
Lincolnshire	117, 118	6
London	119	3
Norfolk	120-124	7
Northamptonshire	125	3
Northumberland	126-129	9
Oxfordshire	130-132	3
Rutland	133	6
Shropshire	134-141	2
Somerset	142-143	2
Suffolk	144-151	4
Surrey	152	3
Sussex	153-157	4
Warwickshire	158-161	3
Wiltshire	162	3
Worcestershire	163, 164	2
Yorkshire	165-176	6

Guide entries	Entry	Map
Wales		
Anglesey	177	5
Carmarthenshire	178	2
Ceredigion	179-181	1, 2
Denbighshire	182, 183	5
Flintshire	184	5
Gwynedd	185-188	5
Monmouthshire	189-193	2
Pembrokeshire	194, 195	1
Powys	196-206	2
Swansea	207	2
Scotland		
Aberdeenshire	208	9
Argyll & Bute	209-212	8, 10
Ayrshire	213, 214	8
Dumfries & Galloway	215, 216	8, 9
Edinburgh	217	9
Fife	218	9
Highland	219-223	8, 10
Perth & Kinross	224	9
Scottish Borders	225-227	9
Stirling	228	8

Back	Page
Dog treats at a glance!	246
Quick Reference Indices	258
Wheelchair accessible	258
Pets live here	258
Licensed	259
Bikes	259
Is social networking going to the dogs?	260
Other titles from Sawday's	266
Town index for dog-friendly places to stay	269
Town index for dog-friendly pubs	271
What's in each Special Place to Stay entry	272

'Dogs welcome inside, horses outside, and ferrets in the garden,' says the sign. They even serve Dog Beer. Are some of our pub owners slightly mad, or utterly sensible?

My favourite dog-with-human scene was in the film Tom Jones, where the sozzled squire fell off his horse into his pack of hounds and went instantly to sleep among the drooling animals. Brian Sewell is known for bringing his dogs to bed. I do sympathise; our two toy poodles were often put into my bed when I was young. They were as clean as whistles, surely? We are engagingly bonkers about the beasts: Mrs Pat Campbell, caught by Customs smuggling her pet Pekinese in her ruff, claimed it was a 'rough-haired canary'.

Dogs cheer us and generally make us less stuffy. It is also true that many dog owners speak more easily to other people's dogs than to their owners.

Photo: Mark Bolton

I once had a whippet-like dog, with some Jack Russell thrown in, and she was often borrowed by a friend who worked in an old folks' home. Annie's spaniel grew up in our Yanley office. Sadly, our new offices don't allow dogs, so we don't have Rhiannon's sheepdog or Rosie's little mongrel padding about anymore. We are all the poorer for the missing dogs.

Within these pages you will find, applied to dogs, the generosity expected for humans. Many of these places we count among our most special. They can be pretty resourceful too. One owner with two terriers received a charming, toupeed, vicar as a guest. Early the next morning her terriers rushed about the garden with an unusual hairy object. Urgent retrieval of the dilapidated object, rapid transformation by hair-dryer, and the vicar descended for breakfast looking, well, just a touch more 'bouffed'. Nothing was said.

Back to the book. It is a compendium of delight for those who want to go away with their dogs. Be prepared to be upstaged, and to be treated as mere poodles to your dogs. But a touch of scepticism is never amiss. Dorothy Parker, whose dog was malingering, said, "He claims he caught it from a lamp-post." Let us not be fooled all the time.

Alastair Sawday

It's simple. There are no rules, no boxes to tick. We choose places that we like and we are subjective in our choices. We look for comfort, originality, authenticity, and a genuine welcome. The way guests — and their pets! — are treated comes as high on our list as the setting, the atmosphere and the food.

Inspections

Our inspectors know their patch. They don't take a clipboard and they don't have a list of what is acceptable and what is not. Instead, they chat with the owner and look round — closely — and if the visit happens to be the last of the day, they stay the night. It's all very informal, but it gives us an excellent idea of who would enjoy staying there; our simple aim is to match places with guests. Once in the book, properties are re-inspected every four years so that we can keep things fresh and up to date.

What to expect

This new edition of our best-selling Dog-friendly guide contains a wonderful mix of places that welcome you and your dog (or dogs — many allow more than one). Some have specific bedrooms that are set aside for guests with a dog in tow, others welcome dogs in all their rooms. There are a few places where dogs may sleep downstairs but not in the bedroom; do check before you book. Dogs may not, anywhere, sleep on the bed!

The 'pub' entries welcome you for a pint with your dog; the 'inn' entries have dog-friendly bedrooms too. All have bar areas that welcome dogs, and often gardens too; most pubs draw the line at allowing dogs into dining rooms (although some have a special table set aside for visitors with a dog). If you want to check the details beforehand just give them a call. Dog treats at the pubs and inns might include a juicy bone, roast beef tidbits or even dog 'beer'!

There's a fascinating mix inside these pages of B&Bs, hotels, self-catering escapes, inns, pubs and Canopy & Stars outdoor retreats. Remote and simple, or wrapped in luxury,

Photo: Quentin Craven (Elsie's puppies)

there's something for every pooch and its owner here.

Map

If you know which region you want to stay in, our maps are your best guide. Lozenges flag up properties in colours denoting whether they are catered (red), self-catering (blue) or pubs (dark grey). Our quirky outdoor retreats are also listed, under Canopy & Stars CANOPY&STARS . The maps are the perfect starting point for planning a stay – but please don't use them for navigation.

Types of places to stay

B&Bs

B&Bs, however grand, are people's homes, not hotels. You'll most probably have breakfast and dinner with your hosts and/or fellow guests, and the welcome will be personal. Some owners give you a front door key so you may come and go as you please; others like to have the house empty between, say, 10am and 4pm.

Do expect
• a personal welcome
• a willingness to go the extra mile
• a degree of informality, and a fascinating glimpse into someone else's way of life

Don't expect
• a lock on your bedroom door
• your room cleaned and your bed made every day
• a private table at breakfast and dinner
• an immediate response to your booking enquiry
• a TV in your room

Hotels

Those we choose generally have fewer than 50 rooms; most are family-run with friendly staff; many are in historic buildings – perhaps a castle or two; others have a boutique feel. All those in this book like dogs!

Inns

Our one-page inns entries vary from swish suites with plasma TVs to sweet simple rooms overlooking the sea. Staying in a pub – above the bar or in the converted barn behind – is often great value for money.

Self-catering places

Perfect independence for couples – and families – with dogs. Cottages, farmhouses, coach houses, studios, mills, barns – each and every one has been visited by us and found to be special. We don't include places we wouldn't stay in ourselves.

Photo above: Alec Studerus (Chao)
Photo right: Jake Eastham

Canopy & Stars

For those who love to be at one with nature, welcome to our collection of beautiful, simple, quirky (and sometimes luxurious) places to sleep under the stars. Treehouses, shepherd's huts, yurts, gypsy caravans and romantic log cabins – the choice is inspiring.

Bedrooms

We tell you if a room is a single, double, twin/double (with zip and link beds), suite (a room with space for seating), family (a double bed + single beds), or triple (three single beds).

Bathrooms

The vast majority of bedrooms in this book are en suite. Only if a bedroom has a shared or a private-but-separate bathroom do we say so.

Photo: Alec Studerus (Jax)

Sitting rooms

Most hotels have one or two communal areas, while most B&Bs offer guests the family sitting room to share, or provide a sitting room just for guests.

Meals

Unless we say otherwise, breakfast is included, simple or extravagant. Some owners are fairly unbending about breakfast times, others are happy just to wait until you want it, or even bring it to you in your room.

Many B&Bs offer their guests dinner, usually an opportunity to get to know your hosts and to make new friends among the other guests. Note that meal prices are per person. Always book in advance.

Prices

Self-catering prices are mostly quoted per week. Each other entry gives a price PER ROOM per night for two. The price range covers a night in the cheapest room in low season to the most expensive in high season. Some owners charge more at certain times (during regattas and festivals, for example) and some owners ask for a minimum two nights at weekends. Others offer special deals for three-night stays. Prices quoted are those given to us for 2014–2015 but are not guaranteed. Double-check when booking.

At many of these places dogs go free, at others where there's a charge, we say so.

Bookings and cancellations

Sometimes you will be asked to pay a deposit. Some are non-refundable; some people may charge you for the whole of the booked stay in advance; and some cancellation policies are more stringent than others. It is also worth noting that some owners will take the money directly from your credit/debit card without contacting you to discuss it. So ask them to explain their cancellation policy clearly before booking to avoid a surprise. Always make sure you have written confirmation of all you have discussed.

Payment

All our owners take cash and UK cheques with a cheque card, and those who take credit cards have our credit card symbol. Check that your particular credit card is acceptable.

Tipping

Owners do not expect tips – but if you have been treated with extraordinary kindness, drop your hosts a line. If you are on Facebook or Twitter, you can sing their praises from our website www.sawdays.co.uk. Find their Special Place, then 'share' or 'tweet.'

Arrivals and departures

Say roughly what time you will arrive (normally after 4pm; for inns, after 6pm), as most hosts like to welcome you personally. Be on time if you have booked dinner. If, despite best efforts, you are delayed, phone to give warning.

Photo: Stanley Richardson (Luna)

Closed

When given in months this means the whole of the month stated.

Feedback

The accuracy of our books depends on what you, as well as our inspectors, tell us. Your feedback is invaluable and we always act upon comments. Tell us whether your stay has been a joy or not, if the atmosphere was great or stuffy, the owners cheery or bored. Importantly, a lot of new places come to us via our readers, so keep telling us about new places you've discovered. Just visit our sites:

www.sawdays.co.uk/recommend

for hotels, inns, B&Bs and self-catering properties

www.canopyandstars.co.uk

for outdoor retreats.

Complaints

Please do not tell us if the bedside light was inadequate, the hairdryer was broken or the bedroom was cold. Tell the owner instead, and ask them to do something about it. Most owners are more than happy to correct problems and will bend over backwards to help. If you think things have gone seriously awry, do tell us.

Symbols

There is an explanation of the symbols used for our Special Places to Stay on the inside back cover of the book. Use them as a guide, not as a statement of fact. However, things do change: bikes may be under repair or a new pool may have been put in. If an owner does not have the symbol that you're looking for, it's worth discussing your needs.

Note that the ⚓ symbol shows places that are happy to accept children of all ages; it does not mean that they will have cots and high chairs. Many who say no to children do so not because they don't like them but because they may have a steep stair, an unfenced pond or they find balancing the needs of mixed age groups too challenging.

The 🐕 symbol is given when the owners have their own pet on the premises. It may not be a cat! But it is there to warn you that you may be greeted by a dog, serenaded by a parrot, or indeed sat upon by a cat.

The symbols used at the foot of the pub entries apply to the bar and not (should the pub have them) to its bedrooms.

Quick reference indices

At the back of the book we list properties that are licensed, have pets of their own, are wheelchair-friendly or that have bikes to hire or borrow.

Treats

Dog treats provided by owners are shown on each entry and listed at the back of the book for a bit of fun. How about local sausage and bacon cooked to perfection with a splash of milk to wash it down, or a coastal walk straight from the door? Or a tour of the grounds from the resident lab, and a bone from the village butcher? Many dogs like to share their favourite treats and walks, and some owners are willing dog sitters so you can have a night out at a non-dog-friendly place.

Membership

Owners pay to appear in this guide. Their membership fee goes towards the

Photo left: Rhiannon Farrow (Dylan)
Photo right: Alec Studerus (Jago)

costs of inspecting, publishing, marketing, and maintaining our websites. It is not possible for anyone to buy their way onto these pages as we only include places that we like. Nor is it possible for owners to write their own description. We say if the bedrooms are small, the stairs are steep or if a main road is near. We aim not to mislead you!

Disclaimer

We make no claims to pure objectivity in choosing these places. They are here simply because we like them. Our opinions and tastes are ours alone and this book is a statement of them – we do hope you will share them. We have done our utmost to get our facts right but apologise unreservedly for any mistakes that may have crept in.

You should know that we don't check such things as fire regulations, swimming pool security or any other laws with which owners of properties receiving paying guests should comply. This is the responsibility of the owners.

We hope you enjoy our dog-friendly selection – we're almost 100% sure that you and your hound will have a brilliant holiday.

Photo above: Rhiannon Gardiner-Bateman (Lily)
Photo right: Withyfield Cottage, Sussex, entry 154

Alastair
Sawday's

'More than a bed
for the night…'

Britain
France
Ireland
Italy
Portugal
Spain

www.sawdays.co.uk

Self-Catering | B&B | Hotel | Pub | Treehouses, Cabins, Yurts & More

When we wanted a handsome hound to star on the cover of this book we launched a competition, asking our readers to enter their dogs. Hundreds of good-looking dogs were entered, so our judges had a tough time choosing their favourite. We just had to include as many as possible, so we picked some runners up and have featured some of our other favourites throughout the book, too. We loved Stanley's eager face!

Stanley's favourite spot is running in the long grass on the meadow in Bradway, near where he lives in Sheffield.

Huxley's favourite place to visit is the seaside, particularly Whitby where he loves having a paddle, chasing sticks and eating fish.

Winston is pretty happy at his local pub, The Abbeville in Clapham after a big ol' run around the common.

Millie is a Pointer Shar Pei cross. She is never happier than when she is off in the woods exploring!

This is **Elsa**. Her favourite place in the world (apart from sitting on her owners' laps and having a tummy rub) is at a sausage sizzle on the beach.

Grendel loves Dartmoor for river swimming, streams to bound, stepping stones to dash across, bracken to dive in, and bunny poo snacks!

Alfie the pooch loves roaming the grounds of Rievaulx Abbey in Yorkshire.

Daisy, the soft-coated wheaten terrier enjoying a day on her favourite beach at Watergate Bay in Cornwall.

Hello, I'm **Herbert**! I celebrated my 1st birthday by chasing round the rolling hills of the Holme Valley and posing on rocks.

Harris's favourite place is definitely his bed (of which he has 3 including his owners!). A goose down duvet or a reindeer skin suits him perfectly

Dogs don't appreciate cultural breaks. They want beaches, woods, puddles and fields. Here's our pick of places that welcome dogs with open paws.

ENGLAND

St Ives, Cornwall

Stride the coastal path to Zennor (six miles), on to The Gurnard's Head pub (three miles) for lunch, then bus it back to St Ives.

Bodmin Moor, Cornwall

Trek up to the two highest points in Cornwall (OS Exp 109) and look to both coasts on a clear day. The remains of an iron age hill fort rewards you at the summit.

Daymer Bay, Cornwall

Lovely large sandy bay, one of the few open to dogs all year round, with proper waves.

Branscombe, Devon

Unspoilt pebble beach in pretty Branscombe where dogs can romp lead-free 50m in either direction of the car park and café. From here, a coastal walk.

Durdle Door, Dorset

Dogs on leads permitted all year round; also at Lulworth Cove and Worbarrow Bay. Dogs off-lead (except May-September) at Studland Shell Bay, a short drive east.

Camber Sands, East Sussex

When the tide is out dogs get a brilliant run on the sand. Well-managed beaches with Minnis Bay the favourite – but no dogs May-September.

Cotswold Water Park, Gloucestershire

Criss-crossed by miles of flat foot and cycle path, this massive water park has been created from dozens of quarries filled with water and linked by canals. Keep dogs on leads in the bird nesting areas, otherwise, let them bound.

Saxon Shore Way, Kent

On the long-distance footpath to the white cliffs of Dover you cross four wonderful nature reserves: Conver Creek, Harty Ferry, the village of Oare and Faversham. Dogs on leads please.

Botany Bay, Broadstairs, Kent

Big old-fashioned sandy beach with rock pools and famous chalk stacks, off limits

Photo: Rosie Leighton

to dogs in summer (May-September 10am-6pm). Dogs welcome all year on Dumpton Gap beach. And gallops on the top for drying wet dogs off.

Greenwich Park, London

A really old park (1427) stuffed full of heritage (Anglo-saxon burial mounds; the Meridian Line), with amazing views across the Thames to St Paul's. Open 6am-6pm (later in summer) for good dogs that are off-lead. Park near the Pavilion Tea House and Royal Observatory.

Groton Wood, Suffolk

Ancient woodland, enchanting walks: bluebells, nightingales, toads, newts and brimstone butterflies.

Wells-next-the-Sea, Norfolk

One area is dog-friendly all year round but at nesting time dogs are on leads. Big dogs go mad for the wide open spaces of

nearby Holkham; at low tide the sands reach to the horizon.

Worcester Woods Country Park, Worcestershire

Acres of oak woodland, wildflower meadows and two gentle, circular walks perfect for elderly pooches.

Danes Dyke, Yorkshire

A small, away-from-it-all, award-winning beach – sand, pebbles, rock pools, clean water – reached from the car park down a steep road one mile west of Flamborough Head.

Rievaulx to Byland, Yorkshire

Not one but two ruined and magnificent abbeys in the North York Moors with a beautiful and varied six-mile walk between them.

Cautley Spout, Cumbria

Take the obvious path behind the inn at Low Haygarth and walk downstream along the beck (passing the famous wild horses of the Howgill Fells) towards the magnificent 'spout'. Dogs must be under control at the top as there's a mighty drop down, and a bit of a scramble to get there. Short, wild, remote and exhilarating.

Keswick, Cumbria

Lots of wag-friendly shops, pubs and cafés in town, and fells, woodland and lakes beyond – meaning clever Keswick won the Kennel Club's 2012 Open for Dogs Awards in the Dog Friendly Town category.

St Bees, Cumbria

A great family beach three miles from Whitehaven – be sure to scoop every poop. For serious walkers, link up with the Coast to Coast Walk that runs from St Bees on the west to Robin Hood's Bay on the east – glorious.

Bamburgh, Northumberland

A vast, big skies, dog-happy beach with dunes, overlooked by magnificent Bamburgh Castle.

Attingham Park, Shropshire

Luscious parkland for dogs with a nose for the high life, at this 18th-century, National Trust mansion. A hidden gem four miles south-east of Shrewsbury, it is blessed with large parkland that borders the river. Keep dogs on leads near the deer.

Baggeridge Country Park, Staffordshire

Between Wombourne and Sedgley, a much-loved Green Flag park, created over a former colliery. There are four trails in all, from a circular Easy Access trail, perfect for wheelchairs and buggies, to a 90-minute romp through Baggeridge Wood.

WALES

Conwy Mountain, Conwy

There's walking here as adventurous as anywhere in Snowdonia – but on a smaller scale.

Elan Valley, Powys

From Rhayader to Devil's Bridge, and some of the remotest hiking south of the Cairngorms. Miles of peaty plateaus, a few sheep, wheeling red kites and five larch-lapped Victorian reservoirs with associated viaducts and dams.

Rhossili Bay, Swansea

Miles of pristine sand at the tip of the Gower Peninsula, reached via many steps. There's enough space for dogs to run free all year – and a colourful selection of kites to bark at.

St David's Head Walk, Pembrokeshire

Circular three-hour walk from Whitesands Bay, the first bit inland, the second along the wind-buffeted coastal path. Thrill to the Hats and Barrels – the rocks and reefs that still pose a threat to boats passing through these tidal races.

Usk Valley Walk, Monmouthshire

One gorgeous stretch of this 48-mile route from Brecon to Caerleon and the sea, is along the fish-rich river bank between Usk and Abergavenny. Every bit as pretty as the Wye.

Glanusk Estate, Crickhowell

Luscious acres roll as far as the eye can see – plus ancient Celtic standing stones, a bridge over the river Usk, a private chapel, farm buildings and stables, 120 different species of oak, opera (though not for the dog), and country shows galore.

Broad Haven, Bosherston, Pembs

Beautiful sheltered sand and dune bay reached via boardwalks across the famous lily ponds. Bow-wow heaven.

SCOTLAND

Culzean Castle & Country Park, Ayrshire

A 'castle in the air' perched high above the crashing waves of the Firth of Clyde, with miles of woodland walks. Leads on please for the deer park and swan pond.

Craigower, near Pitlochry, Perthshire

High-up open heathland with stunning long views, rare butterflies and scattered Scots pines. Dogs on the lead when crossing the golf course.

Hermitage, near Dunkeld, Perthshire

A woodland walk though huge Douglas firs to a folly overlooking the crashing Black Linn waterfall – best keep dogs and toddlers on leads.

Barry Mill, Carnoustie, Angus

It is a lovely walk with the dog up to Barry Mill, for the splash of the waterwheel and the smell of grinding corn: milling demos on Sundays.

Calgary Bay, Isle of Mull

Silver sands and crystal waters, exquisite on a fine day, atmospheric on a misty one. Unrestricted romps for dogs – but please think of humans too. (And the gulls and waders.)

Photo: Jake Eastham

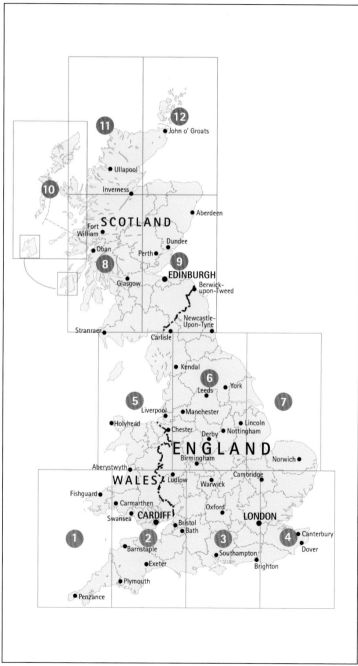

© Maidenhead Cartographic, 2014

Map 2   27

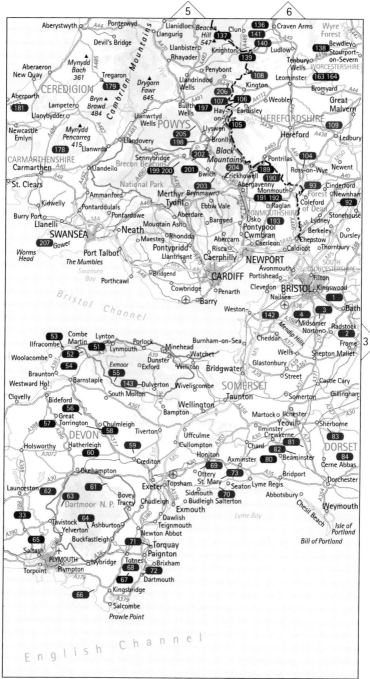

© Maidenhead Cartographic, 2014

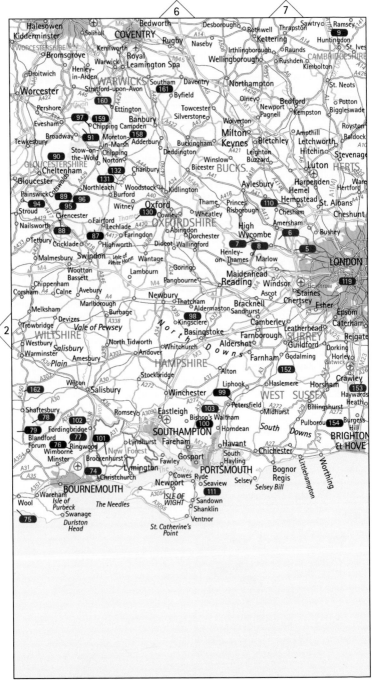

Map 4

29

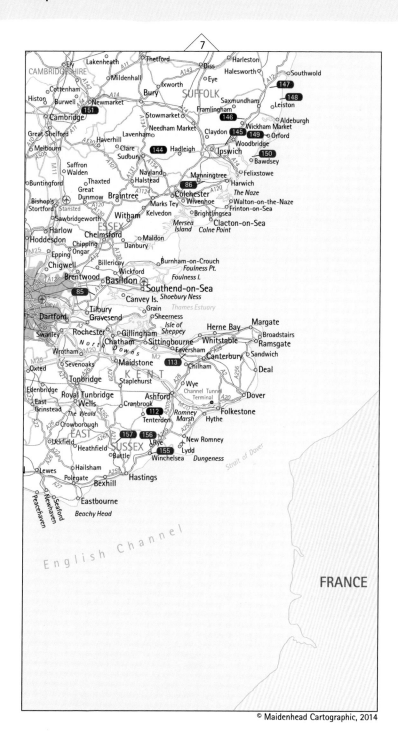

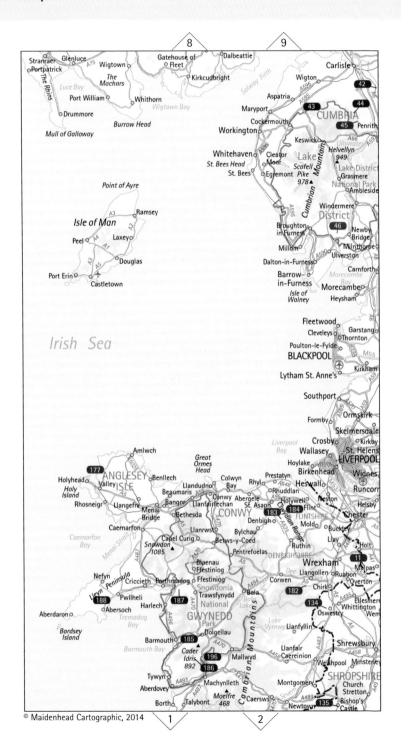

Map 6   31

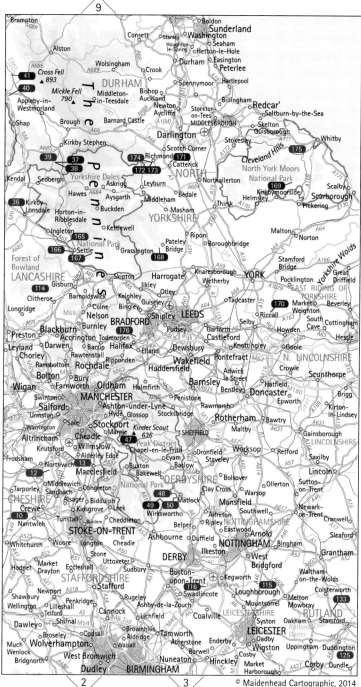

© Maidenhead Cartographic, 2014

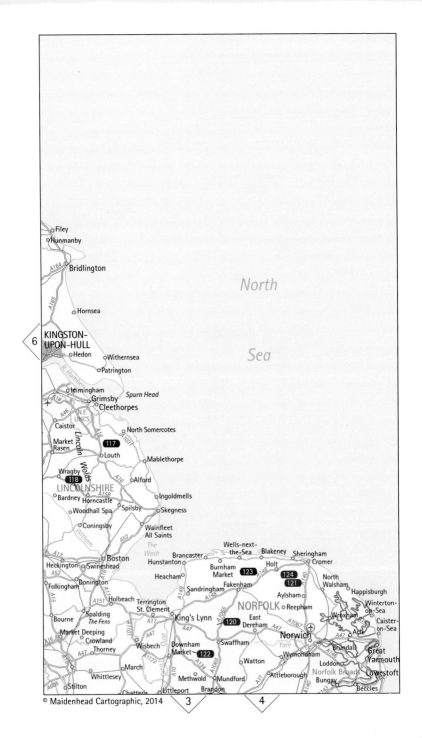

Map 8

33

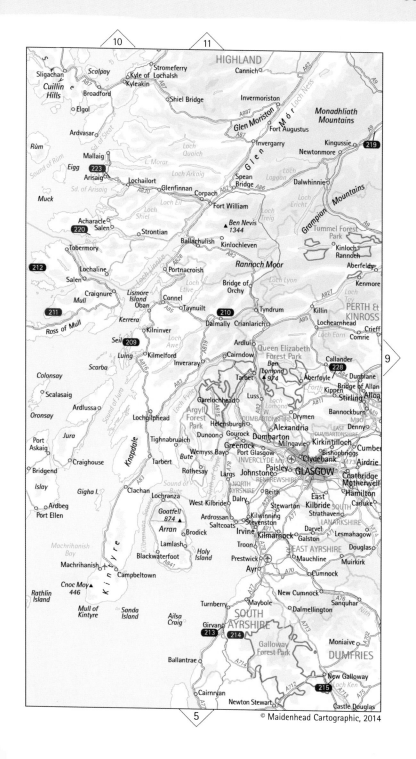

10 11

HIGHLAND

Sligachan Scalpay Stromeferry Cannich
Cuillin Kyle of Lochalsh
Hills Kyleakin
Broadford Shiel Bridge Invermoriston
Elgol Glen Moriston Fort Augustus
Ardvasar Invergarry Monadhliath
Mountains
Rùm Kingussie 219
Mallaig Newtonmore
Eigg 223 Loch Quoich Loch Arkaig
Arisaig Spean Dalwhinnie
Lochailort Glenfinnan Corpach Bridge
Muck Fort William
Acharacle Ben Nevis Grampian Mountains
220 Salen 1344
Tobermory Strontian Tummel Forest
212 Ballachulish Kinlochleven Park
Lochaline Kinloch
Salen Portnacroish Rannoch Moor Rannoch
Craignure Lismore Bridge of Aberfeldy
Mull Island Orchy Loch Lyon Kenmore
Connel Oban
Ross of Mull Kerrera Taynuilt 210 Tyndrum Killin
Kilninver Dalmally Crianlarich Lochearnhead Crieff
Seil 209 Luing Kilmelford Ardlui Comrie
Scarba Inveraray Cairndow Queen Elizabeth Callander
Colonsay Forest Park 228 Dunblane
Scalasaig Ben Aberfoyle Bridge of Allan
Oronsay Ardlussa Lomond Kippen Stirling Alloa
Jura Lochgilphead Tarbet Luss Bannockburn
Port Garelochhead Drymen Dennys
Askaig Argyll Helensburgh Alexandria
Craighouse Forest Dunoon Gourock Dumbarton Kirkintilloch Cumber
Bridgend Park Wemyss Bay Port Glasgow Milngavie Bishopbriggs Airdrie
Islay Tarbert Bute Greenock Paisley GLASGOW Coatbridge
Gigha I. Rothesay Largs Johnstone Motherwell
Ardbeg Clachan Lochranza Beith East Hamilton
Port Ellen West Kilbride Dalry Stewarton Kilbride Carluke
Goatfell Ardrossan Kilwinning Strathaven Darvel
874 Saltcoats Stevenson Lesmahagow
Arran Brodick Irvine Kilmarnock Galston
Machrihanish Lamlash Holy Troon Mauchline Muirkirk
Bay Blackwaterfoot Island Prestwick Douglas
Machrihanish Campbeltown Ayr Cumnock
Cnoc Moy 446
Rathlin New Cumnock Sanquhar
Island Mull of Sanda Turnberry Maybole Dalmellington
Kintyre Island Ailsa SOUTH
Craig AYRSHIRE Moniaive
Girvan 213 214 DUMFRIES
Galloway
Ballantrae Forest Park
New Galloway
215 Loch Ken
Cairnryan Castle Douglas
Newton Stewart

5

© Maidenhead Cartographic, 2014

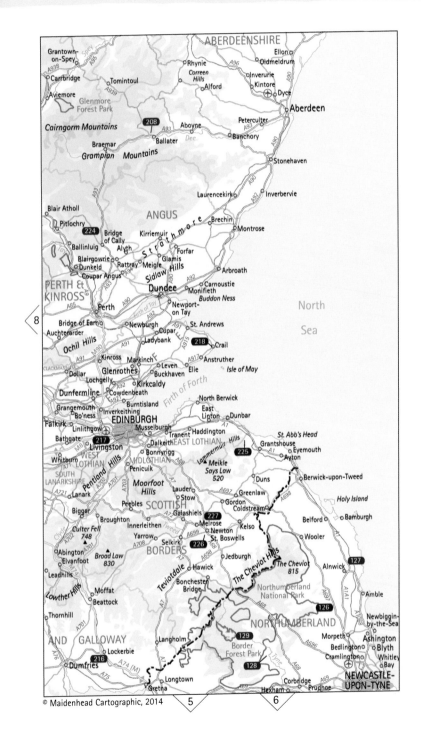

© Maidenhead Cartographic, 2014

Map 10

35

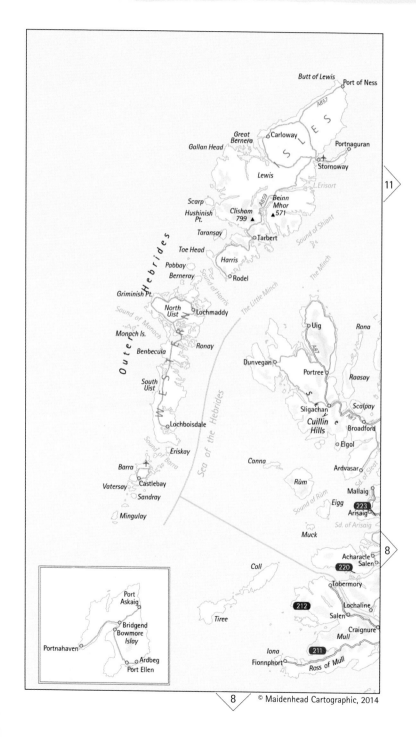

© Maidenhead Cartographic, 2014

Cape Wrath

Durness

Butt of Lewis Port of Ness

A857

221 A836 Bettyhill

A838 Tongue

Scourie

A894 A838 Altnaharra Kinbrace

A836

Portnaguran

Stornoway

L.Erisort

Lochinver Inchnadamph

Loch Shin

Sound of Shiant

Lairg A839 A9

10 Cromalt Hills A835 A837 Invercassley Golspie

Ullapool Bonar Bridge

Easter Ardgay A949 Dornoch

The Minch Ross A836 Tain

Poolewe A832

Loch Maree A835 Ben Wyvis A9 Invergordon

Wester ▲1046 Cromarty

Uig Rona L.Torridon A832 Kinlochewe A832 Garve Dingwall Black Isle Fortrose

Torridon Achnasheen Strathpeffer

Shieldaig A890 Ross Muir of Ord A9 A96

Beauly

Portree Raasay Inverness

Lochcarron

8

Map 12

37

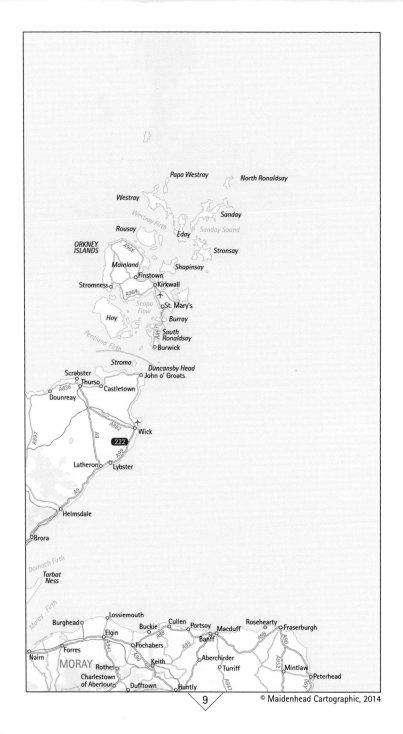

England

Photo: Alec Studerus

The Power House

On top of Bath's highest hill lies Rikki's Bauhaus-inspired home, its glass walls making the most of a magical spot and a sensational view; on a clear day you can see the Welsh hills. In the vast open-plan living space downstairs – homely, inviting, inspiring – are treasures from a lifetime of travels: ancient Tuareg camel sacks, kitsch Art Deco pots, gorgeous Persian chests. Bedrooms are big, airy and light, with doors onto a huge balcony – and those views. Rikki is an incredible chef and uses the freshest and finest ingredients from Bath's farmers' market, ten minutes away. Breakfasts are superb. *Dog heaven! Miles and miles of beautiful walks, woodland, open fields, streams.*

Rooms	1 double; 1 double (Studio): £100–£120. 1 single: £70. 2 further small doubles available, sharing bathrooms. Max. 2 dogs. 2 dog-friendly bedrooms.
Meals	Dinner £25. Pubs/restaurants 3-min drive.
Closed	Rarely.

    Dog biscuits

Rikki Howard
The Power House
Brockham End,
Lansdown,
Bath BA1 9BY
Tel   +44 (0)1225 446308
Email   rikkijacout@aol.com

Entry 1 Map 2

Hollytree Cottage

Meandering lanes lead to this 16th-century cottage, with roses round the door, a grandfather clock in the hall and an air of genteel tranquillity. The cottage charm has been updated with Regency mahogany and sumptuous sofas. The bedrooms have views over undulating countryside; pretty bathrooms have oils and lotions. On sunny days breakfast is in the lovely garden room looking onto a colourful ornamental patio, sloping lawns, a pond, flowering shrubs and trees. A place to come for absolute peace, birdsong and walks; the joys of elegant Bath are 20 minutes away and Julia knows the area well; let her help plan your trips. *Gate out of dog-proofed garden onto fields, footpaths, lanes. 20-minute drive to The Vale of The White Horse.*

Rooms	1 double; 1 four-poster; 1 twin: £75–£90. Singles £45–£50. Dogs £5 per dog per night. Max. 2 dogs. 3 dog-friendly bedrooms.
Meals	Pub/restaurant 0.5 miles.
Closed	Rarely.

    Dog biscuits and bowls

Julia Naismith
Hollytree Cottage
Laverton, Bath BA2 7QZ
Tel   +44 (0)1373 830786
Mobile   +44 (0)7564 196703
Email   jnaismith@toucansurf.com
Web   www.hollytreecottagebath.co.uk

Entry 2 Map 2

The Hunters Rest Inn

Astride Clutton Hill with fine views over the Cam valley the inn began life in the 1750s – as a hunting lodge. Eighty years later it became a smallholding and tavern. It's a big place, rambling around a large central bar, part wood, part stone, its bar topped with copper. There's plenty of jostling space so get ready to order from the Butcombe, Otter and guest ales and the Original Broad Oak and Pheasant Plucker ciders. Get cosy amongst the old oak and pine settles, the odd sofa and the tables to fit all sizes, the quirky wine-label wallpaper, the horse and country paraphernalia, the fires crackling away. Food is hale and hearty: shepherd's pie, pickled beetroot, crusty bread, wild mushroom risotto. Children are well looked after and there's a miniature railway in the garden. The fun continues upstairs with rooms that range from traditional four-poster with antiques to contemporary chic. All are distinctive, all have views, several look south to the Mendips; others have private terraces. Stylish bathrooms have bold tiles, roll top baths and thick towels. A most enjoyable 'sprack and spry' Somerset hideaway. *Walks from front door: fields, forests abound.*

Rooms	4 doubles; 1 twin: £95–£130. Singles £67.50–£77.50. Dogs £10 per dog per stay. If owners know their dogs are well behaved they may be left alone in bedrooms.
Meals	Lunch & dinner £8.25–£17.95.
Closed	Rarely.

   Treats, towels and water bowls

Paul Thomas
The Hunters Rest Inn
King Lane, Clutton Hill,
Clutton BS39 5QL
Tel   +44 (0)1761 452303
Email   info@huntersrest.co.uk
Web   www.huntersrest.co.uk

Entry 3 Map 2

Ring O Bells

Listed in the Domesday Book and rescued from decline by energetic quartet, Miles, Luca, Matt and Fiona this lovely pub is now the local not only for Compton Martin but neighbouring Ubley, whose villagers have their own bar, complete with one of Somerset's biggest inglenooks. A second bar serves locals who want a quiet quaff while the main dining area is abuzz with families, especially at weekends when the roast lunches do a roaring trade. Rightly so, since the food here is something special – Harlequin squash soup, Cornish sardines, smokey cheese burger with chilli jam – children are encouraged to order small portions from the main menu, great for little gourmets who can romp it off in the big gardens at the back. Two nicely simple bedrooms overlook the carpark, thick-walled for peace and quiet with comfy beds and spotless shower rooms. Your room key comes with its own cow bell, so you ring sweetly as you retire after sampling the pub's terrific range of single malts. Miles, music guru, may persuade a famous artist or two to perform (Kylie Minogue did) while lovely Luca welcomes locals and visitors alike. A gem. *Large garden, woodland walks, open fields on the doorstep; large lake to jump in nearby, Weston-super-Mare beach 20 minutes.*

Rooms	2 doubles: £90.
	Max. 1 dog. Can be left unattended in the bedrooms only if well behaved.
Meals	Bar snacks from £4.
	Lunch, 2 courses, £12. Dinner £10–£17.
Closed	Open all day.

'Ring O Bones' dog treats on the bar, towels, dog cushion/basket for room if required, and advice on dog-friendly walks

The Manager
Ring O Bells
The Street,
Compton Martin BS40 6JE
Tel   +44 (0)1761 221 284
Email   ring_o_bells@btconnect.com
Web   www.ringobellscomptonmartin.co.uk

Entry 4 Map 2

The Swan Inn

Swap the bland and everyday for the picture-book perfection of Denham village and the stylish Swan. Georgian, double-fronted, swathed in wisteria, the building has had a makeover by David and Becky (of the Alford Arms, the Old Queens Head and the Royal Oak). It's inviting and charming with rug-strewn boards, chunky tables, cushioned settles, log fire and a fabulous terrace for outdoor meals. Food is modern British. If pressed for time, choose from the 'small plates' list – Grimsby smoked haddock fish cake with Indian spiced cauliflower cream. If you've nothing to rush for, enjoy slow-roast pigs' cheeks with black and white pudding and pea mash, accompanied by a pint of Rebellion IPA or one of 22 wines by the glass. The owners have thought of everything, and the gardens are big enough for the kids to go wild in. *Garden; Buckinghamshire Golf Club and Denham Country Park next door.*

The Jolly Cricketers

When the Jolly Cricketers came on the market, Seer Green residents Chris and Amanda couldn't resist. Now pretty plants clamber up the brickwork outside, while behind the bar, optics have been replaced by sweet shop jars filled with roasted nuts, olives and lollipops – a picture of individuality matched by a freehouse ale selection that shows off the best of local breweries. Ornate fireplaces, oddment-cluttered shelves and pine tables create an unpretentious backdrop for cider-braised ham, crispy poached egg, pineapple chutney and triple-cooked chips; or succulent beef rump, tongue and cheek with potato purée. Coffee mornings, book clubs and pub quizzes contribute to a community spirit but do nothing to dilute this pub's new-found dining status. *Wonderful walks in the Chiltern Hills from the pub.*

| Meals | Lunch, bar meals & dinner £11.75–£19.75. |
| Closed | Open all day. |

 Doggie treats on the bar

Meals	Lunch from £6.50.
	Bar meals from £10.50.
	Dinner from £12.50.
Closed	Open all day.

 Homemade dog biscuits with proceeds to Search Dogs Buckinghamshire, & freshly topped up water bowls

David & Becky Salisbury
The Swan Inn
Village Road, Denham,
Uxbridge UB9 5BH
Tel   +44 (0)1628 488611
Email   info@swaninndenham.co.uk
Web   www.swaninndenham.co.uk

Entry 5 Map 3

Amanda Baker & Chris Lillitou
The Jolly Cricketers
24 Chalfont Road, Seer Green,
Beaconsfield HP9 2YG
Tel   +44 (0)1494 676308
Email   amanda@thejollycricketers.co.uk
Web   www.thejollycricketers.co.uk

Entry 6 Map 3

The Old Queens Head

David and Becky's mini-empire contains this pub by the green. Dating from 1666 it oozes character and charm: old beams and timbers blend perfectly with a stylish and contemporary décor in both the rambling bar and the dining rooms. Find rug-strewn flags, polished boards, classic fabrics, lovely old oak, and innovative seasonal menus and chalkboard specials. Choices range from 'small plates' – seared Scottish queen scallops with Jerusalem artichoke – to big dishes of slow-cooked lamb's breast with spinach and pine nut stuffing, roast garlic mash and purple sprouting broccoli. For those who have room left, there's a tempting selection of puddings –fancy rhubarb, apple and raisin crumble with local clotted cream ice cream? To top it all, a glorious summer garden and walks in the ancient beech woodlands of Common and Penn Woods. *Gorgeous garden and Common Wood on doorstep.*

Meals	Lunch, bar meals & dinner £11.75–£19.75.
Closed	Open all day.

    Plenty of fresh water & dog biscuits on the bar

David & Becky Salisbury
The Old Queens Head
Hammersley Lane, Penn,
High Wycombe HP10 8EY

Tel	+44 (0)1494 813371
Email	info@oldqueensheadpenn.co.uk
Web	www.oldqueensheadpenn.co.uk

Entry 7 Map 3

The Royal Oak

The old whitewashed cottage stands in a hamlet on the edge of the common – hard to believe that Marlow is just a mile away. It's one of a thriving small group of dining pubs (the Alford Arms, Hertfordshire, and the Swan Inn and Old Queens Head). Beyond the terrace is a stylish open-plan bar, cheerful with terracotta walls, rug-strewn boards, cushioned pews and crackling log fires. Order a pint of local Rebellion or one of the 22 wines available by the glass. Innovative pub grub comes in the form of 'small plates' such as crispy breaded British brie with roast butternut squash, and main meals – braised beef shin and confit onion wellington with mustard mash and soused red cabbage; all is fresh and delicious. The sprawling gardens are perfect for summer. *A couple of generous grassy acres, perfect for letting off steam before a lazy lunch. Marlow Common a mile away, footpath up the hill to dog-friendly countryside.*

Meals	Lunch & dinner £11.75–£19.75.
Closed	Open all day.

    Dog biscuits always kept on the bar

David & Becky Salisbury
The Royal Oak
Frieth Road, Bovingdon Green,
Marlow SL7 2JF

Tel	+44 (0)1628 488611
Email	info@royaloakmarlow.co.uk
Web	www.royaloakmarlow.co.uk

Entry 8 Map 3

The Abbot's Elm

Through force of personality and inspiration in the kitchen, John and Julia Abbey have managed to create a pub that caters for everyone without feeling like a compromise. Enter – passing a display case bearing tribute to John's carrying of the Olympic torch – to be faced with the deliciously tough decision of choosing between stylish pub grub in the bar and French-inspired cuisine in the restaurant. No fewer than 36 wines by the glass, including some made specially for the pub, will help you find something for any occasion: a quick lunch, a fancy evening out. The décor throughout the three-sectioned bar and the restaurant is smart and modern without being showy, while 17th-century character remains in the big beautiful hearth and towering beamed ceiling. The Abbot's Elm pulls a diverse crowd, from villagers to hikers to foodies. And if the brandy snap dessert means you end up wanting to stay, there are three ground-floor bedrooms available. Simple but smart, they have some antique items of furniture but comfort is favoured over grandiosity, especially when it comes to robes and towels! *Secure garden. Extensive local walks.*

Rooms	2 doubles; 1 twin/double: £75–£85. Max. 1 dog (more by prior arrangement).
Meals	Lunch & dinner from £9.50. Not Sunday eve.
Closed	Never.
	Walking maps, and three King Charles Cavaliers to act as guides

John & Julia Abbey
The Abbot's Elm
Abbot's Ripton,
Huntingdon PE28 2PA
Tel   +44 (0)1487 773773
Email   info@theabbotselm.co.uk
Web   www.theabbotselm.co.uk

Entry 9 Map 3

The Cholmondeley Arms

As prim and proper as a Victorian schoolmistress on the outside, as stylish as Beau Brummell within: the sandblasted brick walls of this old school house rise to raftered, vaulted ceilings and large windows pull natural light into every corner. Shelves of gin hover above fat radiators, cartoons and photos nestle amongst old sporting paraphernalia, and oriental rugs sprawl beneath an auction lot of tables, pews and chairs. The glorious carved oak bar dominates the main hall and apart from the malted charms of Cholmondeley Best Bitter and Merlin's Gold there are a staggering 150 varieties of ruinously good gin to discover, with the aid of a well-thumbed guide or one of the many charming staff. And when the dinner bell goes study the menus on antique blackboards and opt for devilled lamb's kidneys on toast, followed by baked cod with brown shrimps and lemon butter, or a spicy sausage and butternut squash hash cake. Rooms in the old headmaster's house behind are calm and civilised with all the comfort you need. Seldom has going back to school been this much fun.
Large gardens; plenty of lovely walks locally.

Rooms	5 doubles; 1 twin: £60–£100. Dogs £10 per dog per night. Max. 2. 3 dog-friendly bedrooms.
Meals	Lunch & dinner £7.25–£17.95. Not Christmas Day.
Closed	Rarely.

Dog biscuits & water bowls; dog beds in the dog-friendly rooms. Dog beer (made from meat stock) for sale!

Steve Davies
The Cholmondeley Arms
Malpas SY14 8HN
Tel   +44 (0)1829 720300
Email   info@cholmondeleyarms.co.uk
Web   www.cholmondeleyarms.co.uk

Entry 10 Map 6

Mulsford Cottage

Delicious! Not just the food (Kate's a pro chef) but the sweet whitewashed cottage with its sunny conservatory and vintage interiors, and the green Cheshire countryside that bubble-wraps the place in rural peace. Chat – and laugh – the evening away over Kate's superb dinners, lounge by the sitting room fire, then sleep deeply in comfy bedrooms: cane beds, a bright red chair, a vintage desk. The double has a roll top bath, the twin a tiny shower-with-a-view. Step out to birdsong and the 34-mile Sandstone Trail to Shropshire. Wales starts just past the hammock, at the bottom of the large and lovely garden. *Large fenced dog-proof garden (or nearly dog proof depending on intelligence). Lovely walks, a big wood with a perfect stick-fetching river flowing through it. Prefer dogs to stay by the fire in the sitting room, or in the conservatory in the summer.*

The Three Greyhounds Inn

The bright, many-bottled bar winks and glows as you enter, while host James has a welcome for all. Fat purple cushions soften wooden benches around a huge dual-facing fireplace; reach for the 'Brandy Bible' and settle in. The clever layout makes the space cosy and intimate, with snugs around every corner – four with firesides – and nooks and crannies aplenty. James is proud of the atmosphere, and rightly so. Families nibble and natter with relish, while walkers and couples take their time over delicious smoked haddock and leek tart or pan-fried lamb's kidneys. During annual Cheshire Game Week you can tuck into dishes such as pheasant breast with sautéed white pudding and red leg partridge croquette.... Deep in the Cheshire countryside, this well-restored pub is conveniently close to the M6. *Large garden, and pretty Shakerley Mere opposite, which is ideal for exercising the dog before refreshment at the pub.*

Rooms	1 double; 1 twin with separate shower: £80–£85. Singles £55. Dogs £10 per stay. Max. 2 dogs.
Meals	Dinner from £18. Pub 1.5 miles.
Closed	Rarely.

 Dog towels, recommendations for walks, dog-sitting – and a Bonio before bed!

Meals	Lunch & dinner from £10.50. Bar meals from £5.95. Not Christmas Day.
Closed	Please check before you visit.

 Dogs welcome in the Brandy Snug. Dog biscuits on the bar and water bowls outside. Dog Beer (made from meat stock) is for sale here!

Kate Dewhurst
Mulsford Cottage
Mulsford, Sarn,
Malpas SY14 7LP
Tel   +44 (0)1948 770414
Email   katedewhurst@hotmail.com
Web   www.mulsfordcottage.co.uk

Entry 11 Map 5

James Griffiths
The Three Greyhounds Inn
Holmes Chapel Road, Allostock,
Knutsford WA16 9JY
Tel   +44 (0)1565 723455
Email   info@thethreegreyhoundsinn.co.uk
Web   www.thethreegreyhoundsinn.co.uk

Entry 12 Map 6

The Bull's Head

You feel the warmth as soon as you walk through the door. Candles glow on the tables of this pretty village pub and fires crackle but it's the staff who really make you feel at home. Under a low-beamed ceiling, six hand pumps dispense the finest local ales from Storm, Wincle and Redwillow as well as the inimitable Mobberly Wobbly – ale is truly king! Add in a Highland extravaganza of over 70 malts and other tempting brews and you have the makings of a celebration. Chef Lloyd cooks 'pub classics from the heart' with full English flavours. The steak and ale pie is a fully encased masterpiece in itself, and the Irish whisky sticky toffee pudding with vanilla ice cream is too indulgent for words. With outside tables for sunny days, this is as good as it gets for a village local. *Bull's Head Pub Walk with leaflets on the bar – ideal for dogs and owners.*

Chateau Weuf du Pup

In an unspoilt corner of Cheshound, is an unusual cabin perfect for walkers. Retreat into the compact, timber-panelled den where you can curl up in a cosy basket and be attended to by well trained, wet-nosed helpers, who will fetch you anything you need: newspapers, slippers, sticks. Don't be alarmed by the local customs, it is traditional to mark your arrival with an enthusiastic sniff of your derriere. Madame and Monsieur are your French hosts from the beautiful Mastiff Central: she always to be seen in a Parisian couture fur coat, he, a retired Crufts champion who will regale you with tails of his former glories. You may even be treated to a glimpse of his rosette collection. Meals are eagerly anticipated by staff and guests alike; served on the terrace floor in sleek stainless steel dinnerware they are an enthusiastic affair. The coq au spaniel is not to be sniffed at. You can walk into glorious countryside straight from the door.

Meals	Lunch £2.95–£19.95.
	Bar meals £2.85–£12.
	Sunday lunch £13.95.
Closed	Open all day.

 Dogs welcome in the Whisky Snug. Dog biscuits on the bar and water bowls at the entrance. Dog Beer (made from meat stock) is for sale!

Rooms	1 double basket: £10–£15.
Meals	Dinner, 3 courses, £20 (includes whine).
	Begging at the table encouraged.
	Puppy-dog eyes guarantee extra large portions.
Closed.	Never.

 Madame and Monsieur Weuf du Pup happily share their (chewed) tennis balls with well behaved owners. Stick retrieval service also included for butterfingered two-legged friends

Ben Redwood
The Bull's Head
Mill Lane, Mobberley,
Knutsford WA16 7HX
Tel   +44 (0)1565 873395
Email   info@thebullsheadpub.co.uk
Web   www.thebullsheadpub.co.uk/wordpress

Entry 13 Map 6

Madame & Monsieur Weuf du Pup
Chateau Weuf du Pup
Houndsville DOG 4UU
Tel   +44 (0) w a l k i e s
Email   wooflala@dogslife.com
Web   www.dogtired.woof

Entry 14 Map K9

The Look Out & Sheep to Shore Shepherd's Hut

You'll linger along the scenic route to this spot, a stone skim away from one of Cornwall's dog-friendly bays. Your greeting will be a warm one, perhaps by a pet donkey or curious Highland cow, as well as by the bright and breezy owners. This is the perfect coastal hideout: barbecue, decking, and bright blue picnic table all await relaxed al fresco dinners after a day's surfing. Inside it couldn't be sweeter with a well-stocked wood-burner surrounded by sofas in an all-in-one living and dining space; the pine kitchen fits neatly along one wall, and there are quirky nautical touches to catch the eye. The seaside theme continues upstairs, the master double is a delight: a telescope will please stargazers, the remote lighting and sound system adding to the romance. The cutesy Shepherd's Hut is cosy, warm and perfect for two plus a waggy-friend; and best of all you're on the coastal path. Head out to see what's on the horizon: there are 20 acres of private land around you, Bude and Padstow are close and great walks start from the door. With all of this, you'll be as happy as a clam. *Min. three nights on weekdays; seven in high season. Short breaks available. Secure decking, garden and paddock. Wood with river to jump in, South West Coastal Path, own private beach.*

Rooms	1 cottage for 4: £750–£1,350.
	1 shepherd's hut for 2: £525–£665.
	Dogs free for 1; if more, £10 per dog p.w.
	Max. 2 large dogs or 4 small in Lookout;
	1 large or 2 small in Shepherd's Hut.
Meals	Self-catering; two dog-friendly pubs
	within walking distance.
Closed	Never.
	Bag of chews on arrival, towels for drying off, outside hot/cold shower. Dog-sitting available. Dog walking itinerary on request (and doggie bags)

Jane Montague
The Look Out &
Sheep to Shore Shepherd's Hut
Wanson Mouth, Bude EX23 0DF

Mobile	+44 (0)7880 798111
Email	thelookoutincornwall@gmail.com
Web	www.thelookoutincornwall.co.uk

Entry 15 Map 1

The Mill House Inn

Coast down the steep winding lane to a 1760s mill house in a woodland setting. Trebarwith's spectacular beach — all surf and sand — is a ten-minute walk away. It's quite a spot. Back at the inn, the bar combines the best of Cornish old and Cornish new: big flagged floor, wooden tables, chapel chairs, two leather sofas by a wood-burning stove. The swanky dining room overlooking the burbling mill stream is light, elegant and very modern. Settle down to some rather good food: fish chowder; rib-eye steak with wild mushroom and pink peppercorn fricassée; rose, jasmine and orchid panna cotta. Bar meals are more traditional, they do great barbecues in summer and (be warned) a band often plays at the weekend. In keeping with the seaside setting, bedrooms are simple and uncluttered, with good shower rooms in the smaller standard rooms. Note that room character and comfort have been raised following some essential upgrading. Coastal trails lead to Tintagel, official home of the Arthurian legends, there's biking, surfing, crabbing... you couldn't possibly be bored. *A few acres for roaming, and ten minutes to beach.*

Rooms	7 doubles; 1 family room for 4: £75–£130. Dogs £7.50 per dog per night. Dogs not allowed in 'new' restaurant; welcome in bar and 'old' restaurant.
Meals	Lunch from £7.50. Dinner from £12. Sunday lunch, 3 courses, £17.85.
Closed	Rarely.

A perfect place for mutts to stay, often frequented by 'Dodger', star of TV programme *Doc Martin*; water bowls in bar

Mark & Kep Forbes
The Mill House Inn
Trebarwith,
Tintagel PL34 0HD

Tel +44 (0)1840 770200
Email management@themillhouseinn.co.uk
Web www.themillhouseinn.co.uk

Entry 16 Map 1

Upper & Lower Tregudda

Such a lovely little bay – and these two apartments, on a small hillside, one above the other, have Atlantic views to die for. Nothing particularly swish or stylish inside, but they are light, warm and comfortable and, taken together, are perfect for a big gathering. Upper Tregudda is especially light, its spacious sitting room and huge windows overlooking the sea. A balcony stretches along the sea-facing side of the house, replete with sunloungers for sunsets and views; the sitting room, dining room and master bedroom all have French windows that open onto it. Lower Tregudda – just below – has a much larger kitchen with seating for eight, opening straight onto the lovely shared garden; there are surf boards, fishing nets and croquet too. The area is owned by the National Trust, so walks are special and the coastline is dramatic. There's safe swimming and rock pools on the pebbly beach below, famous Port Isaac is around the headland and the bustling Port Gaverne Inn is at the bottom of the (very steep, very narrow!) hill. Drift off at night to the lap of the sea. *Minimum stay three nights, seven nights in high season. Short breaks available. A stone's throw from the beach which allows dogs year round. Direct access to North Cornish Coastal Path.*

Rooms	1 apartment for 8 (1 double en suite, 1 double, 1 twin, 1 bunk room; 1 bath/shower room); 1 apartment for 8 (1 double en suite, 1 double, 1 twin, 1 bunk room; 1 bath/shower room, 1 shower room): £565–£1,390. Short breaks £293–£515. Dogs £20 per stay. Max. 2 in each apt.
Meals	Self-catering.
Closed	Never.

A dog walker's paradise!
Dog bowls provided

Green Door Cottages
Upper & Lower Tregudda
Port Gaverne,
Port Isaac PL29 3SQ

Tel	+44 (0)1305 789000
Email	enquiries@greendoorcottages.co.uk
Web	www.greendoorcottages.co.uk

Entry 17 Map 1

The Seafood Restaurant

In 1975 a young chef called Rick Stein opened a restaurant in Padstow. These days he has four more as well as a deli, a pâtisserie, a seafood cookery school and 40 beautiful bedrooms. Despite this success, his homespun philosophy has never wavered: buy the freshest seafood from fisherman on the quay, then cook it simply and eat it with friends. It is a viewpoint half the country seems to share – the Seafood Restaurant is now a place of pilgrimage – so come to discover the Cornish coast, walk on the cliffs, paddle in the estuary, then drop into this lively restaurant for a fabulous meal, perhaps hot shellfish with garlic and lemon juice, Dover sole with sea salt and lime, apple and quince tartlet with vanilla ice cream. Book in for the night and a table in the restaurant is yours, though flawless bedrooms are so seductive you may find them hard to leave. They are scattered about town, some above the restaurant, others at the bistro or just around the corner. All are immaculate. Expect the best fabrics, stunning bathrooms, the odd terrace with estuary views. *Minimum stay two nights at weekends. Overlooking the harbour; the coastal walks are fabulous.*

Rooms	32 doubles; 8 twin/doubles: £100-£290. Dogs £20 per night.
Meals	Lunch £38.50. Dinner £58.50.
Closed	25-26 December.

A fleecy blanket to snuggle in – perfect after a run to the lighthouse

Jill & Rick Stein
The Seafood Restaurant
Riverside,
Padstow PL28 8BY

Tel	+44 (0)1841 532700
Email	reservations@rickstein.com
Web	www.rickstein.com

Entry 18 Map 1

Woodlands Country House

A big house in the country, half a mile west of Padstow, with long views across the fields down to the sea. Pippa and Hugo came west to renovate and have done a fine job. You get an honesty bar in the sitting room, a croquet lawn by the fountain and stripped floors in the airy breakfast room, where a legendary feast is served each morning. Spotless bedrooms are smart and homely, some big, some smaller, all with a price to match, but it's worth splashing out on the bigger ones, which are away from the road and have watery views. Expect lots of colour, pretty beds, floral curtains, Frette linen. One room has a four-poster, another comes with a claw-foot bath, there are robes in adequate bathrooms. All have flat-screen TVs and DVD players, with a library of films downstairs. WiFi runs throughout, there's a computer guests can use, taxis can be ordered – but make sure you book restaurants in advance, especially Rick Stein's or Jamie Oliver's Fifteen. Hire bikes in town and follow the Camel Trail, take the ferry over to Rock, head down to the beach, walk on the cliffs. Dogs are very welcome. *Large lawn for morning walks; beaches and bays and dog walking map of the area.*

Rooms	4 doubles; 1 four-poster; 3 twin/doubles: £98–£138. Singles from £74. Dogs £10 per stay.
Meals	Picnics £18. Restaurants in Padstow, 0.5 miles. Breakfast for non-residents £15.
Closed	20 December to 1 February.

For dog walking there's the refreshing pooch-tastic coastal path, plus local pub & restaurant maps

Hugo & Pippa Woolley
Woodlands Country House
Treator, Padstow PL28 8RU
Tel   +44 (0)1841 532426
Email   info@woodlands-padstow.co.uk
Web   www.woodlands-padstow.co.uk

Entry 19 Map 1

Bedruthan Hotel & Spa

A family-friendly hotel that delights parents and children alike. It has beautiful interiors, delicious food, sea views and an inexhaustible supply of distractions. There's a football pitch, surf school, a zip wire, then a cool spa with a couple of pools. If you can think of it, it's probably here, and younger children can be supervised by lovely, qualified staff. There's lots for adults, too, who get the run of the place during school time: a sitting room that hogs the view, a wood-burner to keep things cosy and colourful art on every wall. There are three restaurants (one for children's parties). Younger children have early suppers, adults return later for a slap-up meal, perhaps hand-picked crab, chargrilled steak, hazelnut tart with pistachio ice cream. There's a beach below, but you may spurn it for the indoor pool or a game of tennis. Lovely bedrooms have warm retro colours, blond wood, sparkling bathrooms, then separate rooms for children. Some open onto private terraces, lots have sea views, a few overlook the car park. Impeccable eco credentials and fantastic staff, too. *Walking on the beach, coastal footpaths, fields, woodlands.*

Rooms	38 twin/doubles: £135-£270. 27 suites for 4: £205-£490. 30 family rooms for 4: £175-£305. 6 singles: £75-£125. Dinner, B&B from £95 p.p. Dogs £12 per dog per night. Max. 2 per room (limit of 4 for whole hotel). Dogs can be left in room only at supper time. 5 dog-friendly bedrooms.
Meals	Lunch from £7. Dinner £30-£35. Sunday lunch from £15.
Closed	Christmas & 3 weeks in January.
	Bowls, blankets and beds

Matthew Burns
Bedruthan Hotel & Spa
Mawgan Porth, Newquay TR8 4BU

Tel	+44 (0)1637 860860
Email	stay@bedruthan.com
Web	www.bedruthan.com

Entry 20 Map 1

The Scarlet

A super-cool design hotel which overlooks the sea; a vast wall of glass in reception frames the view perfectly. The Scarlet does nothing by halves – this is a serious contender for Britain's funkiest bolthole – but it also offers a guilt-free destination as it's green to its core. Cutting-edge technology here includes a biomass boiler, solar panels and state-of-the-art insulation. You'll find a couple of swimming pools to insure against the weather, then log-fired hot tubs in a garden from which you can stargaze at night. There's a cool bar, a pool table in the library, then a restaurant that opens onto a decked terrace, where you eat fabulous Cornish food while gazing out to sea. Exceptional bedrooms come with huge views and all have balconies or terraces, private gardens or viewing pods. Expect oak floors from sustainable forests, organic cotton, perhaps a free-standing bath in your room. Some are enormous, one has a dual-aspect balcony, another comes with a rooftop lounge. If that's not enough, there's an ayurvedic-inspired spa, where tented treatment rooms are lit by lanterns. Amazing. *Minimum stay two nights at weekends. Masses of walking: coastal footpaths, fields, woodland and year round dog-friendly beach at the bottom of the garden.*

Rooms	21 doubles; 8 twin/doubles: £195–£405. 8 suites for 2: £270–£460. Dinner, B&B from £127.50 p.p. Dogs £15 per night per dog. Max. 2 per room (limit of 4 for whole hotel). Allowed in bedroom alone at supper time only. 5 dog-friendly bedrooms.
Meals	Lunch, 3 courses, £22.50. Dinner, 3 courses, £42.50.
Closed	4 January to 12 February.
	Homemade dog biscuits on arrival; bowl, blankets and towels.

	Emma Stratton The Scarlet Tredragon Road, Mawgan Porth, Newquay TR8 4DQ
Tel	+44 (0)1637 861800
Email	stay@scarlethotel.co.uk
Web	www.scarlethotel.co.uk

Entry 21 Map 1

Marver House

Chill out by the fire pit at the bottom of the garden, or soak in the hot tub above. Either way, you are accompanied by an unbeatable panorama. In a private gated drive, with houses all around but an unimpeded view, this is a grand site for a grand Victorian house. Through the porch packed with boots is the hall, off which a games room (toys, computer) and a living room lie, and a kitchen off that. All is big, beautiful and filled with light. The décor is eclectic with period furniture and modern pieces; sofas and beanbags are there to sink into, the sun-streamed kitchen is simple and classy. Further treats await up the sweeping stair: six bedrooms, six bathrooms and amazing sea views. Bathrobes, beach towels, handmade soaps and oils spoiling at every turn. The fridge is stocked with drinks including Cornish beer, there are books, board games and huge stacks of logs, surf boards, wetsuits and a Victorian croquet set. Have a massage, a sauna or a splash in the pool at Mawgan Porth Park, then fire up the barbecue – it's huge! Dine at Rick Stein's, Jamie Oliver's or the Scarlet Hotel whose grounds adjoin yours. Fabulous. *Late availability deals and short breaks available. Minimum stay three nights. Beachside location with coastal paths and woodland walks.*

Rooms	1 house for 12 (4 doubles en suite, 2 doubles; 2 bathrooms): £3,750-£7,350. Short breaks available. Max. 2 dogs. Dogs must please stay downstairs.
Meals	Self-catering.
Closed	Rarely.
	Bacon fat biscuits, half-baked pigs' ears and gravy biscuits

Philip Niemand
Marver House
Mawgan Porth, Newquay TR8 4BL
Tel   +44 (0)1637 861820
Mobile   +44 (0)7841 953434
Email   lindsey@mawganporth.co.uk
Web   www.marverhouse.co.uk

Entry 22 Map 1

5 & 6 Porth Farm Cottages

The beach is a five-minute stroll, the cliff path crosses National Trust coastline, the quiet village has a surf school, shop and fish 'n' chips: all the ingredients for a terrific seaside holiday. The cottages are part of a horseshoe of stone barns with communal gardens, art hut, swings and zip wire, all tucked into a hillside with views over the Vale of Lanherne and out to sea. The conversions are impressive, with underfloor heating, elm floorboards and wonderful woodwork. No. 5's staircase spirals up to a gallery landing, comfy bedrooms and a large slate-tiled bathroom. Soak in a roll top bath; blast away sand under a huge shower head. Downstairs: cosy up by the fire in an open-plan living room; the kitchen and dining table catch the morning sun. Outside: sit with a sunset drink and gaze up at the 'living roof' of flowers. It's a short drive to the Eden Project or St Ives, but mostly you can leave the car behind. The coastal path stretches to Newquay, Watergate Bay and Padstow (good bus service, too), there are farm shops and horse riding, and you can head down the valley to St Mawgan's convent and a gastropub lunch. *Dog-friendly Mawgan Porth beach ten-min walk. Footpath through woodland, fields and across a stream to the picturesque village of St Mawgan.*

Rooms	1 cottage for 4 (1 double, 1 twin; 1 bathroom); 1 cottage for 6 (1 double, 2 singles, 1 bunkroom; 1 bathroom, 2 shower rooms): £365–£1,002. Short breaks available out of season. Dogs £20 per stay. Max. 2. Downstairs only.
Meals	Self-catering.
Closed	Never.

Advice on walks, provision of a dog basket on request, and heated floorboards in winter

Carol & Peter Misch
5 & 6 Porth Farm Cottages
Mawgan Porth,
Newquay TR8 4BP

Mobile	+44 (0)7812 574131
Email	enquiries@5and6porthfarmcottages.com
Web	www.5and6porthfarmcottages.com

Entry 23 Map 1

The Gurnard's Head

The coastline here is utterly magical and the walk to St Ives hard to beat. Secret beaches appear at low tide, cliffs tumble down to the water and wild flowers streak the land pink in summer. As for this inn, you couldn't hope for a better base. It's earthy, warm, stylish and friendly, with airy interiors, colour-washed walls, stripped wooden floors and fires at both ends of the bar. Logs are piled up in an alcove, maps and art hang on the walls, books fill every shelf; if you pick one up and don't finish it, take it home and post it back. Rooms are warm, cosy and spotless, with Vi-Spring mattresses, crisp white linen, throws over armchairs, Roberts radios. Downstairs, super food, all homemade, can be eaten wherever you want: in the bar, in the restaurant or out in the garden in good weather. Snack on rustic delights – pork pies, crab claws, half a pint of Atlantic prawns – or tuck into more substantial treats, maybe salt and pepper squid, braised shoulder of lamb, pineapple tarte tatin. Picnics are easily arranged, there's bluegrass folk music in the bar most weeks. *Miles of coastal walks; 3.5 miles to dog-friendly beach.*

Rooms	4 doubles; 3 twin/doubles: £100–£170. Dinner, B&B from £75 p.p.
Meals	Lunch from £12. Dinner, 3 courses, from £26.50. Sunday lunch, 3 courses, £21.
Closed	24–25 December & 4 days in mid-January.
	Welcome biscuits, dog towels & bowls

Charles & Edmund Inkin
The Gurnard's Head
Zennor,
St Ives TR26 3DE
Tel   +44 (0)1736 796928
Email   enquiries@gurnardshead.co.uk
Web   www.gurnardshead.co.uk

Entry 24 Map 1

Wheal Rose

Just above the sandy cove of Portheras, on Britain's most scenic coast, a tiny lane leads down to a beautifully refurbished, detached farmhouse with stunning views. The old part of the cottage has all the charm you would expect: a cosy but surprisingly spacious sitting room with painted beams in muted colours, a log-burner and Cornish art in alcoves and on walls and window sills. This is a great cottage for family get-togethers as there is plenty for everyone to do: take the 15-minute walk down to the cove for a bracing early morning dip, or idle away an afternoon watching the seals. If you fancy spoiling yourself with a Cornish cream tea, take a gentle stroll across the fields to The Old School House and Gallery at Morvah. Or stride out along wild stretches of coastal path through historic mining landscapes dotted with ancient field systems towards Zennor and St Ives. As the sun begins to sink in the sky, light the barbecue, pour a glass of your favourite tipple, and watch the sun's descent into the Atlantic Ocean and the comforting presence of the Lighthouse at Pendeen Watch. *Short breaks available. Secure garden; ten-minute walk to the Cornish coastal path & local sandy cove where dogs may frolic all year round.*

Rooms	1 cottage for 7 (1 double, 1 twin/double, 1 twin, 1 single; 1 bath/shower room, 1 shower room, separate wc): £615–£1,570. Dogs £20 per week. Max: 2 per bedroom. Dogs downstairs only; may be left unattended in conservatory.
Meals	Self-catering.
Closed	Rarely.

 Bed, blanket, towels & bowls

Nicky Gregorowski
Wheal Rose
Higher Chypraze, Morvah,
Pendeen, Penzance TR19 7TU

Tel	+44 (0)1386 881454
Email	gregorowski@hotmail.com
Web	www.whealrose.co.uk

Entry 25 Map 1

33 Chapel Street

The position is perfect, opposite St Mary's Church, between the Promenade and the centre, on the most historic street in town. It's a peaceful, handsome, listed, end-of-terrace house, with a big suntrap courtyard (barbecue, Buddha) and glimpses of the sea. Enter to find cosy rooms with Georgian features and a cool stylish décor. There's a small dining/sitting room (one of two) with a plum velvet armchair and a deep soft sofa, and a smart, white, light kitchen with an ice-blue worktop, a Gaggia coffee machine, good china. (Washing machine and drying room are in the basement below.) Then it's up to three bedrooms, on the first floor or under the eaves, with wool carpets in dusky rose, big romantic hearts over the beds, and duvets and pillows as light as a cloud. The owners leave a lovely welcome pack and useful guides: go Wild Wood Foraging along the coastal paths, dive into the local galleries and shops, discover the Penzance Arts Club six doors down, fall in love with St Ives. Return to a cosy fire, Pecksniffs lotions by a roll top tub and an enchanting collection of local art on pure white walls. *Secure rear garden suitable for even little dogs – who like to try and escape! A mile long beach five-minute walk away.*

Rooms	1 house for 5 (2 doubles, 1 single; 1 bathroom): £500–£980. Max. 3 dogs.
Meals	Self-catering.
Closed	Never.

🚶 🐾 Booklet with dog-friendly pubs, places to visit and walks. A bag of dog treats and bowls

Philippa Penney
33 Chapel Street
Penzance TR18 4AQ
Tel   +44 (0)1326 555555
Email   enquiries@classic.co.uk
Web   www.threeseaviewspenzance.com

The Old Coastguard

The Old Coastguard stands bang on the water in one of Cornwall's loveliest coastal villages. It's a super spot and rather peaceful – little has happened here since 1595, when the Spanish sacked the place. Recently, the hotel fell into the benign hands of Edmund and Charles, past masters at reinvigorating lovely small hotels; warm colours, attractive prices, great food and a happy vibe are their hallmarks. Downstairs, the airy bar and the dining room come together as one, the informality of open-plan creating a great space to hang out. There are smart rustic tables, earthy colours, local ales and local art, then a crackling fire in the restaurant. Drop down a few steps to find a bank of sofas and a wall of glass framing sea views; in summer, doors open onto a decked terrace, a lush lawn, then the coastal path weaving down to the small harbour. Bedrooms are lovely: sand-coloured walls, excellent beds, robes in fine bathrooms, books everywhere. Most have the view, eight have balconies. Don't miss dinner: crab rarebit, fish stew, chocolate fondant and marmalade ice cream. *Coastal path right on the doorstep, miles of walking and all year dog-friendly beach 20-minute drive.*

Rooms	9 doubles; 3 twin/doubles: £110–£185. 1 suite for 2: £195. 1 family room for 4: £170–£220. Dinner, B&B from £75 p.p.
Meals	Lunch from £6. Dinner, 3 courses, about £27. Sunday lunch from £12.50.
Closed	1 week in early January.
	Blankets, bowls and towels, and a designated area especially for dogs in the entrance

Charles & Edmund Inkin
The Old Coastguard
The Parade, Mousehole,
Penzance TR19 6PR
Tel   +44 (0)1736 731222
Email   bookings@oldcoastguardhotel.co.uk
Web   www.oldcoastguardhotel.co.uk

Entry 27 Map 1

The Cabin

Up the hill from the village – and from the atmospheric Halzephron Inn – is a big clifftop house with four acres of land and a panorama of the sea. Here live Lucy and Roger who do laid-back B&B; across the walled garden is your cosy nest, an enchanting cottage for two. It's narrow, snug and beautifully put together: a squashy sofa and rug in front of a woodburner, a kitchen with breakfast bar, a romantic roll top bath. White walls and a big mirror give the illusion of more space, there are thick towels, fresh flowers, a porthole window that looks onto the garden, and you drift off to the waves lapping below from a delicious goosedown bed. Outside: herbs you may plunder, a secret garden overlooking the cove below – magical – and a gate that opens straight onto the coastal path. It's blissful on a summer's day, exhilarating in a gale, and a perfect launch pad for the secluded, outstanding beaches of this part of Cornwall, which offer both drama and golden sand. There's even a smugglers' tunnel up from the cove... all you need is a dog called Timmy, a mystery to solve and lashings of ginger beer. *Secure walled garden. Coastal path runs through grounds; two beaches open all year to dogs ten-minute walk. Good dog-friendly pub five-minute walk.*

Rooms	1 cottage for 2 (1 double; 1 bathroom): £500–£700. From £100 per night. Low season 3 nights £250. Dogs £20 per dog per stay. Max. 2. Can be left in the cottage unattended but not in bedroom.
Meals	Self-catering.
Closed	Rarely.

 Advice on walks

Lucy & Roger Thorp
The Cabin
Gunwalloe,
Helston TR12 7QD

Mobile	+44 (0)7899 925816
Email	info@halzephronhouse.co.uk
Web	www.halzephronhouse.co.uk

Little White Alice

What a treat. Rosie and Simon always dreamt of transforming an old farmstead into something special, and here they are, at the end of the high-hedged lanes, perfectly positioned between the north and south coasts. This is a place where the buildings are a work of art in themselves and energy comes from the wind and the sun – with ground-source heating thrown in for good measure, and water from 25 wild acres. Clustered around The Studio – the arts and crafts hub of Little Alice – are six stone and cedar-clad cottages: two for romancers, four for families. Inside: hand-carved kitchens and woven-willow headboards, wood-burning stoves and heated floors, hampers of local honey and bread from Falmouth, and stunning canvasses of Cornish art (for sale!). All this and private decks, beechwood tables, freeview TV, books, DVDs and a natural swimming pool. There's watersporting at Stithians Lake, surfing beaches ten miles away, views all the way to St Austell. You can even sip Camel Valley champagne in the wood-burning hot tub beneath the stars... It's easy being green! *Short breaks available. Twenty nine acres to explore, and many footpaths running through.*

Rooms	2 houses for 2; 3 houses for 4; 1 house for 8 : £302–£2,218. Dogs £25 per stay. Max. 2. 2 dog-friendly cottages.
Meals	Self-catering.
Closed	Never.

Blankets, towels, dog bags and a tasty treat. Advice on walks and beaches

Rosie Hadden
Little White Alice
Carnmenellis,
Redruth TR16 6PL
Tel   +44 (0)1209 861000
Email   rosie@littlewhitealice.co.uk
Web   www.littlewhitealice.co.uk

Entry 29 Map 1

Round House East

Standing like sentries guarding the village pub and green below are two whitewashed 1820s roundhouses with thatched roofs and crosses – believed to keep the devil away. Ingenious how everything fits so neatly within the curving walls, from solid wood floors to fitted wardrobes, in this warm, quirky bolthole. Local art and retro touches – a tide clock, a 50s sideboard, bold beetroot upholstery – rub shoulders with a vast TV (in both sitting room and cosy upstairs bedroom; WiFi too). In the kitchen extension, past the lime green fridge, find a glass dining table and windows to the pretty cottage garden. Take a morning espresso out to your lounger and watch the seagulls swoop. When night falls, soak in the roll top bath, then retire to a gothic super king-sized bed under a vaulted ceiling; Art Deco mirror, quirky lamps and pink-and-purple rug continue the fun retro theme. Bring bicycles, dogs, flip flops for the beach and walking boots for the South West Coast Path; the Roseland Peninsula is awash with secret coves and seaside restaurants. The King Harry Ferry to Truro is voted one of the world's most scenic ferry routes. *Secure garden, river, woodland and coast. Dogs can also watch the world go by from the garden gate or just sleep on the sofa!*

Rooms	1 cottage for 2 (1 double; 1 bathroom, 1 shower room): £375-£880. Dogs £20 per stay. Max. 2 (but may accommodate more on request).
Meals	Self-catering.
Closed	Never.

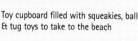 Toy cupboard filled with squeakies, balls & tug toys to take to the beach

Ian Rose
Round House East
Pendower Road,
Veryan, Truro TR2 5QL
Tel   +44 (0)20 7483 4630
Email   enquiries@roundhousecornwall.co.uk
Web   www.roundhousecornwall.co.uk

Entry 30 Map 1

The Hideaway Hut

The Hideaway Hut is a wonderful way to explore a fabulous area of Cornwall. Treworgey Farm is Holly and Andy's family business, spread over 150 acres overlooking the Looe river valley. It's a lively place, with a riding school on site that runs on weekdays and a few holiday cottages dotted about. The Hut sits in its own corner of the farm, with a private shower and loo twenty metres off. From here you can hit the coastal path – five minutes away! – or ramble down in the woodlands, but you're more than welcome to use the games room, the pool, and the tennis court, which you'll share with the cottages. Cornish cream teas, light suppers and homemade cakes can be delivered to your door. There's a wood-burner in the hut to keep you warm and a gas hob for cooking along with all the basics, or you could hike out to the local (forty minutes uphill on the way out) and try the local sparkling cider and some good pub food. Take advantage of this delightful spot: the beach is only a few minutes by car and the many attractions of Cornwall await. *Minimum stay three nights. Book through Sawday's Canopy & Stars online or by phone.*

Rooms	Shepherd's hut for 2 (1 double): from £68 per night. Dogs £5 per night. Max. 1.
Meals	Self-catering.
Closed	December–February.
🐕	One field always kept empty for dogs to run free

Sawday's Canopy & Stars
The Hideaway Hut
Treworgey Farm, Duloe,
Liskeard PL14 4PP

Tel	+44 (0)117 204 7830
Email	enquiries@canopyandstars.co.uk
Web	www.canopyandstars.co.uk/hideawayhut

Entry 31 Map 1

The Buttery, Trussel Barn

Pootle along from Cornish coast to deep valley then up again to Trussel Barn, lapped by a well-tended garden with long rolling views. The Buttery, attached to the main house where the owners do B&B, makes a super-private, one-room bolthole for two. Step in to find... a superb zip-and-link bed under tidy dark beams, a fawn carpet and white walls, chunky pine furniture and leather bucket chairs, a sweet galley kitchen with all you need, and a dining table. Through the kitchen is the bathroom, shiny and white-tiled with a shower. It's well heated throughout, you'll be as snug as a bug on the blowiest nights, and you have games and DVDs to get stuck into. Wake to views shooting off in all directions and gardens that drop to the valley below, where the little branch line runs alongside the river linking Liskeard and Looe... catch that train! Or stay put and enjoy these seven landscaped acres, with a wildlife pond to entertain you and sitting spots for sunshine and views (a barbecue, too). Gardens to visit, pubs to discover, a coastline to walk... it is a wonderful area. *Secure fenced garden and seven acres to roam.*

Rooms	1 annexe for 2 (1 twin/double; 1 shower room): £350–£525. Short stays welcome at £75 per night. Max. 2 dogs. Sheep in field below so dogs must be on a lead in there.
Meals	Self-catering.
Closed	Rarely.
	A box of doggie treats, and towels for wet dogs

Richard Shields & Kathy Williams
The Buttery, Trussel Barn
St Keyne, Liskeard PL14 4QL

Tel	+44 (0)1579 340450
Mobile	+44 (0)7785 350552
Email	trusselbarn@btinternet.com
Web	www.trusselbarn.com

Entry 32 Map 1

Spring Park

Each of these four gleaming wagons at Spring Park has an individual charm. There's 'Duke', a classic 1940s showman's wagon, with bright vibrant paintwork on the outside and interior furnishings to match. Next, 'Maiden', a restored railway wagon has been paired up with a large modern cabin, 'Wisteria Cottage'. Then there's 'Pip', a sturdy 1930s steam roller living van with spacious cabin alongside. Finally, 'Hercules', a large cedar living van, holds an eclectic mix of antique and vintage finds put together by owners Kitty and Paddy. They used to own two vintage boutiques, so this is right up their street! Each wagon has a fifth of an acre of private garden, perfect for just lying back and daydreaming in the Cornish countryside. If you do want to go adventuring, Kitty and Paddy have thoughtfully provided a hamper for you to pack up a picnic and go off for the day, maybe down to the beach for surfing, walking across Dartmoor or wandering through the local villages and visiting the markets. *Minimum stay two nights. Book through Sawday's Canopy & Stars online or by phone.*

Rooms	4 wagons for 2 (1 double): from £60 per night. Dogs £20 per stay. Max. 1 (more by arrangement).
Meals	Self-catering.
Closed	Rarely.

Resident dogs Brook and Peggy always leave a tin of treats for guest dogs along with towels and a blanket

Sawday's Canopy & Stars
Spring Park
Rezare,
Launceston PL15 9NX

Tel	+44 (0)117 204 7830
Email	enquiries@canopyandstars.co.uk
Web	www.canopyandstars.co.uk/springpark

Entry 33 Map 2

Cornwall

B&B

Landewednack House

The pug dogs will greet you enthusiastically and Susan will give you tea and biscuits in the drawing room of this extremely pretty and immaculate house. Antony the chef keeps the wheels oiled and the food coming – treat yourself to green crab soup or succulent lobster; the wine cellar holds over 2,000 bottles so there's plenty of choice. Upstairs to smart, sumptuous roomy bedrooms and tip-top bathrooms; the twin room is smaller and not all have sea views, but everything you could possibly need is there, from robes to brandy. The pool area is stunning, the garden is filled with interest and it's a three-minute walk to the sea. *Minimum stay two nights July/August. Large garden, coastal path and plenty of beaches to explore.*

Rooms	4 doubles; 1 twin: £110–£190.
	Singles £85.
	Dogs £10 per night.
Meals	Dinner, 3 courses, £38.
Closed	Rarely.

A tasty morning sausage in the kitchen, a big welcome from the resident pugs, and a dog-sitting service

Susan Thorbek
Landewednack House
Church Cove, The Lizard,
Helston TR12 7PQ
Tel   +44 (0)1326 290877
Email   luxurybandb@landewednackhouse.com
Web   www.landewednackhouse.com

Entry 34 Map 11

Cornwall

B&B

The Hen House

Greenies will be delighted: Sandy and Gary, truly welcoming, are passionately committed to sustainability and happy to advise on the best places to eat, visit and walk; there are OS maps on loan, too. Enlightened souls will adore the spacious colourful rooms, the bright fabrics, the wildflower meadow with inviting sun loungers, the pond, the chance to try tai chi, the fairy-lit courtyard at night, the scrumptious locally sourced breakfasts, the birdsong. There's even a sanctuary room for reiki and reflexology set deep into the earth in this generous, peaceful retreat. *Minimum stay two nights. Over 12s welcome. Secure garden and wild flower meadow in two acres of fenced grounds. Many great footpaths from door. Within a mile of beach and South West Coastal Path.*

Rooms	3 doubles (3 doubles in 3 barns):
	£80–£90. Singles £70.
	Dogs £5 per night. Dog sitting offered occasionally.
Meals	Pub/restaurant 1 mile.
Closed	Rarely.

Loan of Ordnance Survey maps and walk books of the area; lots of advice on dog-friendly beaches & pubs

Sandy & Gary Pulfrey
The Hen House
Tregarne, Manaccan, Helston TR12 6EW
Tel   +44 (0)1326 280236
Mobile +44 (0)7809 229958
Email   henhouseuk@btinternet.com
Web   www.thehenhouse-cornwall.co.uk

Entry 35 Map 1

The Sun Inn

Extreme pleasure awaits those who book into The Sun. Not only is this ancient inn a delight to behold – thick stone walls, wood-burners, windows onto a cobbled passageway, beer pumps ready for action – but the town itself is a dreamy jewel of the north. The inn backs onto St Mary's churchyard, where wild flowers prosper and bumble bees ply their trade. Potter across and find 'one of the loveliest views in England, and therefore the world' to quote Ruskin. Herons fish the river, lambs graze the fields, hills soar into a vast sky. Turner painted it in 1825. Back at The Sun, all manner of good things: warm interiors, recently refurbished, come in elegant country style. You'll find old stone walls, boarded floors, cosy window seats, newspapers in a rack. Uncluttered bedrooms upstairs are just as good; expect trim carpets, comfy beds, crisp white linen, super bathrooms. Finally, the food – homemade soups, mussels in white wine, loin of local lamb, apple and chocolate pudding. Don't miss it. *Minimum stay two nights if booking Saturday night. Free parking permits provided for all local car parks. River walk, woodland walks, grounds.*

Rooms	8 doubles; 2 twin/doubles: £99–£164. 1 family room for 4: £99–£168. Singles from £76. Dogs £10 per stay. Max. number only restricted by size of room booked and size of dogs! 7 dog-friendly bedrooms.
Meals	Lunch from £10.95. Dinner from £16.95. Not Monday lunch.
Closed	Never.
	Iced water in the bar for visiting dogs, bowls & towels in the bedrooms

Mark & Lucy Fuller
The Sun Inn
6 Market Street, Kirkby Lonsdale,
Carnforth LA6 2AU

Tel	+44 (0)1524 271965
Email	email@sun-inn.info
Web	www.sun-inn.info

Entry 36 Map 6

The Farmhouse at A Corner of Eden

A lovely Georgian farmhouse, set in a glorious valley with infinite sky and distant Cumbrian hills. The wood, the stone, the honesty of the structure create an enveloping, peaceful retreat. Layered on to this lovely house is deep comfort and more than a touch of luxury. The cosy sitting room has a log fire and the beautiful beamed dining room has seating for a small crowd. Bedrooms sport original fireplaces, too, and have polished wooden floors and spoiling fabrics. Richard and Debbie are the loveliest hosts and live in the byre next door but we can hardly think of anything extra you'd need. They've generously left fluffy robes, thick towels, Barbours and wellies to borrow, drinks in the honesty bar in the dairy and for each stay there's a welcome basket with local goodies and champagne. The large range cooker will excite keen cooks and the not too keen can easily find their way to the pub across the fields or just ask Debbie to arrange for meals to be delivered. Simply heaven. Take Angel Barn, too, and come with 14 friends. *Minimum stay three nights at weekends. Short breaks available. Footpaths in all directions, Pennine bridleway just up the lane, river to jump in and 'open access' land close by,*

Rooms	1 cottage for 8 (3 doubles, 1 twin/double; 1 bathroom, 1 shower): £995–£1,680. £720–£900 for a 3-night break. Max. 2 large dogs (contact to discuss other options).
Meals	Self-catering.
Closed	Never.

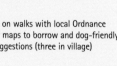 Advice on walks with local Ordnance Survey maps to borrow and dog-friendly pub suggestions (three in village)

Debbie Temple & Richard Greaves
The Farmhouse at A Corner of Eden
Low Stennerskeugh, Ravenstonedale,
Kirkby Stephen CA17 4LL

Tel	+44 (0)1539 623370
Email	enquiries@acornerofeden.co.uk
Web	www.acornerofeden.co.uk

Entry 37 Map 6

The Shepherd's Cabin

Spoil yourselves in the midst of nature in this Cumbrian cabin for two. Wild and wonderful, you can walk straight from the door, with footpaths in all directions – a mile to the pub, or three to the village, and the Pennine Bridleway steps away. Next door, you can take a candlelit soak in the 1920s roll top bath, and there's a separate space with little kitchen. Debbie & Richard have thought of everything, from feather duvets down to fluffy robes and crocs for the bathroom dash, and a damson gin nightcap of their own creation. Pop your iPod in the dock and nestle in the armchairs with a book. There's lighting inside and a campfire just outside. The cabin is tucked away in the grounds of the old farmhouse, with an outside terrace to itself. It is well insulated with a wood-burning stove for year-round toastiness; all flooring, fabric and paints are eco-friendly and made as close to home as possible. There are just two sheep – Lulu & Matilda – at A Corner of Eden, so shepherding duties are light, but you are welcome to say hello. *Minimum stay two nights. Book through Sawday's Canopy & Stars online or by phone.*

Rooms	Cabin for 2 (1 double): from £95 per night. Dogs £5 per night. Max. 2.
Meals	Self-catering.
Closed	Never.

 Local Ordnance Survey maps to borrow for walks and a list of dog-friendly pubs

Sawday's Canopy & Stars
The Shepherd's Cabin
A Corner of Eden, Low Stennerskeugh,
Ravenstonedale, Kirkby Stephen CA17 4LL
Tel   +44 (0)117 204 7830
Email   enquiries@canopyandstars.co.uk
Web   www.canopyandstars.co.uk/shepherdscabin

Entry 38 Map 6

The Black Swan

This fabulous small hotel is hard to fault. Bang in the middle of a pretty village surrounded by blistering country it's all things to all men: a smart restaurant, a lively bar, a village shop; they even hold a music festival here in September. A stream runs through an enormous garden, where you can eat in good weather; free-range hens live in one corner. Inside, warm country interiors fit the mood perfectly. You get fresh flowers, tartan carpets, games on the piano, books galore. There's a locals' bar for local ales and a sitting-room bar with an open fire, but the hub of the hotel is the bar in the middle, where village life gathers. You can eat wherever you want, including the airy restaurant at the front where you dig into delicious country food (the meat is from the fields around you), perhaps smoked trout terrine, steak and venison casserole, lemon and ginger syllabub. Excellent bedrooms are fantastic for the money. Expect pretty colours, beautiful linen, smart furniture, super bathrooms. The Lakes and Dales are close, children and dogs are welcome. A very happy place. *Secure garden, river for swims, excellent walks in woodland and over moors.*

Rooms	12 twin/doubles: £75–£115.
	2 suites for 2: £110–£125. 1 single: £55.
	Dogs £10 per stay.
	3 dog-friendly bedrooms.
Meals	Lunch from £4.50.
	Dinner, 3 courses, £25–£30.
Closed	Never.
	Towels, drying facilities, walks; on-site shop sells dog food

Alan & Louise Dinnes
The Black Swan
Ravenstonedale,
Kirkby Stephen CA17 4NG
Tel   +44 (0)15396 23204
Email   enquiries@blackswanhotel.com
Web   www.blackswanhotel.com

Entry 39 Map 6

George and Dragon

Charles Lowther has found a chef who does perfect justice to the slow-grow breeds of beef, pork and lamb produced on the Lowther Estate – and you'll find lovely wines to match, 16 by the glass. Ales and cheeses are local, berries and mushrooms are foraged, vegetables are home-grown... and his signature starter, twice-baked cheese soufflé with a hint of spinach – is divine. As for the long low coaching inn, it's been beautifully restored by craftsmen using wood, slate and stone, and painted in colours in tune with the period. Bare wooden tables, comfy sofas, intimate alcoves and crackling fires make this a delightful place to dine and unwind; old prints and archive images tell stories of the 800-year-old estate's history. Outside is plenty of seating and a lawned play area beneath fruit trees. Upstairs are 12 bedrooms of varying sizes (some small, some large and some above the bar), perfectly decorated in classic country style. Carpeting is Cumbrian wool, beds are new, ornaments come with Lowther history, showers are walk-in, baths (there are two) are roll top, and breakfast is fresh and delicious. *Garden; lake and mountain walks.*

Rooms	12 twin/doubles: £95–£145.
	Singles from £70.
	Dogs £10 per stay. Dogs may not be left unattended in the restaurant.
Meals	Lunch from £7.95. Dinner from £11.95.
Closed	Boxing Day.

A welcome doggie treat for all hounds

Juno & Charles Lowther
George and Dragon
Clifton,
Penrith CA10 2ER

Tel	+44 (0)1768 865381
Email	enquiries@georgeanddragonclifton.co.uk
Web	www.georgeanddragonclifton.co.uk

The Lodge

Splendidly located on a wide bend of the river Eamont, The Lodge is frontier living at its finest. While the exterior of this timber log cabin blends perfectly into its natural surroundings, the interior comes as a surprise: simple and homely, but beautifully furnished with several stylish touches. From the upstairs 'master' bedroom – with views that make the most of the spot – a wrought-iron spiral staircase drops down into the centre of the well-equipped kitchen/sitting room. Find comfy armchairs around a wood-burner, a double sofabed for extras, and sliding doors that open to a veranda and summer breezes; occasionally deer come to the river bank for a drink. You can catch trout for your supper, then cook up a storm on the four-hob gas oven. Edenhall estate offers plenty of scope for hiking and cycling as well as private stretches of river fantastic for salmon. You can arrange for a chef to come out and cook, book a full hamper before you arrive, or arrange for a masseuse to come and ease away hiker's pains. You're also on the very edge of the Lake District, great yomping territory for you and your dog. *Bookings begin on Monday or Friday. Book through Sawday's Canopy & Stars online or by phone.*

Rooms	Cabin for 4 (1 double, 1 sofabed): from £175 per night.
Meals	Self-catering.
Closed	Never.
	Suggestions for dog-friendly walks; water, food bowl & dog bed all provided for your return

Sawday's Canopy & Stars
The Lodge
Edenhall Estate, The Courtyard,
Penrith CA11 8ST

Tel	+44 (0)117 204 7830
Email	enquiries@canopyandstars.co.uk
Web	www.canopyandstars.co.uk/thelodge

Entry 41 Map 6

Drybeck Farm

Steve and Paula do what they love at Drybeck Farm. A deeply held belief in sustainability is evident in the careful management of land and resources, and the easy, slow pace of life. The farm sits on the banks of the Eden river, and you can eat breakfast while watching the kingfishers, herons and even an occasional otter enjoy the rippling water. Choose between 'Arwen', a cosily decorated 21ft yurt that sleeps up to eight, 'Croglin', an 18ft yurt that sleeps up to six, and 'Evelyn', a bright red wagon just for two. Your first morning's breakfast is taken care of with a lovely welcome hamper of farm produce. Unpack it in your section of the 'cookhouse with a view' overlooking the river, where rough hewn larch planks blend a frontier style with up-to-the-minute fittings. The local area is a hidden gem in the lakes: off the major tourist trail, but with the hub, Carlisle, nearby if you need to drop into town. Round your day off with a dip in the wood-fired hot tub... *Bookings begin on Monday or Friday. Book through Sawday's Canopy & Stars online or by phone.*

Rooms	Yurt for 4 (1 double, 2 single futons): from £95 per night.
	Yurt for 6 (1 double, 4 single futons): from £105 per night. (Extra futons available.)
	Wagon for 2 (1 double): from £56 per night.
	Refundable deposit of £30 per stay, payable on arrival.
	Dogs £5 per night. Max. 2.
Meals	Self-catering.
Closed	January–March.

Pigs' ears from the farm when available

Sawday's Canopy & Stars
Drybeck Farm
Armathwaite,
Carlisle CA4 9ST
Tel   +44 (0)117 204 7830
Email   enquiries@canopyandstars.co.uk
Web   www.canopyandstars.co.uk/drybeck

Entry 42 Map 5

High Houses

Tucked away at the quieter end of the Lake District National Park is this beguiling 17th-century hilltop house – all lime-plastered walls, rustic beams, open fires and original flagstones. Its delightful owners, who live in the house's other half, have resisted smoothing out the rough edges; 1920s graffiti still adorns the stable dividers. The hardships of country living have, however, been banished: find lovely new pink and soft-green 'pineapple' covers on sitting room chairs, delicious bed linen and towels, handmade soaps and piping hot radiators. Bedrooms may prompt some tough decisions – do you choose the room with the roll top bath (semi en suite) and the cockloft for kids, or the four-poster with the sofabed and the log fire? The farmhouse kitchen is cosy with Aga, big fridge and gadgets aplenty, but reluctant cooks can book Jill's homemade meals in advance. Beautiful views reach out from every fine sash window to wildlife-rich farmland beyond – 350 private acres, yours to explore. Venture further and you reach the Lakes and the Solway Plain. Heaven for sybarites and walkers. *Surrounded by sheep, and roaming bantams, but no traffic – brilliant for dog-walking.*

Rooms	1 house for 6 (3 doubles; 2 bathrooms): £600-£800. Max. 2 dogs.
Meals	Self-catering.
Closed	Never.

Water bowl and advice on walks

Jill Green
High Houses
Snittlegarth, Ireby, Carlisle CA7 1HE

Tel	+44 (0)1697 371549
Mobile	+44 (0)7929 397273
Email	enquiries@highhouses.co.uk
Web	www.highhouses.co.uk

Entry 43 Map 5

Scales Plantation

High in the wilds of the North Lakes, in the woods around Scales Farm, Tabitha and Rob Wilson have created a selection of fabulous boltholes. Three shepherd's hut camps with timber kitchens are set in semicircular clearings on the edge of the forest; there's a family safari tent, and a bell tent and cabin camp too. The sites are sheltered and peaceful, with views out towards Bowscale Fell and Mount Skiddaw. As part of the regeneration of the woodland, the once thick canopy has been thinned to allow wildlife such as the resident red squirrels to flourish. The camps have already come to feel like natural extensions of the Lake District, with beautiful walks across the fells on your doorstep. You can get trail advice or hire bikes just down the road and head into the hills, then come back to the rustic comfort of the hut and your toasty wood-burner. Groceries can even be supplied by your hosts: simply choose from the list of supplies in advance and they'll be waiting on your arrival. Keep dogs on leads when sheep are about! *Bookings begin on Monday or Friday. Book through Sawday's Canopy & Stars online or by phone.*

Rooms	3 shepherd's huts for 4 (1 double, 2 singles): from £70. Tent lodge for 6 (1 double, 1 twin, 2 bunks): from £98. Camp for 4 (2 doubles): from £95. Prices per night. Max. 2 dogs.
Meals	Self-catering.
Closed	Rarely.

 Dogs outnumber humans 3 to 1 in the Scales Farm workforce so there would probably be mutiny if canine guests were not welcomed!

Sawday's Canopy & Stars
Scales Plantation
Berrier,
Penrith CA11 0XE
Tel   +44 (0)117 204 7830
Email enquiries@canopyandstars.co.uk
Web   www.canopyandstars.co.uk/scalesplantation

Entry 44 Map 5

Johnby Hall

You are ensconced in the quieter part of the Lakes and have independence in this Elizabethan manor house – once a fortified Pele tower, now a family home. The suites are airy and each has its own sitting room with books, children's videos, squashy sofas, pretty fabrics and whitewashed walls. Beds have patchwork quilts, windows have stone mullions and all is peaceful. Henry gives you sturdy breakfasts, and good home-grown suppers by a roaring fire in the great hall; he and Anna can join you or leave you in peace. Children will have fun: hens and pigs to feed, garden and woods to roam, garden toys galore. Walks from the door are sublime. *Kelly room has attached enclosed garden where owners can let their dogs roam. Ten acres of woodland.*

White Hart Inn

The main counter drips with brass, hops and pumps; walls and shelves are strewn with clay pipes, taxidermy and tankards. It's a sleepy-snoozy village local, friendly too, where regulars mingle with visitors over pints of Coniston and Hawkshead Bitter. There are decent wines and a delicious, no-nonsense menu: rare-breed meat from Aireys of Ayside; steak and Guinness pie; vegetarian chilli… and mallard and pheasant from the shooting parties that gather in the pub car park on winter Saturdays. They source locally, and – yes! – do small portions for children. A sloping flagged floor reflects the light from the window; black leather sofas front wood stoves at each end. The walking's marvellous and the village fits snugly into an ancient landscape of wooded valleys and tight little roads. *National Park on the doorstep, with fields, rivers and streams.*

Rooms	1 twin/double, with sitting room; 1 family room for 4, with sitting room: £110-£125. Singles £80-£90. Dogs max. no limit – within reason!
Meals	Supper, 2 courses, £20. Pub 1 mile.
Closed	Rarely.

 A vast garden for dogs to explore full of exciting whiffs, & ten acres of private woodland

Meals	Lunch & dinner £10.75-£15.75.
Closed	Open all day.

 A whole woodland of new smells to discover

Henry & Anna Howard
Johnby Hall
Johnby,
Penrith CA11 0UU
Tel   +44 (0)1768 483257
Email   bookings@johnbyhall.co.uk
Web   www.johnbyhall.co.uk

Entry 45 Map 5

Nigel & Kath Barton
White Hart Inn
Bouth,
Ulverston LA12 8JB
Tel   +44 (0)1229 861229
Email   nigelwhitehart@aol.com
Web   www.whitehart-lakedistrict.co.uk

Entry 46 Map 5

Cherry Tree Cottage

A brilliant place to come with a pile of children. Pamela and Nick are fun, and stock the place with books and toys. This cottage, a big old hay barn, has outstanding views from its picture window (once the cart doorway) to green hills. No need to worry that the kids will spoil antiques and cream sofas: this is a truly practical base. The open fire is stocked with logs and the kitchen with painted oak units, a table for six and all mod cons, dishwasher included. The jolly pink bathroom has oodles of towels, while bedrooms with velux windows are carpeted and cosy. The bunk room is cheerfully child-friendly and stencils and flowery fabrics abound, as do crooked beams. You have two sitting areas not one, and steep steps outside to a small terrace at the back, and a trampoline in the paddock. In the evenings the games room next door comes into its own: there's TV, ping-pong, an electric organ. A sublime setting at the end of a quiet country lane with walks from the door and an excellent pub down the hill. You're just a mile from Chinley village, with several places to eat. *Quiet sheep farm, great walks from the door with canal and river at the bottom of the valley.*

Rooms	1 cottage for 6 (1 double, 1 twin, 1 bunk room for 2; 1 bathroom, 1 shower room. Cot available): £230–£695. Dogs £5 per stay. Max. 2.
Meals	Self-catering.
Closed	Never.

Water bowls, towels, poop scooper and bags

Pamela & Nick Broadhurst
Cherry Tree Cottage
Buxworth,
High Peak SK23 7NP
Tel +44 (0)1663 750566
Email cotebank@btinternet.com
Web www.cotebank.co.uk

Entry 47 Map 6

The Peacock at Rowsley

You rise leisurely, breakfast indulgently, then follow the river three miles north to Chatsworth House, not a bad way to arrive at one of Britain's most beautiful stately homes. As for the Peacock, it dates to 1653 and was once the dower house to Haddon Hall. It stands by the bridge in the middle of the village and opened as a coaching inn 200 years ago. Its lawns run down to the river, where you may spot the odd fisherman trying his luck. Inside, old and new mix harmoniously: mullioned windows, hessian rugs, aristocratic art, then striking colours that give a contemporary feel. French windows in the restaurant open onto the terrace in summer, a fire smoulders in the bar all year. Stylish rooms have crisp linen, good beds, Farrow & Ball colours, the odd antique. One has a bed from Belvoir Castle, the new suite is open to the eaves. As for the food, it's serious stuff, perhaps squab pigeon with fruit and nuts, monkfish with a coconut sauce, chocolate marquise with barley ice cream. Circular walks start from the front door, so you can walk off any excess in beautiful hills.
Minimum stay two nights at weekends. Secure garden, river to jump in, woodland and coastal walks.

Rooms	10 doubles; 2 four-posters: £160–£260.
	1 suite for 2: £275–£450.
	2 singles: £90–£122.
	Dinner, B&B from £112.50 p.p.
	Dogs £10 per night.
Meals	Lunch from £4.50.
	Sunday lunch £22.50–£29.50. Dinner £60.
Closed	Rarely.

Towels on offer for muddy paws, tasty leftovers & bones at bedtime

Jenni MacKenzie
The Peacock at Rowsley
Bakewell Road,
Rowsley, Matlock DE4 2EB
Tel   +44 (0)1629 733518
Email   reception@thepeacockatrowsley.com
Web   www.thepeacockatrowsley.com

Entry 48 Map 6

The Barn at Dale End House

The countryside here is so ridiculously pretty it's like a child's play scene. Idyllic country lanes lead you through picture-perfect Derbyshire dales, past graceful oaks and fields of sheep to these sandstone converted barns. The old courtyard quacks with a team of ducks, the clucks of the fluffiest chickens and gliding peacocks. There are two contemporary, cleverly renovated barns that allow bookings for two, four, six, eight or ten. In the large barn, there's a huge funky farmhouse kitchen with turquoise glass tiles that cooks will love. An open-plan sitting/dining room with high beamed ceilings is decorated in creams, taupes and soft greys with a chunky long dining table for unhurried dinners and modern pieces of bold art decorating the walls. The bedrooms are light, with subtle colours, plush new bathrooms and views of the surrounding fields. The Lodge is separate with equally sumptuous beds, calming colours and modern twists. There's walking galore straight from the door, heavenly country pubs, historic houses to explore and, of course, Bakewell tart to scoff! *Min. stay two nights. Discounts for four+ nights. Endless signposted country walks from the door, over hills and along rivers to dog-friendly pubs. Peak District National Park to explore.*

Rooms	The Barn for 8 (4 doubles, all en suite): £1,400–£1,780; £300 per night. The Lodge for 2 (1 double, en suite): £445; £85 per night. Max. dogs: no limit within reason. 4 dog-friendly bedrooms.
Meals	Self-catering.
Closed	Rarely.
	Dog bowls and beds

Sarah & Paul Summers
The Barn at Dale End House
Gratton,
Bakewell DE45 1LN

Tel	+44 (0)1629 650380
Email	thebarn@daleendhouse.co.uk
Web	www.daleendhouse.co.uk

Entry 49 Map 6

Ruby loves
holidaying
in Devon.

The Lodge at Dale End House

One of those places where you get your own annexe – in this case, the former milking parlour of the listed farmhouse. It certainly has scrubbed up nicely. The ground-floor bedroom has a finely dressed antique bed and magnificent chandelier while the well-equipped kitchen is a boon if you don't fancy venturing out for supper. Friendly, helpful Sarah takes orders for breakfasts – eggs from her hens, local sausages and bacon – and delivers to your door. No open fire but cosy underfloor heating warms you after a blustery yomp in any direction. Bring your four-legged friends – canine or equine – to this happy house. *Endless signposted country walks from the door, over hills and along rivers to dog-friendly pubs. Peak District National Park to explore.*

Chester's favourite
place is to lie in
front of his owner.

Rooms	1 double with kitchen/dining/sitting room: £85.
Meals	Pubs/restaurants 2.5 miles.
Closed	Rarely.

Dog bowls and baskets

Sarah & Paul Summers
The Lodge at Dale End House
Gratton,
Bakewell DE45 1LN

Tel	+44 (0)1629 650380
Email	thebarn@daleendhouse.co.uk
Web	www.daleendhouse.co.uk

Entry 50 Map 6

Garden Studio, North Walk House

Ramblers may feel they've reached nirvana: a clifftop apartment overlooking the sea that sits on the coastal path to Exmoor. There's a collection of guest houses on the North Walk promenade and Ian and Sarah snapped up a B&B and transformed it into a calm retreat, building in a self-catering space at the same time. Inside is sweet and simple. The walls have been freshly painted in white and the shower room is bedecked in gleaming red tiles. The bedroom sits behind a wooden half wall, brightened cheerfully in blushing pink, in contrast with the dark brass bed. Living and kitchen spaces come together, one corner stocked with all the white goods you could need, the other hosting a sofabed, stacks of books and a library of walking maps. Wind-blasted wanderers can return to privacy, take a drink to the terrace or get cosy with a DVD. In the morning you may prefer to seek out Sarah's fabulously local and organic breakfasts in the B&B above (your hosts couldn't be nicer). There are miles of coast, wood and moorland to explore, so come to discover your inner Akela. *Minimum stay four nights on weekdays, three nights at weekends. Short breaks available. Pets by arrangement. Coast walks (cliffs – so be careful!). Dog-friendly pubs and restaurants nearby.*

Rooms	1 apartment for 2 (1 double, sofabed; 1 shower room): £280-£349. Dogs £10 per night. Max. 2 per room.
Meals	Self-catering.
Closed	Rarely.
	Tin of dog treats on arrival, doggie towels & tips for dog-friendly walks and pubs

Ian & Sarah Downing
Garden Studio, North Walk House
North Walk,
Lynton EX35 6HJ

Tel	+44 (0)1598 753372
Email	walk@northwalkhouse.co.uk
Web	www.northwalkhouse.co.uk

Entry 51 Map 2

Longlands

The five Longlands lodge tents jut impressively out of the hillside on raised wooden decks, in a wide open field near the North Devon coast. They're the perfect haven for big family escapes, sleeping six each. The lodge tents are beautifully made, with a king-sized bed, two single beds and a cabin double, all with thick duvets, spare blankets and hot water bottles. Each has a fully equipped kitchen, private loos and showers and a spacious living area. Tire the little ones out on beach excursions or coastal walks, or explore the enticing 'blanket box' – full of games and other treasures. The on site honesty shop can take care of the basics, you can have meals organised for arrival or those occasional lazy evenings, the games room has plenty to offer in any weather and there are even two boats on the lake for racing round the island! On the edge of Exmoor – with moorland walks aplenty for your dog – a stay at Longlands is packed full of every kind of adventure. *Bookings begin on Monday or Friday; Friday only in peak season. Book through Sawday's Canopy & Stars online or by phone.*

Rooms	5 safari tents for 6 (2 doubles, 2 bunks): from £117 per night. Dogs £25 per dog per stay. Max. 2 per lodge. Dog-sitting can be arranged.
Meals	Self-catering.
Closed	December–March.

🚶 🐕   Dog bed, towel and bowls

Sawday's Canopy & Stars
Longlands
Coulsworthy,
Combe Martin EX34 0PD

Tel	+44 (0)117 204 7830
Email	enquiries@canopyandstars.co.uk
Web	www.canopyandstars.co.uk/longlands

Entry 52 Map 2

The Quarry

Skip back from seaside rock pools to your giant Victorian house, built for an Admiral, now a fantastic place for messing around with friends and family. So much space: in the vast living room, find a huge dining table, log fire, bright paintings and cushions, funky lamps, 42-inch Sky TV, a trunk of games. The yellow-walled kitchen has colourful Victorian tiles and is kitted out to cook up a feast: two-oven Aga, separate cooker, heaps of pots and pans. On sunny days, spill out to the terrace, from which you can spy the sea. Seven simple, uncluttered bedrooms are scattered about the two upper floors, two with their own showers, others sharing big bathrooms with deep baths and sparkling showers. With mostly wooden or Victorian-tiled floors, no precious ornaments, a safe, fenced terrace and large natural garden (with Wendy house) you can let kids loose. Escape to the 'vine room' conservatory (dripping with grapes and nectarines in season) or a secluded garden halfway up the drive. The South West Coast Path runs right past; Ilfracombe is on your doorstep; Woolacombe beach is a ten-minute drive; the moors just a little further. *Coastal path, fields, beaches in Woolacombe.*

Rooms	1 house for 13 (2 doubles en suite, 3 doubles, 1 twin, 1 single, 2 single sofabeds; 2 bath/shower rooms): £1,600–£3,500. 3-night weekends from £1,200. Max. 3 dogs. Prefer dogs to stay downstairs.
Meals	Self-catering.
Closed	Never.
	Dog walk guide

Kirstie Jackson
The Quarry
Torrs Park,
Ilfracombe EX34 8AZ

Mobile	+44 (0)7979 306079
Email	info@bighousedevon.co.uk
Web	www.bighousedevon.co.uk

Entry 53 Map 2

Little Comfort Farm Cottages

Deep in Devon hills and way way down a grass-tufted lane is a slice of green heaven. The usual dose of urban din is replaced by the sound of a gurgling stream and odd squeak of very happy children. Five sturdy stone cottages blend into the landscape and have been gently updated over the years. You're made very welcome on Jackie and Roger's working organic farm; their passion makes this place. Slip off walking boots at your door and escape into a homely haven – an easy mix of lived-in sofas, wooden furniture, log-burner, TV and DVD for lazy nights in. Bathrooms are simple, bedrooms cosy with flowery curtains and country views. The local shop will stock your fridge and freezer, and you can buy the farm's organic sausages, bacon, lamb, beef, eggs and apple juice (Jackie also makes delicious homemade meals). This place is a gift for young families: morning trailer rides, lamb feeding and a barn filled with toys and crafty stuff. A blissful retreat for couples too, outside of the busiest times. Walk miles, fish in the lake, switch off... Remote, yet close enough to Barnstaple and the endless sands of Saunton, Putsborough and Woolacombe. *All cottages have enclosed gardens.*

Rooms	2 cottages for 4; 1 cottage for 5; 1 cottage for 6: £320–£1,153. 1 house for 10: £481–£1,604. Short breaks £240–£354. Dogs £25 per dog per week, £15 per dog per short break.
Meals	Self-catering.
Closed	Never.

Lots of advice on dog-friendly walks, beaches and places to eat out. Towels can be provided for drying soggy dogs & plenty of doggie accessories – just ask!

Roger & Jackie Milsom
Little Comfort Farm Cottages
Braunton EX33 2NJ
Tel   +44 (0)1271 812414
Email   info@littlecomfortfarm.co.uk
Web   www.littlecomfortfarm.co.uk

Entry 54 Map 2

Heasley House

A beautiful house in a sleepy village lost in an Exmoor valley – the sort of place you return to again and again. It's a lovely spot, blissfully lost to the world. A river runs below, tree-clad hills rise above. As for this 1760 dower house, it stands in the middle of the village with a sun-trapping terrace at the front and big views from the garden behind. Inside, old and new mix stylishly. You find stripped boards, stone walls, timber frames, a rather lovely bar. Warm colours run throughout, fires burn in the sitting rooms, you get original art and fresh flowers everywhere. Airy bedrooms are more than comfy with big beds, good linen and lovely bathrooms. Those at the front have the view, those in the eaves have beams. All have flat-screen TVs, fluffy bathrobes and armchairs. Spin down to the restaurant for a feast of local produce, perhaps Brixham scallops with pea purée, pork stuffed with apricots, walnut and praline parfait with maple syrup. Paths lead out, so follow the river into the woods or head north for cliffs at the coast. House parties are very welcome, as are dogs. Brilliant. *Saunton Sands 30-minute drive; lots of walks right outside the door.*

Rooms	6 twin/doubles: £150.
	1 suite for 2: £170.
	Singles from £110.
	Dinner, B&B from £100 p.p.
	6 dog-friendly bedrooms.
Meals	Dinner £26–£32.
Closed	Christmas, New Year & February.

   Towels, blankets, bowls, leads and dog treats

Paul & Jan Gambrill
Heasley House
Heasley Mill,
South Molton EX36 3LE

Tel	+44 (0)1598 740213
Email	enquiries@heasley-house.co.uk
Web	www.heasley-house.co.uk

Entry 55 Map 2

Barn Cottage

A vast landscape surrounds this traditional Devon barn with resplendent hill views that stretch to Dartmoor and Exmoor. Tracy and her husband live in the attached farmhouse and are fast filling their nine acres with a prolific allotment. Their passion for everything local shines through. Tracy taught at Leith's School of Food & Wine so knows her onions and can tantalise your taste buds with a home-grown meal popped in your fridge: enjoy it round the big table in a pretty farmhouse-style kitchen complete with Aga. Try out the new games room with table tennis, table football and darts. Retreat to your lounge with big squashy sofa, contemporary country décor, low beams, and wood-burner. Sweet cottage bedrooms are effortlessly coordinated with vintage florals and patchwork – and there's a good peppering of antique furniture throughout. Hop on the Tarka Railway line; explore the Tarka Trail; picnic at Westward Ho!; or plunder the farmers' market and set up camp in the pretty wee garden with a view. Heaven for foodie-loving walkers and doggie families. *Short breaks available (minimum stay three nights). Enclosed private garden.*

Rooms	1 cottage for 6 (2 doubles, 1 twin; 1 bathroom, 1 shower room): £530–£980. Dogs £5 per dog per night. Max. 2.
Meals	Self-catering.
Closed	Rarely.

Dog treats, poop bags and lots of information on local dog walks, dog-friendly pubs and the best beaches all year round

Tracy Ford
Barn Cottage
Week Parks, High Bickington,
Umberleigh EX37 9BN
Tel +44 (0)1769 560888
Email barncottage@weekparks.com
Web www.weekparks.co.uk

Entry 56 Map 2

The Woodland Retreat

From the cream tea on arrival to the moment you leave, you'll find The Woodland Retreat fits its name perfectly. The shack itself is one of our wilder retreats, small and rustic, but with a big double bed and bunks occupying each wall. The wood-burner in the middle does its best to keep out the chill, but you'd be well advised to take a chunky jumper if you're going in autumn. The kitchen and shower are outdoor but covered, meaning that the terrace acts as a lounge and dining room, with big sofas and wicker recliners as well as a table and chairs for more organised meals. The bell tent is a sort of lounge and extra day space, perfect for taking yourself off to read or nap. There's also the recording studio. Owners Lydia and Alex have a long history in the arts, and their label Candyland Studios is run from the on site recording suite which you can hire. If you don't feel like making music, then head out to the coast at nearby Bude and pick up some surfing tips or rack up some miles hiking the stunning scenery all around. *Bookings begin on Monday or Friday. Book through Sawday's Canopy & Stars online or by phone.*

Rooms	Cabin for 4 (1 double, 2 bunks):
	from £80 per night.
	Max. 4 dogs. Pond is out of bounds.
Meals	Self-catering.
Closed	October-May.
	Biscuits and blanket

Sawday's Canopy & Stars
The Woodland Retreat
Stapleton Farm, Langtree,
Torrington EX38 8NP
Tel   +44 (0)117 204 7830
Email   enquiries@canopyandstars.co.uk
Web   www.canopyandstars.co.uk/woodlandretreat

Entry 57 Map 2

Horry Mill

Pied fly-catchers, a babbling brook, 20 acres of natural woodland, wild flowers, ducks, hens, Aberdeen Angus cattle lowing, birds singing... and no mobile signal. This was once a miller's cottage, destroyed by fire in the 18th century, then rebuilt using the old beams and timbers. Sonia has accentuated the original features (the big fireplace in the beamed sitting room with its plentiful supply of logs, the wide oak stairs, the gleaming floor boards upstairs) and added solid cottage furniture, games, books, a flat-screen TV. In one bedroom is an old iron bedstead with crisp white linen, nice china and a pretty window seat that overlooks the cottage garden. The welcoming owners in the Millhouse nearby are on hand should you need anything. There are walks in all directions, for as long as you feel able. Peaceful and untouched, it's the perfect place for stargazing. And you'll like Simon's *pièce de résistance*: a beautiful wooden thatched summer house a step from your door. *Woodland walks from the door.*

Rooms	1 cottage for 4 (1 double, 1 twin; 1 bath/shower room): £330–£600. Max. 1 dog. In living areas only, not in bedrooms.
Meals	Self-catering.
Closed	Rarely.

Twenty acres of woodland for wonderful walks

Simon & Sonia Hodgson
Horry Mill
Hollocombe,
Chulmleigh EX18 7QH
Tel   +44 (0)1769 520266
Email   horrymill@aol.com
Web   www.horrymill.com

Entry 58 Map 2

The Lamb Inn

This 16th-century inn is nothing short of perfect, a proper local in the old tradition with gorgeous rooms and the odd touch of quirkiness to add authenticity to earthy bones. It stands on a cobbled walkway in a village lost down Devon's tiny lanes, and those lucky enough to chance upon it leave reluctantly. Outside, all manner of greenery covers its stone walls; inside there are beams, but they are not sandblasted, red carpets with a little swirl, sofas in front of an open fire and rough-hewn oak panels painted black. Boarded menus trumpet award-winning food – carrot and orange soup, whole baked trout with almond butter, an irresistible tarte tatin. There's a cobbled terrace, a walled garden, an occasional cinema, an open mic night, and a back bar where four ales are hand-pumped. Upstairs, seven marvellous bedrooms elate. One is large with a bath and a wood-burner in the room, but all are lovely with super-smart power showers, sash windows that give village views, hi-fis, flat-screen TVs, good linen and comfy beds. Dartmoor waits but you may well linger. There's Tiny, the guard dog, too. *Walks within 200 yards, through fields, and village green nearby.*

Rooms	5 doubles; 1 twin/double: £65–£120.
	1 suite for 3: £170–£190.
	Dogs £5 per dog per stay. Max. 2 per
	bedroom. 3 dog-friendly bedrooms.
Meals	Lunch from £9.
	Dinner, 3 courses, £20–£30.
	Sunday lunch from £8.90.
Closed	Rarely.
	Bonio biscuit to keep tails wagging

Mark Hildyard & Katharine Lightfoot
The Lamb Inn
Sandford,
Crediton EX17 4LW

Tel	+44 (0)1363 773676
Email	thelambinn@gmail.com
Web	www.lambinnsandford.co.uk

Entry 59 Map 2

Self-catering   Devon

Culverhayes

On a hill above the thatched village of Sampford Courtenay is a rectory on a gravel driveway with two cottages at the far end. It's a grand setting, the gardens are lovely and you are off the tourist trail; four miles from Dartmoor, a half hour from Exeter. Each cottage has its own outdoor area – a terrace with oak tables and chairs, a lawn with sunloungers. 'Hopetown Cottage' was once the carriage house, 'Spice Cottage' the stables; both are of 18th-century cob and stone. Now they are immaculate inside, with Laura Ashley furniture and well-lit kitchens and not a thing out of place. In airy bedrooms upstairs are pocket sprung beds, down pillows and pretty baskets of toiletries. Once you've explored the North Devon coast or the gardens of Rosemoor, how delightful to return to Culverhayes' own lovely acres, with a large pond and croquet lawns, a greenhouse and a restored kitchen garden – help yourselves to surplus in season. You are welcomed by a Devon cream tea (tuck in by the log fire!) and can book in for supper at the pub, a mere stroll down the hill. *Mid-week breaks available. Ten acres secured with field fences and hedges including two ponds, wooded areas and three paddocks.*

Rooms	1 cottage for 5 (1 double, 1 twin, 1 single; 1 separate wc); 1 cottage for 6 (1 double en suite, 1 double, 2 singles; 1 shower room, 1 bath/shower room): £425–£1,050. Max. 2 dogs.
Meals	Self-catering.
Closed	Never.

 Drying towels, carpet runner for the entrance when wet

Eleanor Channing
Culverhayes
Rectory Hill, Sampford Courtenay EX20 2TG
Tel   +44 (0)1837 89150
Mobile   +44 (0)7816 470068
Email   info@culverhayes.co.uk
Web   www.culverhayes.co.uk

Entry 60 Map 2

Mill End

Another Dartmoor gem, Mill End is flanked by the Two Moors Way, one of the loveliest walks in England. It leads along the river Teign, then up to Castle Drogo – not a bad way to follow your bacon and eggs. As for the hotel, inside is an elegant country retreat with timber frames, nooks and crannies, bowls of fruit, pretty art, vases of flowers on plinths in the sofa'd sitting room and smartly upholstered dining chairs in the airy restaurant. Bedrooms come in country-house style: white linen, big beds, moor views, the odd antique. You might find a chandelier, a large balcony or padded window seats. All come with flat-screen TVs, some have big baths stocked with lotions. Back down in the restaurant, where the mill wheel turns in the window, you find delicious food, perhaps mushroom and tarragon soup, Dartmoor lamb with fondant potato and rosemary jus, chocolate tart. Little ones have their own high tea at 6pm. In the morning there's porridge with cream and brown sugar, as well as the usual extravagance. Dogs are very welcome. *Great walks on the Moors, swimming in the river and woodland walks.*

Rooms	10 doubles; 2 twins: £90–£160.
	2 suites for 2: £120–£210.
	1 family room for 4: £110–£160.
	Singles from £75.
	Dogs £8 per dog per night.
Meals	Lunch from £5.50.
	Sunday lunch from £15.95.
	Dinner £21–£35.
Closed	2 weeks in January.

Bed, towels and bowls

Peter & Sue Davies
Mill End
Chagford,
Dartmoor TQ13 8JN
Tel   +44 (0)1647 432282
Email   info@millendhotel.com
Web   www.millendhotel.com

Entry 61 Map 2

Lewtrenchard Manor

A magnificent Jacobean mansion, a wormhole back to the 16th century. Sue and James have returned to this fine country house, which they established 20 years ago as one of the loveliest hotels in the land. Inside, the full aristocratic monty: a spectacular hall with a cavernous fireplace, a dazzling ballroom with staggering plasterwork. There are priest holes, oak panelling, oils by the score. Best of all is the 1602 gallery with its majestic ceiling and grand piano; *Onward Christian Soldiers* could have been written in the library. Bedrooms are large. Most tend to be warmly traditional (the four-poster belonged to Queen Henrietta Maria, wife of Charles I), but some are contemporary with chic fabrics and fancy bathrooms. All have jugs of iced water, garden flowers and robes. Delicious food waits – perhaps lemon sole, loin of venison, peanut parfait with banana sorbet – and there's a chef's table where you can watch the kitchen at work on a bank of TVs. Outside, a Gertrude Jekyll garden and an avenue of beech trees that make you feel you're in a Hardy novel. *Minimum stay two nights at weekends. Big garden, river and woodland. Dartmoor and coastal paths within one hour.*

Rooms	4 doubles; 6 twin/doubles: £155–£220. 4 suites for 2: £220–£235. Singles from £120. Dinner, B&B from £122.50 p.p. Dogs £15 per stay. Can be left alone in bedroom if in a cage; dining room off limits.
Meals	Lunch: bar meals from £5.25; restaurant from £19.50. Dinner, 3 courses, £49.50. Children over 7 welcome in restaurant.
Closed	Rarely.
	Blankets, towels, biscuits, water bowl

Sue, James, Duncan & Joan Murray
Lewtrenchard Manor
Lewdown,
Okehampton EX20 4PN
Tel   +44 (0)1566 783222
Email   info@lewtrenchard.co.uk
Web   www.lewtrenchard.co.uk

The Elephant's Nest Inn

Visitors look happy as they enter the main bar, all dark beams, flagstone floors and crackling fires... you almost imagine a distant Baskerville hound baying. This is an atmospheric inn that serves delicious home-cooked food – local, seasonal and British with a twist. Tuck into antipasto of pastrami, rosette saucisson and Black Forest ham; South Devon sirloin with mushrooms, vine tomatoes and French fries; and Mrs Cook's fabulous lemon posset with blueberry compote. When suitably sated, slip off to the annexe and a nest of your own in one of three peaceful, very comfortable rooms, with gleaming oak floors heated underfoot; one room has its own private patio. Wake to a pretty garden with views to Brentor church and the moor, an exceptional breakfast and perhaps a cricket match to watch: the pub has its own ground and club. Settle back to the thwack of willow on leather with a pint of Palmer's IPA. There's Doom Bar too, Jail Ale from Princetown, and guest ales from Otter, Cotleigh, Teignworthy, Butcombe. What's more, the pub is a dog-friendly zone – check out their website for photos of the residents. *Right on the moors, large garden and 23 acres to roam.*

Rooms	3 twin/doubles: £88.
	Dogs £5 per dog per night.
Meals	Lunch & dinner £8.95–£19.95.
Closed	Never.

Pigs' ears & assorted treats

Hugh & Denise Cook
The Elephant's Nest Inn
Horndon, Mary Tavy,
Tavistock PL19 9NQ
Tel +44 (0)1822 810273
Email info@elephantsnest.co.uk
Web www.elephantsnest.co.uk

Entry 63 Map 2

Prince Hall Hotel

A small country house lost to the world on beautiful Dartmoor. You spin down an avenue of beech trees, note the majestic view, then decant into this warm and friendly bolthole. It's one of those places that brilliantly blends informality with good service: lovely staff look after you during your stay. Potter about and find a sitting room bar where you can sink into sofas in front of a wood-burner; binoculars in the drawing room where long views are framed by shuttered windows; then a smart white restaurant where you gather for delicious local food, perhaps pea soup with poached asparagus, rack of Dartmoor lamb, vanilla panna cotta with rhubarb soup. Bedrooms are all different, but it's worth splashing out on the big ones at the back which have the view. They're altogether grander and come with smart beds, warm colours, excellent bathrooms, perhaps a sofa, too. Those at the side are simpler, but earthy walkers will find much rest here. Outside, lawns run down to fields, the river passes beyond, then moor and sky. *Minimum stay two nights at weekends. From the hotel miles and miles of river walking, woodland and wild areas.*

Rooms	4 doubles; 4 twin/doubles: £135–£190. Singles from £95. Dinner, B&B from £85 p.p. Max. 2 dogs (may be a charge if more). Only allowed to be left alone in rooms at supper time.
Meals	Lunch from £5.95. Dinner £33.95–£39.95.
Closed	Never.

 A Bonio in your room, dog biscuits at reception; towels, hose, spare leads – and emergency dog food & water bowls just in case

Fi & Chris Daly
Prince Hall Hotel
Two Bridges, Princetown,
Yelverton PL20 6SA
Tel   +44 (0)1822 890403
Email   info@princehall.co.uk
Web   www.princehall.co.uk

Entry 64 Map 2

South Hooe Count House

It's lovely here, so peaceful in your own private cottage perched above the Tamar; the views over the river are glorious and steep steps lead to the shore and a little jetty – borrow a canoe and paddle up stream. Rowers, geese and herons glide by on misty mornings; the woodland garden is full of spring bulbs, vegetables you can pick, free-range hens, chatting guinea fowl and Arabella and Willow the new donkeys. Settle on the cushioned window seat in the pretty sitting room with toasty wood-burner, books, art and family photos; copper urns and pewter jugs on a deep slate sill brim with flowers. The cosy kitchen has a lived-in, charming feel with old pine, pretty china, coffee grinder, Belfast sink and cosy Rayburn. Sip coffee on the sheltered terrace that catches the morning sun. The light-filled bedroom has a comfortable bed, thick curtains and that view to wake to; the double ended roll top bath is a treat. Delightful Trish can give you routes for good walks, lend you a map and suggest places to visit, boat trips to take. Nearby Tavistock has independent shops, galleries and a lively Saturday market. Live by the tide and emerge refreshed. *Babes in arms welcome. Direct access onto a network of footpaths. Short drive to Dartmoor and an expanse of wonderful walking.*

Rooms	1 house for 3 (1 double, 1 single in attic – access via ladder; 1 bath/shower room): £495-£595.
	Short breaks of 3+ nights.
	Dogs free for 1; 2nd dog £15 per week.
Meals	Self-catering.
Closed	Rarely.
	Down path to river – swimming from jetty for you and your dog. Hose for washing off (for both of you!). Basket, water and food bowls

Trish Dugmore
South Hooe Count House
South Hooe Mine,
Hole's Hole, Bere Alston,
Yelverton PL20 7BW
Tel   +44 (0)1822 840329
Email   trishdugmore@googlemail.com

Entry 65 Map 2

The Henley Hotel

A small hotel above the sea with fabulous views, super bedrooms and some of the loveliest food in Devon. Despite such credentials it's Martyn and Petra who shine most brightly, and their kind, generous approach makes this a memorable place to stay. Warm Edwardian interiors come with stripped wood floors, seagrass matting, Lloyd Loom wicker chairs, the odd potted palm. Below, the Avon estuary slips gracefully out to sea: at high tide surfers ride the waves; at low tide you can walk on the sands. There's a pretty garden with a path tumbling down to the beach, binoculars in each room, a wood-burner in the snug and good books everywhere. Bedrooms are a steal (one is huge). Expect warm yellows, crisp linen, tongue-and-groove panelling and robes in super little bathrooms. As for Martyn's table d'hôte dinners, expect something special. Fish comes daily from Kingsbridge market, you might have warm crab and parmesan tart, roast monkfish with a lobster sauce, then hot chocolate soufflé with fresh raspberries. Gorgeous Devon is all around. Don't miss it. *Minimum stay two nights at weekends. Coastal walks from the garden.*

Rooms	2 doubles; 3 twin/doubles: £120–£145. Singles from £85. Dinner, B&B £85–£95 p.p. (min 2 nights).
Meals	Dinner £36.
Closed	November–March.

Your hosts love dogs, beaches are right outside & lovely countryside is all around

Martyn Scarterfield & Petra Lampe
The Henley Hotel
Folly Hill, Bigbury-on-Sea,
Kingsbridge TQ7 4AR

Tel	+44 (0)1548 810240
Email	thehenleyhotel@btconnect.com
Web	www.thehenleyhotel.co.uk

Entry 66 Map 2

Jackson's Cabin

A rustic, quirky cabin in the orchard garden – everything here is handmade or handed down. Nick and Dolly's favourite books and eclectic items collected on their travels dot the wood-panelled interior of this cosy cabin. The living space, sleeping two in the double and the children in bunks, gives neatly into an open-plan kitchen and dining area, and outside is a secure garden all your own, screened from the main house by a weeping willow. Jackson's Cabin isn't the only gem on the acre of land that makes up The Brake: there's a cob oven in which Nick and Dolly bake their own sourdough bread, a wood-fired sauna, Nick's carpentry workshop (where the cabin's furniture has its origins) and Dolly's art studio. The resident pets are friendly, and yours will feel right at home. Hop in the car and explore further afield: potter round bohemian Totnes, or head for the coast close by – the river Dart and the Kingsbridge Estuary are idyllic spots for spending some time on the water. A year-round dog-friendly beach is a ten-minute drive away. *Minimum stay two nights, three in peak season. Book through Sawday's Canopy & Stars online or by phone.*

Rooms	Cabin for 4 (1 double, 2 children's bunks): from £80 per night. Dogs £15 per stay. Max. 1. Dogs can be left in the cabin as long as they don't chew anything!
Meals	Self-catering.
Closed	Rarely.

Advice on walks

Sawday's Canopy & Stars
Jackson's Cabin
The Brake, Blackawton,
Totnes TQ9 7DE

Tel	+44 (0)117 204 7830
Email	enquiries@canopyandstars.co.uk
Web	www.canopyandstars.co.uk/jacksonscabin

Entry 67 Map 2

Fingals

People love the individualism of Fingals with the easy-going among us happiest there. Richard runs things in a rare laissez-faire style; Sheila is impossibly kind. Guests wander around as if at home, children and dogs potter about. Dinner (local and mostly organic) is served a couple of times a week in one of the panelled dining rooms and you can choose to eat with fellow guests. You may find yourself next to an earl, a comedian or an ambulance driver, all drawn by the charm of this place. Breakfast is served until 11am – a nice touch if you've stayed up late making friends in the honesty bar. The setting is a handsome Queen Anne farmhouse next to a stream with a small indoor pool, sauna and grass tennis court. With books and art everywhere, the rooms are full of personality in a mix of styles. Generous, engaging, occasionally chaotic... If you want to stay longer and look after yourselves, there are three lovely self-catering boltholes in the garden; the eco suite with its sunken bath overlooking the stream is impeccable. Don't miss Greenway by the Dart – Agatha Christie's atmospheric home. *Min. stay two nights at weekends. On the SouthWest Coast Path.*

Rooms	8 doubles; 2 twins: £75-£220. 1 suite for 2: £300-£700. 1 barn for 5; 1 barn for 6: £400-£1,200. Extra bed/sofabed available £15 per person per night. Dogs £5 per dog per night. Max. 2 per bedroom.
Meals	Dinner £36.
Closed	Mid-January to mid-March.
	Miles and miles of coastal walks

Richard & Sheila Johnston
Fingals
Dittisham,
Dartmouth TQ6 0JA

Tel	+44 (0)1803 722398
Email	info@fingals.co.uk
Web	www.fingals.co.uk

Entry 68 Map 2

Combe House Devon

Combe is matchless, an ancient house on a huge estate, the full aristocratic monty. You spin up a long drive, pass the odd Arabian horse dawdling in the fields, then skip through the front door and enter a place of architectural wonder. A fire smoulders in the vast panelled hall, the muralled dining room gives huge country views, the sitting room bar in racing green opens onto the croquet lawn. Best of all is the way things are done: the feel is more home than hotel with a battalion of lovely staff on hand to attend to your every whim. Wander around and find medieval flagstones, William Morris wallpaper, Victorian kitchen gardens that provide much for the table; expect home-buzzed honey and fresh eggs from a roving band of exotic chickens. Rooms are stately with wonderful beds, stunning bathrooms and outstanding views, while the vast suite, once the laundry press, is the stuff of fashion shoots. There are 3,500 acres to explore, then ambrosial food waiting on your return, but it's Ruth and Ken who win the prize; they just know how to do it. Dogs are very welcome. *Min. stay two nights at weekends. So many miles of wonderful walking here, a dog-walking guide has been produced — written by Toby the dog!*

Rooms	10 twin/doubles; 1 4-poster: £215–£375. 4 suites for 2; 1 cottage for 2: £425–£450. 1 house for 8: £720–£780. Dogs £12 per dog per night. Max. 2 per bedroom. Dogs welcome in 4 rooms in main house, Combe Cottage and Combe Thatched House.
Meals	Lunch from £29. Cream tea from £10. Dinner £54. Sunday lunch £39.
Closed	Rarely.
	Welcome biscuit for all dogs, poop bins, bowls, and dog survival kit (anything and everything for a dog on holiday!)

Ruth & Ken Hunt
Combe House Devon
Gittisham,
Honiton EX14 3AD

Tel	+44 (0)1404 540400
Email	stay@combehousedevon.com
Web	www.combehousedevon.com

Entry 69 Map 2

Masons Arms

Lose yourself in tiny lanes, follow them down towards the sea, pass the Norman church, roll up at the Masons Arms. It stands in a village half a mile back from the pebble beach surrounded by glorious country, with a stone terrace at the front from which to gaze upon lush hills. It dates back to 1350 – a cider house turned country pub – and the men who cut the stone for Exeter Cathedral drank here, hence the name. Inside, simple, authentic interiors are just the thing: timber frames, low beamed ceilings, pine cladding, whitewashed walls and a roaring fire over which the spit roast is cooked on Sundays. Some bedrooms are above the inn, others are behind on the hill. Those in the pub are small but cosy (warm yellows, check fabrics, leather bedheads, super bathrooms); those behind are bigger, quieter and more traditional; they overlook a garden and share a private terrace with valley views that tumble down to the sea. Footpaths lead out – over hills, along the coast – so follow your nose, then return for super food: seared scallops, lamb cutlets, saffron and honey crème brûlée. *Minumum stay two nights at weekends in summer. Wonderful walks along the Jurassic coast.*

Rooms	8 doubles; 6 twin/doubles; 6 four-posters: £80-£180. 1 family room for 4: £165-£195. Dogs £10 per dog per night. Max. 3 per bedroom.
Meals	Lunch from £7.50. Bar meals from £9.95. Dinner, 3 courses, £20-£25. Sunday lunch from £9.95.
Closed	Never.
	Bowls, baskets and poop bags

Helen Mashiter
Masons Arms
Branscombe,
Seaton EX12 3DJ

Tel	+44 (0)1297 680300
Email	masonsarms@staustellbrewery.co.uk
Web	www.masonsarms.co.uk

The Cary Arms at Babbacombe Bay

The Cary Arms hovers above Babbacombe Bay with huge views of water and sky that shoot off to Dorset's Jurassic coast. It's a cool little place – half seaside pub, half dreamy hotel – and it makes the most of its position: five beautiful terraces drop downhill towards a small jetty where locals fish. The hotel has six moorings in the bay, you can charter a boat and explore the coast. Back on dry land the bar comes with stone walls, wooden floors, rustic-chic tables and a fire that burns every day. In good weather you eat on the terraces, perhaps seared Brixham scallops, roast partridge, elderflower and lime crème brûlée. Dazzling bedrooms come in New England style. All but one open onto a private terrace or balcony (perfect for dogs), you get decanters of sloe gin, flat-screen TVs, fabulous beds, super bathrooms; one has a claw-foot bath that looks out to sea. Back outside, you can snorkel on mackerel reefs or hug the coastline in a kayak. If that sounds too energetic, head to the treatment room (pre-book) or sink into a deckchair on the residents' sun terrace. *Minimum stay two nights at weekends. Hotel overlooks an all year round dog-friendly beach. Right on the coastal path: perfect for long walks around Torbay.*

Rooms	6 doubles; 1 twin/double: £175–£375. 1 family room for 4: £320–£370. 4 cottages for 2-8: £850–£3,000. Dogs £20 per night. Max. usually 2 (sometimes 1 more in cottages). 2 dog-friendly bedrooms and 4 cottages.
Meals	Lunch from £7.95. Dinner £25–£35.
Closed	Never.
	Dog's dinner of meat and rice (£5); dog bed and bowl with treats as a welcome to the room

Felicia Crosby
The Cary Arms at Babbacombe Bay
Beach Road,
Babbacombe, Torquay TQ1 3LX

Tel	+44 (0)1803 327110
Email	enquiries@caryarms.co.uk
Web	www.caryarms.co.uk

Entry 71 Map 2

Devon

Campbells

Above the hurly-burly of Dartmouth is a reassuringly traditional B&B. Captain Campbell is charming, looks after you beautifully and is dedicated to your getting the most out of your stay. The entrance at the rear doesn't prepare you for the lovely estuary scene that spreads out on the southerly, terraced side. Inside: thick carpets, good family furniture, silverware in glass-fronted cabinets and two bedrooms with watery views. Breakfast is bolstering – full English, with good Devon ingredients. You are just across the way from the Naval College, and five minutes' walk from shops, boats, restaurants and cafés. *Plenty of space for free running in the enclosed garden, or in the public orchard just 170 yards away.*

Devon

Glebe House

Set on a hillside with fabulous views over the Coly valley, this late-Georgian vicarage is now a heart-warming B&B. The views will entice you, the hosts will delight you and the house is filled with interesting things. Chuck and Emma spent many years at sea – he a Master Mariner, she a chef – and have filled these big light rooms with cushions, kilims and treasured family pieces. There's a sitting room for guests, a lovely conservatory with vintage vine, peaceful bedrooms with blissful views and bathrooms that sparkle. All this, two sweet pygmy goats, wildlife beyond the ha-ha and the fabulous coast a hike away. *Min. two nights July/August weekends & bank holidays. A poodle parlour nearby. Fifteen acres around house where dogs can run free; walks on beach in winter.*

Rooms	2 doubles: £80–£100.
Meals	Pubs/restaurants 0.5 miles.
Closed	October–March.

 A plethora of good country walks (and dog-friendly pubs); hose and indoor drying-off space with towels galore. Multi-coloured bribery biscuits; evening pooch-sitting too!

Colin Campbell
Campbells
5 Mount Boone,
Dartmouth TQ6 9PB
Tel   +44 (0)1803 833438

Rooms	1 double; 1 twin/double: £80.
	1 family room for 4: £80–£110.
	Singles £50.
Meals	Dinner, 3 courses, £25.
	Pubs/restaurants 2.5 miles.
Closed	Christmas & New Year.

 Dog biscuits, and afternoon tea for guests comes with a Bonio for the dogs

Emma & Chuck Guest
Glebe House
Southleigh, Colyton EX24 6SD
Tel   +44 (0)1404 871276
Mobile   +44 (0)7867 568569
Email   emma_guest@talktalk.net
Web   www.guestsatglebe.com

Captain's Club Hotel and Spa

A sparkling hotel on the banks on the Stour, where a tiny ferry potters along the river dodging swans and ducks. The hotel has its own launch and those who want to skim across to the Isle of Wight can do so in style. Back on dry land, locals love the big bar which hums with happy chatter, and they sink into sofas, sip cocktails or dig into a crab sandwich. There's live music on Sunday nights, newspapers at reception and doors that open onto a pretty terrace, perfect in good weather. Bedrooms all have river views and come in an uncluttered contemporary style, with low-slung beds, crisp white linen, neutral colours and excellent bathrooms. None are small, some are huge with separate sitting rooms, while apartments have more than one bedroom, thus perfect for families and friends. Residents have free access to the spa (hydrotherapy pool, sauna, four treatment rooms). Dinner is in an ultra-airy restaurant, where you dig into tasty brasserie-style food, perhaps goats' cheese soufflé, Gressingham duck, pear mousse with Kir royale sorbet. Christchurch is a short walk upstream. *Minimum stay two nights at weekends. River walk, local sandy beaches five-minute drive, New Forest 20 minutes.*

Rooms	17 doubles: £199–£259.
	12 apartments for 2-6: £289–£649.
	Max. 3 dogs.
	Dogs welcome in 3 bedrooms.
Meals	Bar meals all day from £6.
	Lunch from £15. Dinner £30–£35.
Closed	Never.

 Dog bed and bowls

Timothy Lloyd & Robert Wilson
Captain's Club Hotel and Spa
Wick Ferry, Wick Lane,
Christchurch, BH23 1HU
Tel   +44 (0)1202 475111
Email   reservations@captainsclubhotel.com
Web   www.captainsclubhotel.com

Entry 74 Map 3

Bishops Cottage

A homespun restaurant with rooms on the side of a hill above Lulworth Cove. The house was once home to the Bishop of Salisbury, Wordsworth's grandson. Outside: a swimming pool in the garden where you can soak up the sun while watching walkers pour off the hill. Inside: smart interiors have low beamed ceilings, painted wood floors, Farrow & Ball colours and a couple of sofas in front of the fire. Philip, larger than life, studied art at Goldsmiths and his work appears on a wall or two; he also made the bar from a hatch recovered from a military vessel sunk by a U-boat. Three lovely bedrooms wait upstairs: one has the view, the others have sofas in sitting rooms, then big comfy beds and lovely bathrooms. You get toppers, bathrobes, duck down duvets – Liesl's determination to pamper you rotten is unstinting. Outside, the coastal path weaves past one sandy cove after another, a rollercoaster ride through this magnificent World Heritage landscape. Come back for lovely food, perhaps seared scallops, wild sea bass, chocolate tart with vanilla ice cream. *Minimum stay two nights at weekends. Jurassic coast to explore.*

Rooms	2 doubles; 1 twin/double: £120–£150. Singles from £110. Small dogs free (charges made if extra cleaning is required). Max. 2 per stay. Allowed in bedroom alone for short times only. Dogs welcome in Bar Room Suite and Boat House room.
Meals	Lunch from £6.50. Dinner, 3 courses, £25–£30.
Closed	1 November to mid-March.
	Dog bowls

Liesl & Philip Ashby Rudd
Bishops Cottage
West Lulworth,
Wareham BH20 5RQ
Tel   +44 (0)1929 400552
Email   bishopscottagelulworth@gmail.com
Web   www.bishopscottage.co.uk

Entry 75 Map 3

2 Old Down Cottages

Wend your way through woodland and hit big skies and harvested fields. You're in the heart of Thomas Hardy country with Horton Tower on the horizon where scenes from *Far from the Madding Crowd* were filmed. Approach this semi-detached cottage through swathes of anemone and towering purple verbena. Once an 18th-century barn, now a well-decorated and uncluttered space; an open fire steals the show in a cosy sitting room with squidgy sofas and TV. Seat six around a farmhouse table in a smart kitchen groaning with good quality cutlery and pristine white china. Pretty country bedrooms have beams and fabulous views of fields. You're spoilt for spotless and contemporary bathrooms – three in all. Sit long enough on the small terrace out the back or in the pretty front garden and you're sure to spot a deer or an owl. Walk to Cranborne Chase, once King John's hunting ground and one of England's last ancient woodlands. Expect a thoughtful welcome from garden-loving Phillipa who lives in the nearby farmhouse: homemade cake and flowers. A bucolic bolthole within easy reach of Dorset's market towns and beaches. *Secure front garden, woods right next door; loads of good walks in a very rural spot (dogs on leads if livestock around).*

Rooms	1 cottage for 6 (1 double en suite, 1 twin en suite, 1 twin; 1 bath/shower room): £456–£1,221. Short breaks available (min 3 nights). Dogs £25 per stay. Max. 1 (well behaved). Bedrooms out of bounds.
Meals	Self-catering.
Closed	Never.
🐕	Advice on walks, towel for drying and poop scoop. Plenty of space in roomy kitchen & living room

Phillipa Davidson
2 Old Down Cottages
Horton,
Wimborne
Tel   +44 (0)1258 840969
Email   olddown@btinternet.com
Web   www.olddown.co.uk

Entry 76 Map 3

The Inn at Cranborne

Aussie Jane's passion for the great English inn runs deep; she waved goodbye to her jet-setting career to take on the faded Fleur de Lys in the heart of pretty Cranborne. Now the Hall & Woodhouse inn glows. In the cosy bar – all panelled walls, rugs on woodblock or flagstone floors, warm heritage hues – say hello to Mike, Jane's character Jack Russell, then bag the smartly upholstered pew bench by the blazing wood-burner and peruse Edward Cracknell's inviting seasonal menus. In autumn, tuck into a hearty mushroom and bacon soup, then lamb rump with roast root vegetables and rosemary jus, leaving room for sticky toffee and date pudding. Look to the bar menu for sandwiches and pub classics like steak and mushroom pie. Fancy staying the night? Upstairs, rooms have a classy contemporary feel, with cord carpets, fat radiators, painted furniture, and goose down duvets with Welsh blankets on big comfortable beds. Smart tiled bathrooms (the best have roll top baths) with posh Bramley toiletries have village views. Cranborne Chase and the New Forest (for walking and cycling), Salisbury and the Jurassic Coast are close. *Good walks in the heart of Cranborne Chase; 20 minutes from the coast.*

Rooms	8 twin/doubles: £95–£120. Dogs £15 per night.
Meals	Lunch & dinner, 3 courses, £20–£30.
Closed	Rarely.

A 'doggie breakfast': local sausage and bacon cooked to perfection with a splash of milk to wash it down

Jane Gould
The Inn at Cranborne
5 Wimborne Street, Cranborne,
Wimborne BH21 5PP
Tel   +44 (0)1725 551249
Email info@theinnatcranborne.co.uk
Web   www.theinnatcranborne.co.uk

Entry 77 Map 3

The King John Inn

You're on the Dorset/Wiltshire border, lost in blissful country, with paths that lead up into glorious hills. Tumble back down to this super inn. Alex and Gretchen have refurbished every square inch and the place shines. Expect airy interiors, a smart country feel, a sun-trapping terrace and a fire that crackles in winter. Originally a foundry, it opened as a brewery in 1859, and, when beer proved more popular than horseshoes, the inn was born. You'll find three local ales on tap but great wines, too – Alex loves the stuff and has opened his own shop across the courtyard – take home a bottle if you like what you drink. As for the food, it's as local as can be with game straight off the Rushmore estate and meat from over the hill; the sausages are a thing of rare beauty. Country-house bedrooms are the final treat. Some are bigger than others, three are in the Coach House, all come with wonderful fabrics, padded headboards, crisp white linen and super bathrooms (one has a slipper bath). In summer, a terraced lawn gives views over a couple of rooftops onto the woods. A perfect spot. *Miles of walking.*

Rooms	6 doubles; 2 twin/doubles: £120–£170. Dogs £25 per stay. Max. 2. Dogs welcome in Coach House.
Meals	Lunch from £12.95. Bar meals from £8.95. Dinner from £13.95.
Closed	Rarely.
	Tweed bag with dog treats, poop bags and VIP dog beds

Alex & Gretchen Boon
The King John Inn
Tollard Royal,
Salisbury SP5 5PS
Tel   +44 (0)1725 516207
Email   info@kingjohninn.co.uk
Web   www.kingjohninn.co.uk

Entry 78 Map 3

Coach Cottage

Off the village street, up the walkers' track, past a few cottages and there is yours, sweetly 18th-century and fronted by a garden of roses and herbs – just enough space to sit out in summer. Enter an open-plan sitting/dining room bursting with character. Floors are light oak, colours are Farrow & Ball, deep-red cushions and curtains create warmth and a Victorian fireplace holds a trusty wood-burner. There are old cob walls by the staircase and vibrant dried gourds on a ledge; Coach Cottage blends old and new perfectly. A few steps down is the little kitchen, its pine units painted a lovely blue, its racks full of pots and pans. The bathroom is downstairs, too – no space up! – and stocked with luxurious towels. After a day's exploring Studland, Brownsea Island and the fossil-lined coast, wend your way up the narrow stairs to cosy bedrooms behind old latch doors and charming brass beds with bright woollen throws. If the cottage is a treat then so is the village, set in glorious countryside under Hambledon Hill – not too big, not too small, with a cinema in the village hall, several pubs and some great little shops. *Short breaks available. Coach Cottage is on an unmade road leading up to the Iron Age hill fort of Hambledon: fabulous for dogs!*

Rooms	1 cottage for 3 (1 double, 1 single; 1 bath/shower room): £330-£620. Dogs £10 per stay.
Meals	Self-catering.
Closed	Rarely.

Advice on walks, and the river Stour is nearby for a splash

Kate Partridge & Richard Choat
Coach Cottage
Coach Lane,
Child Okeford DT11 8EJ

Mobile	+44 (0)7725 245066
Email	info@coachcottage.co.uk
Web	www.coachcottage.co.uk

Entry 79 Map 3

Laverstock's Herdwick Hut

Laverstock Farm is a family estate where the Herdwick Hut has found a quiet stretch of the Woodland Walk to settle down. You are perfectly positioned for day trips to Lyme Regis and the Jurassic Coast, long hikes up Dorset's highest hills, Lewesden and Pilsdon and days of gentle meandering through the quiet countryside. You'll find an info pack with suggestions of dog-friendly walks and beaches inside the hut. Relax amid cool cream furnishings and a comfy bed, with the kitchen awning outside fitted with gas hobs and a big solid sideboard for prepping and cooking. The gas-powered shower and compost loo are about 100 metres away in a purpose built washroom, just for Herdwick Hut guests, and dogs can bathe in the stream alongside. On arrival at the hut you'll find Laverstock's own apple juice, fresh baked cake and some eggs, if the chickens have been on form. From then on, you can simply relax into gentle Dorset, or head out seeking adventure. *Minimum stay two nights. Book through Sawday's Canopy & Stars online or by phone.*

Rooms	Shepherd's hut for 2 (1 double): from £65 per night. Max. 1 dog.
Meals	Self-catering.
Closed	Rarely.
🐾	Large information pack with maps for walks from the Hut together with towels for drying dogs

Sawday's Canopy & Stars
Laverstock's Herdwick Hut
Laverstock Farm,
Bridport DT6 5PE

Tel	+44 (0)117 204 7830
Email	enquiries@canopyandstars.co.uk
Web	www.canopyandstars.co.uk/laverstockhut

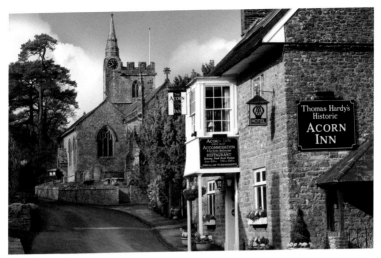

The Acorn Inn

Perfect Evershot and rolling countryside lie at the door of this 400-year-old inn deep in Thomas Hardy country. Hardy called the inn the Sow and Acorn and let Tess rest a night here; had he visited today he might have let her stay longer. Red Carnation Hotels, under the guidance of Alex and chef Jack, are reviving its fortunes. This is very much a traditional inn: as much a place for locals to sup pints of Otter Ale and swap stories by the fire in the flagstoned bar, as for foodies to sample some good food sourced within 25 miles. Walk through to the dining room and the atmosphere changes to rural country house with smartly laid tables, terracotta tiles, soft lighting and elegant fireplaces; food is taken seriously, take scallops with pumpkin and vanilla purée and chorizo dressing and roast pork belly with sherry vinegar jus, or a rare roast beef and horseradish sandwich in the bar. Bedrooms creak with age and style; uneven floors, antiques, bright fabric wall-coverings, beautiful draperies to soften grand four-posters, and smart new bathrooms. Hardy would approve. *Amazing footpaths in all directions, 400-acre deer park in village and dog-friendly beach is a 20-minute drive.*

Rooms	3 doubles; 3 four-posters; 3 twins: £99–£149. 1 suite for 2: £149–£194. Singles £79–£149. Dogs £10 per dog per night. Max. 2 per room.
Meals	Lunch & dinner £4.95–£21.95. Bar meals from £4.95. Sunday lunch, 3 courses, £20.
Closed	Rarely.
	Dog-friendly guide to the village and surrounding area, and all doggie arrivals are given a treat

Jack Mackenzie & Alex Armstrong-Wilson
The Acorn Inn
Evershot,
Dorchester DT2 0JW
Tel   +44 (0)1935 83228
Email   stay@acorn-inn.co.uk
Web   www.acorn-inn.co.uk

Entry 81 Map 2

Old Forge

Snug in a stream-tickled hamlet, deep in Hardy country, this B&B is as pretty as a painting – and wonderfully peaceful. That is, until owner Judy starts to giggle: she is full of smiles and laughter. This is a happy place, a real country home, a no-rules B&B. The one guest double, sharing the former forge with a self-catering pad for two, is neat, warm and cosy with yellow hues, thick carpets and trinkets from travels. The 17th-century farmhouse opposite is where you breakfast: Prue Leith-trained Judy serves a neighbour's eggs and a friend's sausages, in an eclectically furnished room with bucolic views to garden, meadows and hills. *Garden with stream.*

Rooms	1 double: £80–£90.
	Extra person £15.
	Max. 2 dogs.
Meals	Restaurant 1.5 miles.
Closed	Rarely.

 Advice on walks, blankets, doggie towels and Bonio

Judy Thompson
Old Forge
Lower Wraxall Farmhouse, Lower
Wraxall, Dorchester DT2 0HL
Tel   +44 (0)1935 83218
Email   judyjthompson@hotmail.co.uk
Web   www.lowerwraxall.co.uk

Entry 82 Map 2

Dorset   B&B

Munden House

This is a super B&B – a couple of farm cottages and assorted outbuildings beautifully stitched together. It's run with great warmth by Colin and Annie, who buy and sell colourful rugs and have travelled the world to do it. Outside, long views shoot off over open country; inside, airy interiors, pretty bedrooms and lots of colour. The garden studios are bigger and more private; one has a galleried bedroom above a lovely sitting room. Annie cooks fantastic food – local meat, fish from Brixham – and her vegetarian dishes will seduce die-hard carnivores. You eat at smartly dressed tables; breakfast is on the terrace in good weather. *Footpaths, open fields, woodland from front door; coast 30-minute drive.*

Rooms	5 doubles; 1 four-poster;
	1 twin/double: £90–£130.
	Singles from £70.
	Dogs £10 per dog per stay. Max. 2.
	Can stay in cottage unsupervised if
	well behaved.
Meals	Dinner, 3 courses, £27. Pub 0.5 miles.
Closed	Christmas.

 Dog treats – and beds and bowls if needed

Annie & Colin Fletcher
Munden House
Mundens Lane, Alweston, Sherborne
DT9 5HU
Tel   +44 (0)1963 23150
Email   stay@mundenhouse.co.uk
Web   www.mundenhouse.co.uk

Entry 83 Map 2

Tilly on tour: she's a big fan of Canopy and Stars and Alastair Sawday's Special Places to Stay. She loves long autumn walks in the woods!

Lower Fifehead Farm

A passion for cooking here! The dramatic dining room has church pews at an oak refectory table; the log fire will be lit in winter, and you can eat on the terrace in summer. Hearty breakfasts include bacon and sausages from home-reared pigs, devilled mushrooms or eggs Benedict; Jessica makes the bread and preserves, and there's always freshly-squeezed orange juice. It's a gorgeous house too — it's been in Jasper's family for over 20 years and shines with pretty fabrics, antiques, hand-painted furniture, vintage pieces, rich colour — and seriously comfortable brass beds. Don't miss the candlelit dinners. *Minimum stay two nights at weekends. River for playing in runs through the village. Four hundred acres to explore, but mimd the roaming chickens!*

Monty is trying out some new camouflage in The Firs in Bedfordshire. What do you think?

Rooms	2 doubles; 1 twin/double: £75–£95. Singles from £55. Dogs £10 per night. Max. 2.
Meals	Dinner, 2-3 courses, £20–£30. Pubs/restaurants 2 miles.
Closed	Christmas & New Year.

 Pigs' ears, advice on walks, towels and a hose outside the kitchen window for washing muddy paws

Jessica Miller
Lower Fifehead Farm
Fifehead St Quinton, Sturminster
Newton DT10 2AP
Tel   +44 (0)1258 817335
Email   lowerfifeheadfm@gmail.com
Web   www.lowerfifeheadfarm.co.uk

Entry 84 Map 2

The Bell Inn & Hill House

A 600-year-old timber-framed coaching inn, as bustling today with contented locals as it was when pilgrims stopped on their way to Canterbury. Everything here is a delight: hanging lanterns in the courtyard, stripped boards in the bar, superb staff in the restaurant, copious window boxes bursting with colour. This is a proper inn, warmly welcoming, with thick beams, country rugs, panelled walls and open fires. Stop for a pint of cask ale in the lively bar, then potter into the restaurant for top food, perhaps stilton ravioli, grilled Dover sole, orange and passion fruit tart. Christine grew up here, John joined her years ago; both are much respected in the trade, as is Joanne, Master Sommelier and loyal manager of many years. An infectious warmth runs throughout this ever-popular inn. As for the bedrooms, go for the suites above: cosily inviting, individual, quite fancy. In the morning stroll up the tiny high street to breakfast with the papers at elegant Hill House, where further bedrooms, some snazzily refurbished, lie. Then head north into Constable country, or east to the pier at Southend. Wonderful. *Footpath through farmer's field to local village.*

Rooms	9 doubles; 1 twin: £50-£70.
	5 suites for 2: £85.
	Dogs £10 per night. Max. 2.
Meals	Lunch from £11.95.
	Bar meals from £8.95.
	Dinner, à la carte, £27.
	Not bank holidays.
Closed	Christmas Day & Boxing Day.
	Dog bowl; wonderful walking on the doorstep with field & woodland smells

Christine & John Vereker
The Bell Inn & Hill House
High Road, Horndon-on-the-Hill,
Stanford-le-Hope SS17 8LD
Tel   +44 (0)1375 642463
Email   info@bell-inn.co.uk
Web   www.bell-inn.co.uk

Entry 85 Map 4

The Mistley Thorn

This Georgian pub stands on the high street and dates back to 1746, but inside you find a fresh contemporary feel that will tickle your pleasure receptors. The mood is laid-back with a great little bar, an excellent restaurant and bedrooms that pack an understated punch. Downstairs, an open-plan feel sweeps you through high-ceilinged rooms that flood with light. Expect tongue-and-groove panelling, Farrow & Ball colours, blond wood furniture and smart wicker chairs. Climb up to excellent rooms for smartly dressed beds, flat-screen TVs, DVD players and iPod docks; you get power showers above double-ended baths too. Those at the front have fine views of the Stour estuary, all are exceptional value for money. Back down in the restaurant dig into delicious food; Sherri runs a cookery school next door and has a pizzeria in town. Try smoked haddock chowder, Debden duck with clementine sauce, chocolate mocha tart. Constable country is all around. There's history, too; the Witch-Finder General once lived here. Sunday nights are a steal: £100 for two with dinner included. Brilliant. *Near the Essex Way (miles of walking); river opposite.*

Rooms	5 doubles; 3 twin/doubles: £100-£145. Singles from £85. Dinner, B&B, from £72.50 p.p. Dogs £10 per dog per night. Max. 2 medium-sized. 4 dog-friendly bedrooms.
Meals	Lunch from £6.25. Set lunch £12.50-£15. Dinner, 3 courses, about £25.
Closed	Rarely.
🐕	A doggie bag filled with homemade biscuits, towels for muddy paws and a scrumptious sausage for breakfast

David McKay & Sherri Singleton
The Mistley Thorn
High Street, Mistley,
Manningtree CO11 1HE

Tel	+44 (0)1206 392821
Email	info@mistleythorn.co.uk
Web	www.mistleythorn.co.uk

Great Farm

Wend your way along the leafy path through the trees and cross the narrow footbridge over the river — young-at-heart adventurers will find it idyllic. Otter Camp, Nightingale Camp and Barn Owl Camp are close together but secluded; each has its private clearing. Otter and Nightingale are intimate and off-grid, though the swish bathrooms are a step above camping. The river Coln forms a boundary to the front, there's woodland at the rear, and sheep and cattle nearby — keep the dogs on leads! Each spot has its campfire, kitchen with gas hob (some outdoors), flushing loo and shower and many thoughtful touches besides. Leonie leaves the basics, and can provide a hamper of local ingredients for breakfasts and picnics; dinners too can be delivered. You're on a family-run working farm in the rural heart of the Cotswolds, with pretty villages and pubs galore and great walks. Go down river to lovely Lechlade, or the Cotswold Water Park — Leonie will give you a map. If you're lucky, you'll spot an otter... *Minimum stay two nights. Book through Sawday's Canopy & Stars online or by phone.*

Rooms	Shepherd's hut for 2 (1 double); train carriage for 2 (1 double); Gypsy caravan camp for 6 (2 doubles, 2 cubby singles): from £95 per night. Max. 4 dogs. Must be kept on a long lead as sheep and cattle nearby.
Meals	Self-catering.
Closed	Never.

Dog bowls & a mystery treat provided

Sawday's Canopy & Stars
Great Farm
Whelford,
Fairford GL7 4EA

Tel	+44 (0)117 204 7830
Email	enquiries@canopyandstars.co.uk
Web	www.canopyandstars.co.uk/greatfarm

Entry 87 Map 3

The Fleece at Cirencester

Charles II once stayed at this coaching inn – posing as a manservant, the story goes. Now it's had a serious refurb, in classic English style. Bar, lounge and restaurant glow; bedrooms too, spreading across three floors. Open all day, the Fleece has quite a buzz. Drop by for a wake-up coffee and eggs on toast; choose a deli board at lunchtime and a pint of Thwaites. There are daily specials and Sunday roasts; our steak with chips was delicious. As for the staff, they're charming, well-trained and smartly turned out. Set off into the Cotswolds for a hike with the dog, browse the antique shops and the chic little delis, then come back to the Fleece for the night. The 'Character' rooms, with their beamy, up-in-the-roof feeling, are the best, but all are top-notch, with plush carpets and dark boards, beds antique and new, coordinated cushions, feature wallpapers, plump pillows and Crabtree & Evelyn soaps… face the famous market square and watch the world go by, or settle quietly into a room at the back. The Fleece is a crowd-pleaser from start to finish. *Plenty of walks in the Cotswolds.*

Rooms	18 doubles; 4 twin/doubles: £85–£125. 5 suites for 2: £115–£150. 1 family room for 4: £75–£150. Dogs £15 per stay. 2 dog-friendly rooms.
Meals	Lunch from £6.95. Bar meals from £4.95. Dinner from £8.95. Sunday lunch, 2 courses, £11.95.
Closed	Rarely.

Dog beds and treats as well as details of dog-friendly walks. 10% of the overnight charge is donated to Teckels Animal Sanctuaries

Ricardo Canestra
The Fleece at Cirencester
Market Place,
Cirencester GL7 2NZ

Tel	+44 (0)1285 658507
Email	relax@thefleececirencester.co.uk
Web	www.thefleececirencester.co.uk

Entry 88 Map 3

Inn at Fossebridge

Here, on the old Roman road, rusticity and elegance achieve the perfect balance at this gorgeous 17th-century coaching inn run with aplomb by the Jenkins family. Stone archways divide the bar, which is as authentic as they come with flagstone floors, stone walls, open fires, beamed ceilings and a real hubbub at lunchtime. Throw in real ales, roast lunches and a welcome for all and you have somewhere worth going out of your way for. The Georgian style dining room pulls in lovers of good food for local venison haunch steak, celeriac dauphinoise, braised red cabbage and bitter chocolate jus with lavender crème brûlée to finish. The pub garden is one of the largest and most attractive in the Cotswolds with a two-acre lake, mature trees, barbecues in summer, a tyre swing and wooden tractor and train for children. Bedrooms, country-smart, and decorated in Georgian style, range from smallish to spacious, with coordinated fabrics, striped walls, L'Occitane goodies, flat-screen TVs. There's also an elegant residents' sitting room. Walk from the pub up the Coln valley and revel in glorious countryside. *Ask about mid-week offers. Fields, streams, woodland.*

Rooms	8 doubles: £85–£150.
	1 family room for 3: £95–£150.
	Dogs £15 per dog per night. Max. 2.
	5 dog-friendly rooms
Meals	Lunch & dinner £11–£21.50.
	Bar meals £4.50–£9.50.
	Sunday lunch £14.
Closed	Never.

 Dog biscuits and bowls

Robert & Samantha Jenkins
Inn at Fossebridge
Fossebridge,
Cirencester GL54 3JS
Tel   +44 (0)1285 720721
Email   info@fossebridgeinn.co.uk
Web   www.fossebridgeinn.co.uk

Entry 89 Map 3

The Lion Inn

Annie's determination to restore an old inn's charms has been a joyous success. Push open the heavy oak door to reveal a beautiful main bar: rugs on pale-painted floors, candles at mullioned windows, rough stone walls, and a log fire crackling in a 15th-century inglenook. Jugs of fresh flowers, battered leather armchairs and grand gilt-framed paintings enhance the authentic feel. Review the papers over a pint of real ale, play scrabble, cards or one of the selection of games. Order from the seasonal menu: perhaps ham hock and black pudding terrine, monkfish with chorizo piperade, pineapple tarte tatin. In summer, spill onto the peaceful terrace for a platter of seafood. Country-chic rooms upstairs – one with its own small balcony, three with private staircases, one above the noisy snug bar – are toasty-warm and TV-free, with inviting beds and soothing colours, upholstered armchairs and antique furniture. Bathrooms are just as good, with Bramley products and en suite showers. Winchcombe is on the Cotswold Way; Chipping Campden, Broadway and Cheltenham are a short drive. *Courtyard garden with grassed area for dogs to play. Many dog-friendly circular walks starting from the door – on the Cotswold Way.*

Rooms	5 doubles: £90–£140.
	2 suites for 3: £130–£165.
	Dogs £15 per night. Max. 2 per bedroom.
Meals	Lunch & dinner £12–£19.
Closed	Never.

Dog bed, towel for drying off and a cold sausage or two from the kitchen. Free maps on favourite local walks too

Annie Fox–Hamilton
The Lion Inn
North Street, Winchcombe,
Cheltenham GL54 5PS
Tel   +44 (0)1242 603300
Email   reception@thelionwinchcombe.co.uk
Web   www.thelionwinchcombe.co.uk

Entry 90 Map 3

Gloucestershire

Seagrave Arms

A cute little Cotswold inn. The ingredients are simple: lovely Georgian interiors, delicious local food and super rooms with honest prices. Inside, ancient flagstones lead through to the bar; you'll find a roaring fire, local ales, window seats and half-panelled walls. Next door is the charming little restaurant, where you dig into the freshest food. The Seagrave is a founding member of the Sustainable Restaurant Association, and 90% of its meat and vegetables come from local farms. Bedrooms are scattered about, some in the main house, others in the converted stables (dog-friendly). They may differ in size, but all have the same cool style with Farrow & Ball colours, crisp white linen and excellent bathrooms with REN lotions. You'll find a sofa if there's room, perhaps a double-ended bath. Spin back down for some lovely food – in summer you decant onto a gravelled terrace and small lawned garden – perhaps Windrush Valley goats' cheese tart, Madgett's Farm duck with star anise, rhubarb crumble and clotted cream ice cream. The Cotswold Way is close, a good way to atone. *Secure garden, great walks.*

Rooms	8 doubles: £95–£125.
	1 suite for 3: £125–£150.
	Max. 2 dogs. 2 dog-friendly rooms.
Meals	Lunch from £5.95.
	Dinner, 3 courses, about £30.
	Not Monday.
Closed	Never.

 Advice on walks

Kevin & Sue Davies
Seagrave Arms
Friday Street, Weston Subedge,
Chipping Campden GL55 6QH
Tel   +44 (0)1386 840192
Email   info@seagravearms.co.uk
Web   www.seagravearms.co.uk

The Priory Cottages

Down the one-mile lane, left over the cattle grid and onto an unmarked track – keep going! The owners' white farmhouse and the lovely cottages soon pop into view. The position is special and the bird life is extraordinary – so much so that Peter Scott set up Slimbridge on the other side of the water. This well-insulated home is a single-storey outbuilding divided into two wood-clad cottages, and inside has a charming simplicity. Step into a living room with a creamy sofa and armchair, a dining table, a cosy wood-burner and a TV; there are river views, too. To the side is a galley kitchen, brand new and nicely equipped; the white bathroom and separate wet room are simple but appealing. Expect cream bedspreads, white cotton, old pine, fresh paintwork and toasty terracotta floors. To the front are two grassed areas divided by a willow screen and a lovely old orchard; skirt around the Cowans' house and you reach the river beyond. You can walk to the pub in the nearby village for a pint, visit the ancient village of Awre, or cycle in the nearby Forest of Dean. Come for the peace of it all – and the birds. *Dogs can roam in orchards in front of the cottages – if the sheep aren't there! River walks, and Forest of Dean within walking distance.*

Rooms	1 cottage for 2-4 (1 twin/double, sofabed; 1 bathroom); 1 cottage for 4 (1 double, 1 twin/double; both en suite): £260–£523. Mid-week breaks for £500. Dogs £20 per dog per stay. Max. 3 per stay.
Meals	Self-catering.
Closed	Never.
	Advice on walks, outside tap for washing muddy paws

Ian Cowan
The Priory Cottages
Awre,
Newnham GL14 1EQ

Tel	+44 (0)1594 516260
Email	rigc@onetel.com
Web	www.theprestorycottages.co.uk

Entry 92 Map 2

The Ostrich Inn

In the village of Newland the Ostrich is where the beer drinkers go, to sample eight changing ales. Across from All Saints Church, that 'Cathedral of the Forest', you mix with all sorts before a log fire. Huntsmen and trail bikers pile in for massive portions of delicious food, from Newland bread and cheese platter to rack of Welsh lamb with marsala sauce. The nicotine-brown ceiling that looks in danger of imminent collapse is supported by a massive oak pillar in front of the bar where the locals chatter and jazz CDs keep the place swinging. The weekly menu, served throughout the pub, takes a step up in class, and is excellent value. Energetic Kathryn and her team, including Alfie the pub dog, encourage the buzz. To the back is a walled garden – and the loos, 'just by there', beyond the coal sacks. *Dogs can romp in the Forest of Dean and swim in the river Wye then relax in the walled garden.*

Mayfield Studio

A small lane runs past the studio, and oak doors open to a stylish interior. Slate floors are warmed from beneath and the double height ceiling lends an airy feel. A lime-washed staircase leads to a mezzanine bedroom of uncluttered simplicity with views across the valley. Quirky industrial lighting, stone walls, 1930s woodcut prints, and Ercol furniture all marry superbly. There's no garden – although with permission you may use Sara's next door; choose to stay on a B&B or self-catering basis, with breakfasts delivered or left for you as you wish. Walk to Laurie Lee's favourite pub or dine locally, it's all on your doorstep. *Prices during Cheltenham Race Week on request. Self-catering option. Pets allowed downstairs; child or baby welcome, stairs difficult for toddlers. River to jump in, woodland and good walks.*

Meals	Lunch & dinner £12.50–£18.50. Bar meals £5.50–£10.50.	Rooms	1 double (daybed available): £100–£125. Extra bed/sofabed available £40 per person per night. Max. 2 dogs. Downstairs only.
Closed	3pm-6.30pm (6pm Saturday).	Meals	Breakfast arranged on booking. Pubs/restaurants 2-4-minute walk.
		Closed	Rarely.

 A warm welcome for dogs & a sausage for the well-behaved ones

 Advice on walks

Kathryn Horton
The Ostrich Inn
Newland,
Coleford GL16 8NP
Tel +44 (0)1594 833260
Email kathryn@theostrichinn.com
Web www.theostrichinn.com

Entry 93 Map 2

Sara Kirby
Mayfield Studio
Vicarage Street,
Painswick,
Stroud GL6 6XP
Tel +44 (0)1452 814858
Email sara.kirby@mac.com

Entry 94 Map 3

The Guest House

You get your own new timber-framed house with masses of light and space, a terrace, and spectacular valley and woodland views. The living room has wooden floors, lovely old oak furniture and French windows onto the rose-filled garden. Sue brims with enthusiasm and is a flexible host: breakfast can be over in her kitchen or continental in yours. Look forward to the eggs from the hens and delicious dinners with produce from the veg patch. The bedroom is a charming up-in-the-eaves room with oriental rugs, colourful linen and a big comfy bed; your fresh, simple wet room is downstairs. A peaceful, secluded place. *Fenced two-acre garden; excellent and varied walks straight from the door, and to the nearest pub (dog-friendly).*

Rooms	1 double with sitting room & kitchenette: £130-£150; £285-£875 for a 2-7 night break.
Meals	Dinner, 2 courses, from £15; 3 courses, from £20. Pub 1 mile.
Closed	Rarely.

 Walks with resident dogs in the day & friendly dog-sitting at night

Sue Bathurst
The Guest House
Manor Cottage,
Bagendon, Cirencester GL7 7DU
Tel +44 (0)1285 831417
Email heritage.venues@virgin.net
Web www.cotswoldguesthouse.co.uk

Entry 95 Map 3

Calcot Peak House

A treat to stay in such a handsome old house with such relaxed owners — lovely Alex is full of enthusiasm for her B&B enterprise. There's an excellent butcher in Northleach so breakfasts are tip top, and the bedrooms are a sophisticated mix of traditional and contemporary: Farrow & Ball colours, rich florals, fresh flowers, and fluffy white robes for trots to the bathroom. You also have your own charming drawing room: tartan carpet, pink sofas, family oils. Outside: 19 acres for Dexie the dog and a bench on the hill for the view. Tramp the Salt Way, dine in Cirencester, let the owls hoot you to sleep. *Lovely walks, a nine-acre garden, a pond in the garden.*

Rooms	1 double; 1 twin sharing bathroom & drawing room (let to same party only), children's room available: £95. Singles £80. Max. 2 dogs. Very welcome to sleep in utility room (comfortable and warm!) but not in bedrooms.
Meals	Pub 2 miles.
Closed	Rarely.

 Dog biscuits, towels

Tom & Alexandra Pearson
Calcot Peak House
Northleach,
Cheltenham GL54 3QB
Tel +44 (0)1285 721047
Email pearsonalex5@gmail.com

Entry 96 Map 3

The Court

Just off the high street this huge honey-hued Jacobean house has been in the family since it was built in 1624 by Sir Baptist Hicks. Dogs sound the alarm when you knock... step inside to find a relaxed faded splendour. Delicate ornaments sit on exquisite antiques, family portraits and spectacular oils line the walls; up winding stairs, bedrooms (all with TVs) have comfy beds, books, a mix of beautiful and functional furniture and breathtaking views of rooftops or gardens. Jane's friendly housekeeper cooks your Aga breakfast – eggs and jams are from the garden. The walking is superb, Hidcote and Kiftsgate are close. Great value. *Secure large garden; don't scare the free-range flock of hens!*

This is Charlie on his first ever trip to the beach at Wells-next-the-Sea. He was unsure about the sea, but loved the sand dunes!

Rooms	1 double: £70–£80. 1 family room for 3; 1 family room for 4 (separate bath): £60–£100. Singles from £50. Max. 3 dogs.
Meals	Pub/restaurant 30 yds.
Closed	Christmas, Easter, Whitsun bank holiday & half term.

The Court doggie breakfast: a small plate of biscuits; good walks locally – just keep an eye out for sheep!

Jane Glennie
The Court
Calf Lane,
Chipping Campden GL55 6JQ
Tel   +44 (0)1386 840201
Email   j14glennie@aol.com
Web   www.thecourtchippingcampden.co.uk

Entry 97 Map 3

Taffy loves walking in Perthshire countryside and chilling out in one of the many lochs which surround the area.

The Wellington Arms

Lost down a web of lanes, the 'Welly' draws foodies from miles around. Cosy, relaxed and decorated in style – old dining tables, crystal decanters, terracotta floor – the newly extended bar-dining room fills quickly, so make sure you book to sample Jason's inventive modern British cooking. Boards are chalked up daily and the produce mainly home-grown or organic. Kick off with home-grown courgette flowers stuffed with ricotta, parmesan and lemon zest, follow with rack of home-reared lamb with root vegetable mash and crab apple jelly, finish with elderflower jelly, strawberries and raspberry sorbet. Migrate to the huge garden for summer meals and views of the pub's smallholding: bees, four Tamworth pigs, Longwool sheep and 120 rarebreed chickens; the eggs can be bought at the bar. Stay over and cosy up in either the gorgeous New or Old room, housed in the former wine store and pig shed. Expect exposed brick and beams, vast Benchmark beds topped with goose down duvets, fresh flowers, coffee machines, mini-fridges, and slate tiled bathrooms with underfloor heating and walk-in rain showers. Breakfast is a real treat. *Great for walks: public footpaths start straight outside the pub.*

Rooms	2 doubles: £130–£150.
	Dogs £10 per dog per night.
Meals	Set lunch £15.75 & £18.75.
	Dinner £11–£21.
Closed	Rarely.

Lily dog treats, breakfast and dinner treats too! Chews and butcher's bone; real sheepskin rug to flop onto

Jason King & Simon Page
The Wellington Arms
Baughurst Road,
Baughurst RG26 5LP

Tel	+44 (0)118 982 0110
Email	hello@thewellingtonarms.com
Web	www.thewellingtonarms.com

Entry 98 Map 3

Adhurst Wood

The four yurts at Adhurst, in the ancient woodland of the South Downs National Park just an hour and a half from London, are perfect places for getting back to nature and great for larger groups. Owners Guy and Alison are passionate about sustainable living and invite you to set the fire, tramp through the woods and immerse yourself in a slower, more basic, way of life. The site is completely off-grid and the yurts, made from local wood, have been decked out with colourful throws, solar fairy lights and wind-up radios. They share a camp kitchen, a gas-powered hot shower and the compost loo, though one comes with its own wood-fired bath tub. Wood-burners keep the yurts warm, and can be used to make tea, but there is also a storm kettle which can be lit with nothing more than twigs, leaves and a match. Once you've had a cup of tea, you'll be ready to explore the woods (look out for the zip wire), try a bit of horse riding, head over to Cowdray to watch the polo, or admire the beautiful scenery of the South Downs Way. *Bookings begin on Monday or Friday. Book through Sawday's Canopy & Stars online or by phone.*

Rooms	4 yurts for 4 (1 double, 2 child singles): from £95 per night.
Meals	Self-catering.
Closed	November-April.

Endless sticks in the woods and a river to splash through

Sawday's Canopy & Stars
Adhurst Wood
Steep,
Petersfield GU31 5AD
Tel   +44 (0)117 204 7830
Email   enquiries@canopyandstars.co.uk
Web   www.canopyandstars.co.uk/adhurst

Entry 99 Map 3

Wriggly Tin Shepherd's Huts

Wriggly Tin Shepherd's Huts were born out of a family holiday where Alex Evans and his two daughters got out into the countryside and never looked back. Although that defining stay was actually in tipis, Alex's love of all things mechanical has lead him to hand build these lovely off-grid huts in a wooded corner of Hampshire. Butser, a two person hut named after the highest point in the area, is dog-friendly, with enough space under the raised double bed for a dog to sleep in comfort. Showers and loos are shared and housed in, unsurprisingly, an even more cunningly converted shepherd's hut. You're far enough apart to feel on your own, with your personal fire pit, tripod, cast iron griddle and plenty of wood and kindling for some daring experiments in campfire cooking. Wriggly Tin gives you a chance to settle in to the slow lane. Keep a pan of water on the wood-burner for tea and stroll through the surrounding bluebell woods; for more dog-friendly paths head half an hour to the coast or walk along the nearby river Meon. *Bookings begin on Monday, Wednesday or Friday. Book through Sawday's Canopy & Stars online or by phone.*

Rooms	2 shepherd's huts for 2 (1 double); 1 shepherd's hut for 3 (1 double, 1 single): from £75 per night. £15 per extra guest per night. Max. 2 dogs.
Meals	Self-catering.
Closed	November-March.

Packet of sausages in brown paper for the dog

Sawday's Canopy & Stars
Wriggly Tin Shepherd's Huts
Brook Lane,
Hambledon PO7 4TF

Tel   +44 (0)117 204 7830
Email   enquiries@canopyandstars.co.uk
Web   www.canopyandstars.co.uk/wrigglytin

Entry 100 Map 3

Waterfall Cottage

The 1840 cottage is set in gardens planted by a Chelsea gold-medallist; embraced by stream, waterfall and trees, its lawns lead directly to New Forest heathland and forest dotted with ponies and deer... it is quintessentially English, a magical place. John used to paddle in the stream as a boy – his aunt (the gardener) used to live here; now there's a lovely new summer house too, perfect for curling up in with a good book. Inside, the cottage is light and sunny and full of family antiques and some of Naomi's paintings and John's photographs. Restored parquet floors, velvet drapes, fresh flowers, Aga and working coal and log fire create cottage cosiness. Off a big landing are three eiderdowned bedrooms: the master with its own dressing room and tiny, wisteria-clad balcony, the second double with hugely wide floorboards and goatskin rugs, the little single with sloped ceiling and Victorian bed. Pubs, shops, bike-hire and horse-drawn carriages are a mile off; walks are on the spot. And everywhere, the song of birds and stream: it's like stumbling upon a hidden corner of England. *Big garden and field beyond, securely fenced. Stream, open heathland, direct access to the New Forest. All year dog-friendly beaches 20 mins. Dog-friendly pubs nearby.*

Rooms	1 cottage for 6 (2 doubles, 1 single, 1 single on landing, sofabed; 1 bath/shower room. Cot): £500–£1,350.
Meals	Self-catering.
Closed	Never.

 Bow-wow heaven in the woods! Maps & advice on walks. Enclosed porches, dust sheets, dog cage, Aga in kitchen for sleeping against & dog gates between rooms

Naomi King
Waterfall Cottage
Burley,
New Forest BH24 4HR

Tel	+44 (0)1722 334337
Email	naomi4law@btinternet.com
Web	www.newforestcottage.biz

Entry 101 Map 3

October House

Horses graze under ancient oaks and ash, and the loudest thing in this former garden nursery is the year-round parade of colourful shrubs. Take in the peace over home-laid eggs hot from the Aga in Alison's family kitchen, where she and Richard share tips on New Forest trails and Solent sailing. Your little nest stands in its own private garden, with south-facing windows sprinkling sunlight on buttercup walls, and a cerise duvet warming a large pine bed. You can pick from well-stocked bookshelves and snuggle into the sofa, take dogs, horses or bikes through AONB woodland where King John used to hunt… and come and go as you please. *Min. two nights, three nights in high season. Secure garden and paddock to romp around. Streams, the New Forest, coastline and superb local dog-friendly pubs: perfect doggie days out!*

Shafts Farm

The 1960s farmhouse has many weapons in its armoury: a tremendous South Downs thatched-village setting, owners who know every path and trail, comfortable, generous bedrooms and a stunning rose garden designed by David Austin Roses (parterres, obelisks, meandering paths). The two bedrooms are fresh in cream, florals and plaids, each with a shower room with heated floors to keep toes toasty. Homemade granola, garden fruit and the full English make a fine start to the day; the airy, cane-furnished conservatory is the place for afternoon tea and a read. Your hosts are both geographers and have an intriguing display of maps. *Paddocks to play in, walks from the door, the river Meon to paddle in and a dog-friendly pub five minutes' walk away.*

Rooms	1 suite for 2 (with sitting area): £80–£90. Singles £65–£80. Sofabed available. Dogs £5 per night. No limit, but only 1 allowed in guest room. If more, we ask they go in our cosy kennel.
Meals	Pub in village.
Closed	Christmas.

 Bedding, bowls & towels. Laminated maps of local walks & dog-friendly pubs. Medium-sized dog cage on request

Alison Acland
October House
South End, Damerham,
Fordingbridge SP6 3HW
Tel   +44 (0)1725 518810
Email   alison.acland@btopenworld.com
Web   www.octoberhousebandb.com

Entry 102 Map 3

Rooms	2 twins: £90. Singles £50. Dogs £10 per stay. Max. 2.
Meals	Pubs/restaurants 500 yds.
Closed	Rarely.

 Bed time biscuits, a hose for muddy paws, towels for drying and advice on walks

Rosemary Morrish
Shafts Farm
West Meon,
Petersfield GU32 1LU
Tel   +44 (0)1730 829266
Email   info@shaftsfarm.co.uk
Web   www.shaftsfarm.co.uk

Entry 103 Map 3

Glewstone Court Country House Hotel & Restaurant

Those in search of the small and friendly will love it here. The staff are great, many have been here for yonks, and Bill and Christine run it all with great style, instinctively disregarding the bland new world in favour of a more colourful landscape. Their realm is this attractive country house filled with an eclectic collection of art and antiques. Eastern rugs cover stripped wood floors, resident dogs snooze in front of the fire, guests gather in the drawing room bar to eat, drink and relax. Outside, there's croquet on the lawn in the shade of an ancient cedar of Lebanon, while back inside a fine Regency staircase spirals up to a galleried landing. Warmly comfortable bedrooms await, tea trays come laden with homemade biscuits. Two bedrooms are huge, those at the front have long views across the Wye Valley to the Forest of Dean, those at the back overlook cherry orchards. Christine's fabulous food, seasonal and mostly local – Hereford beef, Marches lamb – is served at lunch and dinner every day with traditional Sunday lunch popular with locals. The Brecon Beacons and the Cotswolds are close. *Riverside walks and public footpaths through surrounding countryside.*

Rooms	6 doubles; 1 four-poster: £125-£140. 1 suite for 2: £150. 1 single: £70. Singles £85-£100. Dogs £7 per dog per night.
Meals	Lunch from £14. Dinner, 3 courses, about £30. Sunday lunch £21.
Closed	25-27 December.

 Dog towels, blankets and poop-scoop bags; advice on walks

Christine & Bill Reeve-Tucker
Glewstone Court Country House Hotel
Glewstone,
Ross-on-Wye HR9 6AW
Tel   +44 (0)1989 770367
Email info@glewstonecourt.com
Web   www.glewstonecourt.com

Entry 104 Map 2

Llan y Coed

The magic starts as you pass through the farmyard of Llan y Coed, and across a sheep-grazed common high above the Wye. Then the roof of your cottage, a restored drover's home, appears – to a backdrop of the distant Black Mountains. Buzzards wheel, black sheep bleat, ducks skim the ponds: it's a haven for wildlife! (Badgers, squirrels, foxes, rabbits and chickens, too.) The whole ethos of farmer/owners Kesri and Paul is one of harmony with nature, reflected in the limewashed interiors. The big open-plan living room and kitchen are deliberately spare; there's a cosy sitting room with an open fire; and, upstairs, an uncluttered bathroom and a double and a twin bedroom with wonderful views. Robins, woodpeckers, chaffinches, greenfinches, cuckoos, kestrels and more share these 130 acres; wild orchids flourish. The owners may cook you a curry for your arrival, after that there's home beef, lamb, chicken and eggs to enjoy, all organic: rustle up a feast on the barbecue on the veranda. Heaven for walkers, families and foodies (two Michelin-starred pubs are close by) and all who find richness in the simple pleasures of life. *Short breaks available. Surrounded by 130 acres.*

Rooms	1 cottage for 4 (1 double, 1 twin/double; 1 bathroom): £495-£850. Dogs £15 per week per dog, £10 per short break. Max. 2. Downstairs only; may be left in boot room unattended.
Meals	Self-catering.
Closed	Rarely.

 Dog bowl on request

Kesri Smolas
Llan y Coed
Dorstone,
Hay-on-Wye HR3 6AG

Tel	+44 (0)1497 831215
Email	kesri@llanycoed.co.uk
Web	www.llanycoed.co.uk

Entry 105 Map 2

The Wagon over the Valley

Daphne's individual spirit infuses the whole of the New Inn Brilley – you can't miss the Stupa draped in prayer flags near the shared shower hut, and there's an old barn turned meditation space, where you can arrange guided meditation sessions. She acquired the wagon from a kindred spirit called Dale, who wanted to swap his current life on the roads for a life of wandering the hills with just horse and tent. Dale had fitted the wagon with Gypsy caravan-inspired furnishings: a bed with a white linen and lace canopy, a cosy wood-burner and two Edwardian desks, which, combined with the absolutely magnificent view towards the Black Mountains, are enough to give anyone the urge to write. Daphne herself added the lean-to kitchen and finishing touches like the pretty fairy lights out on the decking, where you'll find handcrafted outdoor furniture and the valley views. During the day you can head to the markets in Hay, explore the stunning scenery by bike, horse, canoe or simply by foot. *Minimum stay two nights. Book through Sawday's Canopy & Stars online or by phone.*

Rooms	Wagon for 2 (1 double): from £75 per night. Max. 3 dogs in the wagon.
Meals	Self-catering.
Closed	Rarely.

Fresh water by the door

Sawday's Canopy & Stars
The Wagon over the Valley
New Inn Brilley, Brilley,
Whitney-on-Wye, Hereford HR3 6HE
Tel   +44 (0)117 204 7830
Email   enquiries@canopyandstars.co.uk
Web   www.canopyandstars.co.uk/wagonvalley

Entry 106 Map 2

New Inn Brilley

Daphne is delightful, and spiritual and kind. Her ancient drovers inn shines brightly in the hills above Hay with its tattered Tibetan flags, wonky overgrown garden and words of wisdom at every turn. Enter a kingdom of peace, sleep in the house or the yurt, help yourself to supper or let yourself be cooked for. Spotless bedrooms (up steep steps) are pink or yellow, one with a teeny, sweet bathroom, one without (but Daphne can provide a potty). Homemade yogurt and plum jam at breakfast with eggs from her bantams, a warm and history-filled house crammed with collectibles and with views from every window. Unusual and uplifting. *Fenced boundaries. Woodland and exciting paths; Offa's Dyke walk beyond.*

The Stagg Inn

On a lonely road lies the first British pub to have been awarded a Michelin star. Gavroche-trained Steve Reynolds took it on and, defying all odds, ended up a Herefordshire food hero. As for provenance: the only thing you're not told is the name of the bird from which your pigeon breast (perfectly served on herb risotto) came. Most of the produce is very local, some is organic, with fresh fruit and vegetables from the kitchen garden, or Titley Court next door. Seductive and restorative is the exceptional food: goat's cheese and fennel tart, saddle of venison with horseradish gnocchi and kummel, bread and butter pudding with clotted cream, a cheese trolley resplendent with 15 regional beauties. The intimate bar is perfect and dog-friendly, there's beer from Wye Valley Brewery, cider from Dunkerton's and some very classy wines. *Titley Pool, a naturally formed kettle lake, for dips!*

Rooms	2 doubles, sharing bathroom: £55–£65. 1 yurt for 6 (separate shower room): £70–£90. Singles £40. Max. 2 dogs per stay in house, 3 in yurt. Sheep and poultry here, so dogs must be supervised.
Meals	Dinner with dessert, £12.50. Pub 4 miles.
Closed	Rarely.

 Fresh water by the door

Daphne Tucker
New Inn Brilley
Brilley, Whitney-on-Wye,
Hereford HR3 6HE
Tel   +44 (0)1497 831284
Email   karmadaphne@onetel.com
Web   www.newinnbrilley.co.uk

Entry 107 Map 2

Meals	Lunch & dinner from £25. Bar meals £9.80. Sunday lunch, 3 courses, £19.30.
Closed	Monday & Tuesday.

 Walking opportunities galore

Steve & Nicola Reynolds
The Stagg Inn
Titley,
Kington HR5 3RL
Tel   +44 (0)1544 230221
Email   reservations@thestagg.co.uk
Web   www.thestagg.co.uk

Entry 108 Map 2

Herefordshire

The Oak Inn

Just west of the Malvern Hills – a freehouse dating from the 1600s, sympathetically refurbished. Farmhouse tables and chairs stand on polished flagstones, hops hang from beams and wood-burners crackle in exposed brick hearths – it's country pub to the core. There are ales from Bathams and Wye Valley and, as you'd expect, good ciders like Robinson's Flagon and Weston's Stowford Press. Traditional home-cooked food with modern twists are the order of the day; try slow-cooked local free-range pork belly with 'boozy' mustard mash or braised venison casserole with spiced red cabbage. Lighter options include deli boards with home-cured meats, soups (try the golden beetroot with horseradish cream) and homemade sandwiches. The pretty garden is backed by apple orchards, while inside the fires and candles in the bar, two snugs and dining area are kept glowing by a bright and attentive team. A super little pub.

Meals	Lunch from £4.25. Dinner £11.50.
Closed	3pm-5.30pm (Monday-Saturday). 3pm-7pm (Sunday).

 Roast beef tidbits & other doggie treats; dogs welcome throughout. Secure garden, walks through the orchards and into woods beyond; Malvern Hills ten-minute drive

Hylton Haylett & Julie Woollard
The Oak Inn
Bromyard Road, Staplow,
Ledbury HR8 1NP
Tel   +44 (0)1531 640954
Email enquiries@oakinnstaplow.co.uk
Web   www.oakinnstaplow.co.uk

Entry 109 Map 2

Hertfordshire

The Alford Arms

It isn't easy to find, so come armed with precise directions before you set out! In a hamlet enfolded by acres of National Trust common land, David and Becky Salisbury's gastropub is worth any number of missed turns. Inside are two interlinked rooms, bright and airy, with soft colours, scrubbed pine tables, wooden and tile floors. Food is taken seriously and ingredients are as organic, free-range and delicious as can be. On a menu that divides dishes into small plates and main meals, find warm confit rabbit and wild mushroom tart, baked smoked haddock and prawn pancake, pan-roasted Buckinghamshire venison haunch with sticky red cabbage, whole baked seabass, homemade ice cream. Wine drinkers have the choice of 22 by the glass; service is informed and friendly. Arrive early on a warm day to take your pick of the teak tables on the sun-trapping front terrace.

Meals	Lunch, bar meals & dinner £11.75-£19.75.
Closed	Open all day.

 Fresh water & dog biscuits in the bar & the garden. Edge of National Park beech woods: lots of wonderful forest walking

David & Becky Salisbury
The Alford Arms
Frithsden,
Hemel Hempstead HP1 3DD
Tel   +44 (0)1628 488611
Email info@alfordarmsfrithsden.co.uk
Web   www.alfordarmsfrithsden.co.uk

Entry 110 Map 3

The Pilot Boat Inn

This amphibious-looking Bembridge Harbour landmark is ship-shape in more ways than one. Behind the nautical portholes and narrow Mackintosh windows of its Art Deco ship, award-winning landlord George has assembled friendly staff, good booze and generous plates of simple, fresh and often fishy pub cuisine. Snatch sea views from the side garden, savouring a speciality crab sandwich. Whether a dog walker, child-festooned parent or beachcomber with sand-tingled toes, warm welcomes await. Bar décor is eclectic, occasionally opulent. Floors and furnishings are dark wood, red walls frame vintage prints. Sofa seating is kitsch and comfy, board games beckon, bright fish somersault in tanks. Try an Island Brewery Yachtsman Ale, something from the wine list (decent mid-range options) or a draft Stowford Press, Grolsch or Guinness. The ranks of banter-fuelled islanders swell in summer with yachty types and holidaymakers – but why stray, with five compact and contemporary rooms upstairs? Find maritime flavours, reassuringly expensive mattresses, compact Art Deco en suites. A happy harbourside base. *Fabulous walks, nature reserve (SSSI) next door and wonderful beaches from the inn.*

Rooms	3 doubles; 2 twin/doubles: £90.
Meals	Lunch & dinner £8–£20.
Closed	Open all day.

 Advice on walks

George Bristow
The Pilot Boat Inn
Station Road,
Bembridge PO35 5NN
Tel   +44 (0)1983 872077
Email info@thepilotboatinn.com
Web   www.thepilotboatinn.com

Entry 111 Map 3

The House

Down a rough track off the Appledore road, at the top of a lawned garden with a veg patch alongside (all safe for children and dogs), is a 15th-century Kentish Weald house, one of the best. Inside: two rambling storeys of sloping ceilings and uneven floors, wonky timbered walls and wooden latch doors, and an artistic, atmospheric décor – bliss to be cocooned here on a wet winter's day! The kitchen is the hub of the house, with shelves spilling cookery books, an espresso machine gleaming, and a red Aga pumping out the heat. More beams in the sitting room and fine old rugs on a painted floor, flowers in an enamel jug, logs in the inglenook, a scattering of vintage lamps and gilded mirrors, a big flat-screen TV. Upstairs are the bedrooms, simple and cosy, with new Roberts radios and old Enid Blytons, a worn teddy bear on the shelf, a charming rustic blanket. There's a walk-in shower in the en suite and a tub in the bathroom. Camber Sands is 12 miles, the Red Lion at Snargate (ancient, authentic) is three, and owner Karen owns the Ship Inn in Rye: browse the papers, drink Kentish cider, tuck into potted shrimps... *Large enclosed garden, woods around the house and a short drive to the beach.*

Rooms	1 house for 9: £850–£1,950.
	2 night breaks from £500.
	Max. 2 dogs.
Meals	Self-catering.
Closed	Never.
	Doggie 'overnight bag' – basket, towels and a pig's ear

Karen Northcote
The House
Cherrycroft,
Kenardington TN26 2NE

Tel	+44 (0)1797 222233
Email	karen@theshipinnrye.co.uk
Web	www.thehouse.so

Entry 112 Map 4

Pippa is a Duck Toller and her favourite place is Wittenham Clumps. She loves leaping into the river Thames to make friends with the ducks!

The Linen Shed

A weatherboard house with a winding footpath to the front door and a pot-covered veranda out the back: sit here and nibble something delicious and homemade while you contemplate the pretty garden with its gypsy caravan. Vickie, wreathed in smiles, has created a 'vintage' interior: find wooden flooring, reclaimed architectural pieces, big old roll tops, a mahogany loo seat. Bedrooms (two up, one down) are painted in the softest colours, firm mattresses are covered in fine linen, cotton or linen, dressing gowns hang in the smart bathrooms. Food is seriously good here, and adventurous – try a seaside picnic hamper! *Orchards, coastal path, woodland and creeks.*

Rafa and Wizard love anywhere that their owner is with them, but they particularly like playing in the woods and posing for pictures.

Rooms	1 double with separate bath (occasionally sharing with family); 2 doubles with separate bath/shower: £85–£110. Singles from £75. Max. 2 dogs. 2 dog-friendly bedrooms.
Meals	Picnic hamper from £20. Pub/restaurant 300 yds.
Closed	Rarely.

    Dog biscuits

Vickie Hassan
The Linen Shed, 104 The Street,
Boughton-under-Blean,
Faversham ME13 9AP
Tel   +44 (0)1227 752271
Email   bookings@thelinenshed.com
Web   www.thelinenshed.com

Entry 113 Map 4

The Inn at Whitewell

It is almost impossible to imagine a day when a better inn will grace the English landscape. Everything here is perfect. The inn sits just above the river Hodder, and doors in the bar lead onto a terrace where guests can enjoy five-mile views across parkland to rising fells. Inside, fires roar, newspapers wait, there are beams, sofas, maps and copies of *Wisden*. Bedrooms, some in the Coach House, are exemplary and come with real luxury, perhaps a peat fire, a lavish four-poster, a fabulous Victorian power shower. All have beautiful fabrics, top linen and gadgets galore; many have the marvellous view – you can fall asleep at night to the sound of the river. There are bar meals for those who want to watch their weight (the Whitewell fish pie is rightly famous) or a restaurant for splendid food, so dig into seared scallops, Bowland lamb, a plate of local cheese (the Queen once popped in for lunch). Elsewhere, a wine shop in reception, seven miles of private fishing and countryside as good as any in the land. Dogs and children are very welcome, the walking is magnificent. Brilliant. *Moorland walks.*

Rooms	17 doubles; 5 twin/doubles: £120–£215.
	1 suite for 2: £210–£240.
	Singles from £88.
	Dogs not allowed in dining room.
Meals	Bar meals from £8. Dinner £25–£35.
Closed	Never.

Lovely dog beds to borrow, water bowls in the bars & river to swim in at the end of the garden

Charles Bowman
The Inn at Whitewell
Dunsop Road, Whitewell,
Clitheroe BB7 3AT
Tel   +44 (0)1200 448222
Email reception@innatwhitewell.com
Web   www.innatwhitewell.com

Entry 114 Map 6

The Gorse House

Passing cars are less frequent than passing horses – this is a peaceful spot in a pretty village. Lyn and Richard's 17th-century cottage has a feeling of lightness and space; there's a fine collection of paintings and furniture, and oak doors lead from dining room to guest sitting room. Country style bedrooms have green views and are simply done. The garden layout was designed by Bunny Guinness, you can bring your horse (there's plenty of stabling) and it's a stroll to a good pub dinner. The house is filled with laughter, breakfasts with home-grown fruits are tasty and the Cowdells are terrific hosts who love having guests to stay. *Secure garden, lots of walks from the door. Dogs welcome in the ground-floor bedroom.*

Rooms	1 double: £65. 1 family room for 4: £65-£120. 1 triple with kitchenette: £65-£98. Singles £35. Dogs £5 per dog per night. Max. no real limit, but if large then 2.
Meals	Packed lunch £5. Pub 75 yds (closed on Sun eves).
Closed	Rarely.

 Advice on walks, towels available and a treat provided on arrival

Lyn & Richard Cowdell
The Gorse House, 33 Main Street,
Grimston, Melton Mowbray LE14 3BZ
Tel +44 (0)1664 813537
Mobile +44 (0)7780 600792
Email cowdell@gorsehouse.co.uk
Web www.gorsehouse.co.uk

Entry 115 Map 6

Breedon Hall

Through high brick walls find a listed Georgian manor house in an acre of garden, and friendly Charlotte and Charles. Make yourselves at home in the fire-warmed drawing room full of fine furniture and pictures; carpets and curtains are in the richest, warmest reds and golds. Charlotte is a smashing cook and gives you homemade granola, jams and marmalade with local eggs, bacon and sausages; you'd kick yourself if you didn't book dinner. Bedrooms are painted in soft colours, fabrics are thick, beds covered in goose down; bathrooms are immaculate. Borrow a bike and discover the glorious countryside right on the cusp of two counties. *Min. two nights at weekends. Large enclosed garden. Excellent walks everywhere; the Cloud Trail and Poppy Wood recommended particularly.*

Rooms	2 doubles: £95-£110. Singles £85. Dogs max. 1 per room. May be left alone in bedroom, for a short time, if house-trained.
Meals	Dinner, 3 courses, £35. Pub/restaurant 1-minute walk.
Closed	Rarely.

 Advice on walks. a 'drying' room for wet dogs and Bullet, our friendly spaniel, never minds sharing his home!

Charlotte Meynell
Breedon Hall
Main Street, Breedon-on-the-Hill,
Derby DE73 8AN
Mobile +44 (0)7973 105467
Email charlottemeynell@btinternet.com
Web www.breedonhall.co.uk

Entry 116 Map 6

Brackenborough Hall Coach House

The charming Coach House to the Hall is reached via a tree-lined drive past fields of cows and calves; this is an idyllic spot. On the ground floor are two apartments, the Stables and the Saddle Room (with hay racks intact and the original brick floors), a communal space in between, then the Granary above, wonderfully raftered, spanning the entire floor, nabbing the best views, and big enough to seat (and feed) a party of 24. All ideal for renting separately. Original features have been adapted throughout, and neatly incorporated into modern living. In the Granary are two spacious and carpeted bedrooms, each sleeping four; those in the Stables and Saddle Room are smaller, with pine floors and furniture, brick and panelled walls. The place is generous to a fault: a welcome hamper of Lincolnshire goodies; umbrellas, sticks and racquets; books, DVDs, maps, walks and wildlife info; games, puzzles and ping-pong. In the fenced garden: a sandpit, barbecue and climbing frames; beyond, a wood with rope swings and stepping logs. All this, and the tallest parish spire in the country two miles away, in the market town of Louth. *Sofa beds, cots and highchairs available. Five hunderd acre farm with walks from door: woods, parkland, stream. Lincolnshire Wolds and sandy beaches nearby.*

Rooms	2 apartments for 4; 1 apartment for 8: £340–£1,280. Short breaks any length, mid-week discounts. Dogs £20 per stay (up to 7 days). Max. 6 (more by arrangement).
Meals	Self-catering.
Closed	Rarely.

 Hose for washing muddy paws, towels provided on request, folders of walks, maps and spare lead; owners on site for advice

Paul & Flora Bennett
Brackenborough Hall Coach House
Brackenborough, Louth LN11 0NS

Tel	+44 (0)1507 603193
Mobile	+44 (0)7974 687779
Email	paulandflora@brackenboroughhall.com
Web	www.brackenboroughhall.com

Entry 117 Map 7

Lincolnshire

Baumber Park

Lincoln red cows and Longwool sheep surround this attractive rosy-brick farmhouse – once a stud that bred a Derby winner. The old watering pond is now a haven for frogs, newts and toads; birds sing lustily. Maran hens conjure delicious eggs, and charming Clare, a botanist, is hugely knowledgeable about the area. Bedrooms are light and traditional with mahogany furniture; two have heart-stopping views. Guests have their own wisteria-covered entrance, sitting room with an open fire, dining room with local books and the lovely garden to roam. This is good walking, riding and cycling country; seals and rare birds on the coast. *Usually min. two nights at weekends in high season. Good walks on and from the farm and in the area. Lovely empty, sandy beaches 35 minutes away.*

Rooms	2 doubles; 1 twin with separate shower: £60-£70. Singles from £45. Dogs £6 per night. Max. 2 per room. Remember to bring dog's own bedding!
Meals	Pubs 1.5 miles.
Closed	Christmas & New Year.

 Much advice on local walks, maps loaned when required

Clare Harrison
Baumber Park
Baumber, Horncastle LN9 5NE
Tel   +44 (0)1507 578235
Mobile +44 (0)7977 722776
Email mail@baumberpark.com
Web   www.baumberpark.com

Entry 118 Map 7

London

Russell's

Be in the thick of edgy, vibrant, multi-cultural London in this pink Victorian terraced house bang on the high street. Lovely Annette gives you imaginative breakfasts: try mushrooms cooked in truffle oil. You enjoy a funky guest sitting room with vintage furniture, a friendly whippet called Reggie, interesting book shelves and an easy-going feel. Lovely uncluttered bedrooms (those overlooking the garden are quieter) have good art and great 60s and 70s pieces. Sparkling bathrooms have powerful showers. Very good cafés on the doorstep, a 20-minute walk to the Olympic Stadium, and near Hackney Marshes, with grazing cows! *Close to parks, marshes and the canal.*

Rooms	2 doubles, 1 twin/double; 1 single; 1 double, 1 twin/double sharing bath: £75-£115. Singles from £75. Max. 2 dogs per room. May be left alone in bedroom if quiet and well behaved. 2 dog-friendly bedrooms.
Meals	Pubs/restaurants 5-minute walk.
Closed	Rarely.

 Dog treats, and advice on walks, dog-friendly pubs and places to eat

Annette Russell
Russell's
123 Chatsworth Road,
Clapton E5 0LA
Mobile +44 (0)7976 669906
Email annette@russellsofclapton.com
Web   www.russellsofclapton.com

Entry 119 Map 3

Heron Cottage

A great little spot for a family break, in the heart of the village of Castle Acre, next to the ruined castle's gateway, strolling distance from pubs, tea room and green. Your cottage is modern, fresh and smartly decorated, its living room warm and inviting with comfy sofas, a sisal rug on a wooden floor, bookshelves laden with novels and a wood-burner that comes with a basket of logs. The kitchen is well-equipped and the dining area bright with candlesticks, objets and pots of scented lavender. Upstairs are painted wooden beds scattered with cerise cushions, all top quality and spotlessly clean. Outside: a small courtyard garden. But you may not be spending much time lazing about... the ancient Peddars Way rambles down the old Roman Road to the Norfolk Coast Path – tempting for walkers. For sightseers, it's a short drive to the 11th-century ruins of Cluniac Priory, the Queen's country retreat at Sandringham, and also historic Houghton Hall. As for ornithologists, the bird-rich salt marshes lining the North Norfolk coast are a must-visit. *The Peddars Way is on the doorstep, lovely walks along the river, marshland.*

Rooms	1 cottage for 4 (1 double, 1 twin; 1 shower room): £290–£420. £75 p.n. (not July & August). Heating £25 p.w., £15 at weekends & short breaks.
Meals	Self-catering.
Closed	Open all year.
	Dog bowls

Marian Sanders
Heron Cottage
6 Bailey Gate,
Castle Acre PE32 2AF
Tel   +44 (0)1485 532918
Email   marianatmoreau@hotmail.com
Web   www.welcometocastleacre.com

Entry 120 Map 7

Saracens Head

Lost in the lanes of deepest Norfolk, an English inn that's hard to beat. Outside, Georgian red-brick walls ripple around, encircling a beautiful courtyard where you can sit for sundowners in summer before slipping into the restaurant for a good meal. Tim and Janie came back from the Alps, unable to resist the allure of this inn. A sympathetic refurbishment has brightened things up, but the spirit remains the same: this is a country-house pub with lovely staff who go the extra mile. Downstairs the bar hums with happy locals who come for Norfolk ales and good French wines, while the food in the restaurant is as good as ever: Norfolk pigeon and pork terrine, wild sea bass, treacle tart and caramel ice cream. Upstairs you'll find a sitting room on the landing, where windows frame country views, and six pretty bedrooms. All have been redecorated and have smart carpets, blond wood furniture, comfy beds and sparkling bathrooms. Breakfast sets you up for the day, so explore the coast at Cromer, play golf on the cliffs at Sheringham, or visit Blickling Hall, a Jacobean pile. Blissful stuff. *Beaches ten-minute drive.*

Rooms	5 twin/doubles: £100–£110.
	1 family room for 4: £110–£140.
	Singles from £70.
	Dogs can be left alone in bedroom if owners are in building; not allowed in restaurant.
Meals	Lunch from £6.50.
	Dinner, 3 courses, £25–£35.
	Not Mon; or Tue lunch October–June.
Closed	Christmas.

 Walks, water bowls, towels for a rub down & wellies for guests who forgot theirs

Tim & Janie Elwes
Saracens Head
Wolterton,
Norwich NR11 7LZ

Tel	+44 (0)1263 768909
Email	info@saracenshead-norfolk.co.uk
Web	www.saracenshead-norfolk.co.uk

The Berney Arms

In a peaceful estate village in open country, by the village green, is a spruced-up inn with candy-coloured tables out front. The sleek feel continues within, and there is much to love, from the the bar areas with their beautiful fires and beams, settles, comfy leather chairs and cheeky Pirelli posters, to the bright restaurant with its linen tablecloths and stylish French-country feel. The menu is good-looking and tempting and attracts Norfolk foodies, so look forward to stilton and pear tart, estate venison with red wine jus, chocolate truffle torte with toffee ice cream. Friendly staff, under landlords the Hirsts, bustle efficiently, while the atmosphere tempts one to linger, as does the promise of afternoon tea. The conversion of the old stables, forge and carriage house is impressive, and holds five stylish rooms and some original features; the suite sports a splendid brick forge. Expect gleaming dark wood floors and clean lines, chunky wood and brass beds, good bathrooms and private terraces – every room has one. Off the beaten track but well worth knowing if visiting the north Norfolk coast. *Walks on the coast and Thetford Forest.*

Rooms	3 doubles; 1 twin: £75–£95. 1 suite for 4: £95–£120. Singles £57.50. Max. 2 dogs per bedroom. Can be left in room during supper as long as well behaved.
Meals	Lunch & dinner £9.50–£19.95.
Closed	Rarely.

Generous garden & big rooms with paw-friendly flooring

Phil & Sue Hirst
The Berney Arms
Church Road, Barton Bendish,
King's Lynn PE33 9GF

Tel	+44 (0)1366 347995
Email	info@theberneyarms.co.uk
Web	www.theberneyarms.co.uk

Entry 122 Map 7

The Manse House

The Virgin Mary appeared in a vision and pilgrims flocked to Little Walsingham, prompting a mushroom-like sprouting of chapels, churches and a priory in this sleepy Norfolk village. Many still tread the path at Easter, though you need not hold a faith to find comfort here. Tucked down a lane behind a chapel is a beautiful spot with a garden that glories in the best view around. The Manse House sits above all else, overlooking the ruins of the friary and the Dutch gable-end buildings, while a conservatory draws the sunlight in to the flagstone-floored kitchen and dining space. If a glut of history surrounds you, the interiors reveal a softly modern bent. Bedrooms come in different sizes, but all have fine beds and furniture with characterful touches (a Mongolian cabinet, a fabulous screened en suite shower in the master, a freestanding claw-foot bath). In the living room are a wood-burner, fresh flowers and bold prints. Better still, the local organic farm shop stocks your welcome hamper, there are well-known walks from the door and you can ask about borrowing Jill's retro beach hut in Wells-next-the-Sea. Hallelujah! *Secure garden, river, North Norfolk coast, 20 miles of dog-friendly walk – dunes and pine forest.*

Rooms	1 house for 5 (1 double en suite, 1 double, 1 single, z-bed; 1 bathroom): £600–£950. Max. 3 dogs. Dogs to sleep downstairs.
Meals	Self-catering.
Closed	Rarely.
	Local organic dog biscuits; towels on request

Jill Payne
The Manse House
High Street, Walsingham NR22 6BY
Tel   +44 (0)1328 862334
Mobile   +44 (0)7887 903372
Email   jillfablady@aol.com
Web   www.themansehouse.co.uk

Entry 123 Map 7

Plumstead Hall Farmhouse

Percy and Emma's large farmhouse has a gently bustling family feel, and you are made to feel at home as soon as you step onto the lovely old Norfolk pamments in the hall. The bedrooms, up higgledy-piggledy stairs, have feather duvets and pretty covers, green views and a huge bathroom; the second room with a sloping ceiling is simpler. Breakfast is a relaxed, do-it-yourself affair on the mini stove: eggs, bacon, cereals, breads and jams, all locally sourced and eaten in the guest dining room. The north Norfolk beaches are close and there are historic homes to visit. Birdwatchers, walkers and cyclists will be happy as Larry. *Minimum stay two nights. Fantastic coastal, woodland and parkland walks nearby.*

Rooms	2 doubles sharing bath (let to same party only): £80–£100. Singles £80–£100. Dogs £20 per stay. Max. 2. Can be left alone in bedroom as long as well house-trained and not in need of babysitting.
Meals	Pub/restaurant 5 miles.
Closed	Christmas & New Year.
	Advice on walks

Percy & Emma Stilwell
Plumstead Hall Farmhouse
Northfield Lane, Plumstead,
Norwich NR11 7PT
Tel   +44 (0)1263 577660
Email   plumsteadhall@gmail.com
Web   www.plumsteadhallfarmhouse.co.uk

Entry 124 Map 7

Bridge Cottage

A hidden gem only a few miles from Peterborough and Oundle. Find pretty bedrooms with sloping ceilings, the purest cotton sheets, proper blankets and lovely bathrooms. Judy and Rod give you scrumptious, locally-sourced breakfasts in their friendly kitchen with that heavenly view. Gardening is a large part of Judy's life and she's created all from scratch over the last decade. Wander down a smooth lawn leading to a pretty summerhouse with decking by the stream; a peaceful place for a doze or a glass of wine watching the sun set over the most beautiful countryside; here is the prettiest of cottage planting in groups for strong impact: honeysuckles, roses and sweet peas waft their scent, perennials give all round pleasure and herbs are grown for the table. There's also a conservatory for a quiet read where, in summer, your breakfast tomatoes burgeon and ripen. *Lots of walks, river in garden, miles of woodland.*

Rooms	2 doubles, 1 with separate bath; 1 twin: £80–£85. Singles £47.50–£60. Dogs £5 per night. Max. 2. Dogs welcome in downstairs twin.
Meals	Pub/restaurant 500 yds.
Closed	Christmas.
	Advice about country walks, maps available

Judy Colebrook
Bridge Cottage, Oundle Road,
Woodnewton, Peterborough PE8 5EG
Tel   +44 (0)1780 470860
Mobile   +44 (0)7979 644864
Email   enquiries@bridgecottage.net
Web   www.bridgecottage.net

Entry 125 Map 6

Brinkburn Northumberland

This is heavenly countryside, and Brinkburn Priory (built in 1135) has an unrivalled position within it. Solitude and peace are yours in a dramatic wooded ravine along the meandering river Coquet – no wonder the monks who built it felt serene. Mark and Emma have renovated (beautifully) two lovely old buildings: The Stables, perfect for a big family or friends' gathering with plenty of outdoor space, and Priory Cottage – a cosy bolthole for two. Both have underfloor heating, superb kitchens and bathrooms, comfortable sofas and chairs by wood-burning stoves, good fabrics and gentle, neutral colours. Nothing is other than generous and all has been thought of, even down to bathrobes and good lotions and potions. It's so romantic you may even be inspired to get married here, in summer on the terrace with a marquee or in the elegant White Room in winter. There are more than 30 acres for you to explore, with woodland walks along the river and lots of wildlife; beaches are peerless and yet you are close to good road and rail links, and the airport. Newbies to Northumberland will fall in love. *Min. stay four nights on weekdays, three at weekends. Short breaks available. Cot available. Long way from main road. Keep dogs on leads if livestock around.*

Rooms	1 cottage for 2 (1 double, 1 sofabed); 1 cottage for 8 (1 double en suite, 1 double, 1 twin/double, 2 singles; 1 bathroom): £425-£1,690. Extra bed/sofabed available £9 per person per night. Dogs £20 per dog per stay. Max. 2 per cottage, ask if more. Can be left alone in room if in cage.
Meals	Self-catering.
Closed	Never.

 Towels, bowls, biscuits on arrival and beds on request

Emma Fenwick
Brinkburn Northumberland
Brinkburn Stables & Brinkburn Priory Cottage,
Longframlington, Morpeth NE65 8AR

Tel	+44 (0)1665 570870
Email	emma@brinkburnpriory.com
Web	www.brinkburnpriory.com

Entry 126 Map 9

Joiners Arms

A cool little inn with fantastic rooms up on the Northumberland coast. You're half a mile back from the sea, where a string of beaches stretch north from Embleton to Bamburgh. As for the Joiners, a recent facelift has propelled it firmly into the 21st-century. Downstairs, you find a funky mix of raw panelling and old stone walls, with low-hanging lamps above the bar and a coal fire smouldering away. There are stripped floors, tables in bay windows, local ales, and cakes on the counter you can't resist. The restaurant comes in chic cabin style with raw wood walls and green leather banquettes. Bedrooms don't hold back. Expect antler chandeliers, low-slung French beds, double-ended baths in the corner of most rooms. Some have Juliet balconies, others exposed brickwork, all have rich colours, flat-screen TVs and robes in fabulous bathrooms. Outside, Alnwick Castle, Holy Island, the magical coast and beautiful hills all wait. As for the food, come home to tasty gastro fare, perhaps smoked haddock chowder, a delicious Northumbrian steak, sticky toffee pudding with ginger ice cream. *Beach walks.*

Rooms	5 doubles: £140–£155.
	Dinner, B&B offers available.
	Dogs £20 per stay. Max. 1 per room.
	2 dog-friendly bedrooms.
Meals	Lunch from £4.95.
	Dinner, 3 courses, £25–£30.
Closed	Never.
	Dog treats at the bar, bed in room, bowl, dog mat and toy

	Robin Freer
	Joiners Arms
	Newton-by-the-Sea NE66 3AE
Tel	+44 (0)1665 576239
Email	accommodation@newton-hall.com
Web	www.joiners-arms.com

Entry 127 Map 9

Battlesteads Hotel

In the land of castles, stone circles and fortified towers is Battlesteads, an old inn given a new lease of life by owners who choose to be 'green'. The boiler burns wood chips from local sustainable forestry, a polytunnel produces the salads, all raw waste is composted; the Slades have won a bevy of awards, from 'Considerate Hotel of the Year' to a Green Tourism gold. Enter a large, cosy, low-beamed and panelled bar with a wood-burning stove and local cask ales. A step further and you find a spacious dining area: leather chairs at dark wood tables and a conservatory dining room that reaches into a sunny walled garden. The menus show a commitment to sourcing locally and the food is flavoursome. The Northumbrian fillet steak with Cumbrian blue cheese is meltingly tender and you must try Dee's award-winning bread and butter pudding! The housekeeping is exemplary so bedrooms are spotless, spacious, carpeted and comfortable, and there's wheelchair access on the ground floor. Hadrian's Wall is marvellously close. *Woodland, field and river walks; secure garden.*

Rooms	16 twin/doubles: £115–£145.
	1 single: £70–£95.
	Dogs £5 per night.
	4 dog-friendly bedrooms.
Meals	Lunch from £8.75. Dinner from £10.75.
	Sunday lunch, 3 courses, £14.50.
Closed	Never.
	Doggie 'welcome pack' with a Bonio biscuit, towel, blanket and poop bags. Dogs may dine with their owners

Richard & Dee Slade
Battlesteads Hotel
Wark, Hexham NE48 3LS
Tel   +44 (0)1434 230209
Email   info@battlesteads.com
Web   www.battlesteads.com

The Pheasant Inn

A super little inn lost in beautiful country, the kind you hope to chance upon. The Kershaws run it with great passion and an instinctive understanding of its traditions. The bars are wonderful. Brass beer taps glow, 100-year old photos of the local community hang on stone walls, the clock above the fire keeps perfect time. Fires burn, bowler hats and saddles pop up here and there, varnished wood ceilings shine. House ales are expertly kept, Timothy Taylor's and Wylam waiting for thirsty souls. Fruit and vegetables come from the garden, while Robin's lovely food hits the spot perfectly, perhaps twice-baked cheese soufflé, slow-roasted Northumberland lamb, brioche and marmalade bread and butter pudding; as for Sunday lunch, *The Observer* voted it 'Best in the North'. Bedrooms in the old hay barn are light and airy, cute and cosy, great value for money. You're in the Northumberland National Park — no traffic jams, no too much hurry. You can sail on the lake, cycle round it or take to the hills and walk. For £10 you can also gaze into the universe at the Kielder Observatory (best in winter). Brilliant. *Min. two nights at weekends. Lots of walks; keep dogs on lead if sheep are in fields.*

Rooms	4 doubles; 3 twins: £75-£95. 1 family room for 4: £90-£130. Singles £65. Dinner, B&B from £70 p.p. Dogs £5 per night. Max. 2 per bedroom. Dogs welcome in ground floor rooms, with access to garden, not bars and lounge areas.
Meals	Bar meals from £8.95. Dinner, 3 courses, £18-£22.
Closed	25-27 December. Monday & Tuesday, November–March.

 Heavenly forest & lakeside walks

Walter, Irene & Robin Kershaw
The Pheasant Inn
Stannersburn,
Hexham NE48 1DD

Tel	+44 (0)1434 240382
Email	stay@thepheasantinn.com
Web	www.thepheasantinn.com

Entry 129 Map 9

The Trout at Tadpole Bridge

A 17th-century Cotswold inn on the banks of the Thames, so pick up a pint, drift into the garden and watch life float by. The Trout is a drinking fisherman's paradise, walls are busy with bendy rods, children are liked and dogs can doze in the flagstoned bars. The downstairs is open-plan and timber-framed, there are gilt mirrors and logs piled high in alcoves. Gareth and Helen have cast their fairy dust into every corner: super bedrooms, fabulous modern food (fish chowder, Kelmscott pork belly, pear frangipane tart), a relaxed style. Bedrooms at the back are away from the crowd and three open onto a small courtyard – but you may prefer to stay put in your room and indulge in funky fabrics, monsoon showers (one room has a claw-foot bath), DVD players, a library of films. Sleigh beds, brass beds, upholstered armchairs… one even has a roof terrace. You can watch boats pass from the breakfast table, feast on local sausages, tuck into homemade marmalade courtesy of Helen's mum. Food is as local as possible, and there are maps for walkers to keep you thin. Bliss! *Min. two nights at weekends May-October. Beautiful riverside garden, access to the Thames path, woods close by.*

Rooms	2 doubles; 3 twin/doubles: £130.
	1 suite for 2: £160. Singles from £85.
	Max. 3 small dogs or 2 large.
Meals	Lunch & dinner £10.95-£19.
	Sunday lunch from £11.95.
Closed	Christmas Day & Boxing Day.

Local walking guides, tennis balls for the garden & a chew for every visiting dog!

Gareth & Helen Pugh
The Trout at Tadpole Bridge
Buckland Marsh,
Faringdon SN7 8RF

Tel	+44 (0)1367 870382
Email	info@troutinn.co.uk
Web	www.trout-inn.co.uk

The Wychwood Inn

With its pretty façade and perfect Cotswold setting, the Wychwood is enticing enough before you discover its cool, bright interiors. Low ceilings with washed wood beams, pale floors and feature wallpapers; there's even a silver rhino head on the funky red-tiled bar. The summer-styled dining room with its green dragonfly paper and country chandeliers is delicious, while outside the long lawn and tangle of trees is irresistible to children. Bedrooms are luxurious and stylish. All are above the pub, two at the back, three at the front, but cunningly sound-proofed and with deeply comfy beds. The four-poster, from a local heiress, is unusually beautiful. Splendid bathrooms have sparkling tilework; all are a good size, the one at the back is huge, with a bath as well as a double-sized shower. Clever zebra blinds at the windows allow the light in while preserving your privacy. Nothing is too much trouble for mother and son, Tracey and Paul, who add features here and there in response to requests from guests. All this and tempting menus too. A gem. *Many lovely walks in the Cotswolds.*

Rooms	5 doubles: £90–£140.
	£5 per dog per night. Max. 2.
Meals	Starters from £4.50. Mains from £9.95.
Closed	Never.

 Advice about walks

Tracey Hunt
The Wychwood Inn
High Street,
Shipton-Under-Wychwood OX7 6DQ
Tel +44 (0)1993 831185
Email tracey.hunt@talk21.com
Web www.thewychwoodinn.com

Entry 131 Map 3

The Kingham Plough

You don't expect to find locals clamouring for a table in a country pub on a cold Tuesday in February, but different rules apply at the Kingham Plough. Emily, once junior sous chef at the famous Fat Duck in Bray, is now doing her own thing and it would seem the locals approve. You eat in the tithe barn, now a splendid dining room, with ceilings open to ancient rafters and excellent art on the walls. Attentive staff bring sublime food. Dig into game broth with pheasant dumplings, fabulous lamb hotpot with crispy kale, and hot chocolate fondant with blood orange sorbet. Interiors elsewhere are equally pretty, all the result of a delightful refurbishment. There's a piano by the fire in the locals' bar, a terrace outside for summer dining, fruit trees, herbs and lavender in the garden. Bedrooms, three of which are small, have honest prices and come with super-comfy beds, flat-screen TVs, smart carpets, white linen, the odd beam; one has a claw-foot bath. Arrive by train, straight from London, to be met by a bus that delivers you to the front door. The Daylesford Organic farm shop/café is close. *Min. two nights at weekends. Walk to nearby villages of Daylesford & Bledington; dog-friendly little stream for frolics. Details of all local walks available at the bar.*

Rooms	7 twin/doubles: £90-£130.
	Singles from £75.
	Dogs £10 per dog per stay.
	Max. 2 per bedroom.
Meals	Lunch from £15. Bar meals from £5.
	Dinner, 3 courses, about £30.
	Sunday lunch from £17.
Closed	Christmas Day.

 Scrumptious pigs' ears at the ready

Emily Watkins & Miles Lampson
The Kingham Plough
The Green, Kingham,
Chipping Norton OX7 6YD
Tel   +44 (0)1608 658327
Email   book@thekinghamplough.co.uk
Web   www.thekinghamplough.co.uk

The Olive Branch

A lovely pub in a sleepy Rutland village, where bridle paths lead out across peaceful fields. The inn dates to the 17th century and is built of Clipsham stone. Inside, a warm, informal rustic chic hits the spot perfectly; come for open fires, old beams, exposed stone walls and choir stalls in the bar. Chalk boards on tables in the restaurant reveal the names of the evening's diners, while the food – seared scallops with black pudding fritter, slow-roast pork belly with creamed leeks and apple sauce – elates. As do the hampers that you can whisk away for picnics in the country. Bedrooms in Beech House across the lane are impeccable. Three have terraces, one has a free-standing bath, all come with crisp linen, pretty beds, Roberts radios, real coffee. Super breakfasts – smoothies, boiled eggs and soldiers, the full cooked works – are served in a smartly renovated barn, with flames leaping in the wood-burner. The front garden fills in summer, the sloe gin comes from local berries, and Newark is close for the biggest antiques market in Europe. A total gem. *Fenced areas, and good walking through woods and open meadows.*

Rooms	5 doubles;
	1 family room for 4: £115–£195.
	Singles from £97.50.
	Dogs £10 per night. Max. 2.
	3 dog-friendly bedrooms.
Meals	Bar meals £10.50. Dinner from £14.50.
	Sunday lunch £24.95.
Closed	Rarely.

Alfie the springer shares treats & walks. His top tip: sit by the youngest family member at meals (they may drop something!)

Ben Jones & Sean Hope
The Olive Branch
Main Street, Clipsham,
Oakham LE15 7SH

Tel	+44 (0)1780 410355
Email	info@theolivebranchpub.com
Web	www.theolivebranchpub.com

Entry 133 Map 6

Pen-y-Dyffryn Country Hotel

In a blissful valley lost to the world, this small, traditional country house sparkles on the side of a peaceful hill. To the front, beyond the stone terraces lush with aubretia, fields tumble down to a stream that marks the border with Wales. Daffodils erupt in spring, the lawns are scattered with deckchairs in summer, paths lead onto the hill for excellent walks. Colourful interiors are attractive: Laura Ashley wallpaper and an open fire in the quirky bar; shuttered windows and super food in the restaurant; the daily papers and a good collection of art in the sitting room. Bedrooms are stylish without being grand. Most have great views, one has a French sleigh bed, a couple have jacuzzi baths for two. All the rooms are dog-friendly and four have their own patios. You get crisp white linen, silky curtains, padded bedheads. There's super food, too: Shetland mussels, Welsh beef, a plate of local cheese; the smoked haddock at breakfast is divine. Offa's Dyke and Powis Castle are close. Spa treatments are available in your room; perfect after a long walk in the hills. *Minimum stay two nights at weekends. Safe garden. Woodland area adjoining hotel entirely open to the public, with no livestock.*

Rooms	8 doubles; 4 twins: £114–£166.
	Singles from £86.
	Max. 2 dogs per bedroom.
Meals	Light lunch (for residents) by
	arrangement. Dinner £30–£37.
Closed	Rarely.

A private patio for pooches, the perfect spot for their sundowner after a hard day's walk. Guide to circular walks

Miles & Audrey Hunter
Pen-y-Dyffryn Country Hotel
Rhydycroesau,
Oswestry SY10 7JD

Tel   +44 (0)1691 653700
Email   stay@peny.co.uk
Web   www.peny.co.uk

Entry 134 Map 5

The Castle Hotel

This thriving medieval market town sits amid some of the loveliest country in the land, a launch pad for walkers and cyclists, with Offa's Dyke, Long Mynd and the Kerry Ridgeway all close. After a day in the hills what better than to roll back down to this quirky hotel for a night of genteel carousing. You'll find heaps of country comforts: hearty food, an impeccable pint, cosy rooms with honest prices. Downstairs, there's a coal fire in the pretty snug, oak panelling in the breakfast room, and Millie the short-haired dachshund who patrols the corridors with aplomb. Spotless bedrooms upstairs have good beds, warm colours, flat-screen TVs, an armchair if there's room. Some are up in the eaves, several have views of the Shropshire hills, two are seriously fancy. Back downstairs you find the sort of food you hanker for after a day in the open air, perhaps broccoli and stilton soup, beef and ale pie, sticky toffee pudding (all for a song). Don't miss the hugely popular real ale festival in July, the beer drinker's equivalent of Glastonbury. There's a lovely garden, too, perfect for sundowners in summer. *Large secure garden, and many walks from the hotel front door.*

Rooms	7 doubles; 1 twin: £85–£130.
	2 family rooms for 4: £85–£105.
	Singles from £60.
	Dinner, B&B from £70 p.p.
	Max. dogs no limit, but require
	notification if over 2.
Meals	Lunch from £4.50.
	Dinner, 3 courses, about £25.
Closed	Christmas Day.

Dog biscuits, water bowls, leads, poop bags, towels, lots of information on walks, attractions and dog-friendly pubs

Henry Hunter
The Castle Hotel
Bishop's Castle SY9 5BN

Tel	+44 (0)1588 638403
Email	stay@thecastlehotelbishopscastle.co.uk
Web	www.thecastlehotelbishopscastle.co.uk

Entry 135 Map 5

Walcot Hall

The Walcot Hall estate is full of unusual features, a vast expanse of sprawling grounds where you can lose yourself for hours. There's a variety of quirky places to stay, hidden in secluded corners. The Chapel is for the hardier visitor to Walcot Hall, nestled in the trees of the large arboretum. It's an incredible, airy bolthole for four, which even has an organ for you to practise! The Dipping Shed's rough exterior, carried over from its former agricultural life, hides a beautiful interior with tall beamed ceiling and dark wood furniture. Recently, two cosy yurts have appeared, perched on a hillside with spectacular views over the lakes and Shropshire's hills and forests. Walcot Hall's understandably popular for weddings, but is Robin and Lucinda's family home too. There's always plenty of room to run around, and you might find one of the Parish children's dens if you go walking in the woods. Bring a fishing rod if you'd like to fish in the lake (children might prefer to fish tiddlers in the Arboretum pools) or on a clear day take one of the boats out. *Bookings begin on Monday or Friday. Book through Sawday's Canopy & Stars online or by phone.*

Rooms	2 yurts for 2 (1 double): from £56 per night.
	2 cabins for 4 (2 doubles): from £82 per night.
Meals	Self-catering.
Closed	Yurts: November-March.
	Cabins: rarely.

 The run of extensive grounds, and a splash in the lake

Sawday's Canopy & Stars
Walcot Hall
Lydbury North,
Bishop's Castle SY7 8AZ

Tel	+44 (0)117 204 7830
Email	enquiries@canopyandstars.co.uk
Web	www.canopyandstars.co.uk/walcothall

Entry 136 Map 2

Criggin Cottage

Ringed by the gentle hills of the Teme valley, this Shropshire hideout is a converted outbuilding of local stone and wood, with a patio overlooking a sunken garden for summer barbecues and starlit nightcaps. Downstairs is open-plan and cottage cosy, with natural fibres, exposed stone walls, old beams and a heated slate floor. Curl up with a book in the sitting area, warmed by the log-burning stove, or gather in the kitchen, whose burr oak units were made by a local carpenter – along with the bedheads and wardrobes of the two bedrooms. These are upstairs – one king, one twin, both fresh and bright, with en suite showers and views worth rising early for. Easy-going, bee-keeping owners Mark and Rita, who live steps away in the main house, greet you with a hamper that includes fresh eggs, homemade jam and their own honey; they can also stock the larder in advance, sparing you a four-mile trip to the nearest shop. Traipse the dales, stroll by the river Teme, and enjoy the silence – broken only by the chirping of songbirds around the feeders or the distant growl of a tractor. *Secure private garden, walks from the door, a brook perfect for dogs to jump in and advice on nearby river (Cocker Spaniel Aggie loves getting wet!).*

Rooms	1 cottage for 4
	(1 double, 1 twin/double): £450–£750.
	Dogs £10 per stay. Max. 2 per stay.
Meals	Self-catering.
Closed	Never.

 A comfy dog bed large enough for 2! Welcome jar of homemade dog biscuits (whilst owners enjoy homemade Victoria sponge). Book of dog-friendly local walks, and advice

	Rita Hughes
	Criggin Cottage
	Melin-y-Grogue,
	Llanfairwaterdine LD7 1TU
Tel	+44 (0)1547 510341
Email	rita@criggin.co.uk
Web	www.criggin.co.uk

Entry 137 Map 2

Lakeside Retreat

Off-piste drivers will delight in the approach – down a bumpy farm track, over an open field, across a ford and through grassy woodland. You land in a dreamy, bucolic setting with an arboretum and views over two deep water lakes (yes you may swim, yes you may use a little boat) with island, waterfalls, a small summerhouse that revolves, and a stream teeming with wildlife. A veranda and patio with table and chairs face south so you won't miss a thing; writers, artists and those clutching a large drink may take root here on less chilly days. Your wooden cabin is comfortable and very cosy: find one fresh and airy living/dining room with a fully formed kitchen area and plenty of good seating; glass doors open out to the terrace. The main bedroom has a giant bed with a pretty rose-strewn bedspread and a cream rug; the bunk room is fine for adults or children but it's all so romantic you may want to farm them out! Owner Victoria, who lives nearby, leaves you jam from her damsons and raspberries, local apple juice, something baked, and fresh flowers. A gorgeous little watery retreat. *Weekly bookings (Fri-Fri) or three night weekend (Fri-Mon). Additional night's stay on request. Children over five welcome. Secure 15 acres of garden & woodland, two lakes and a brook to swim in!*

Rooms	1 cabin for 4 (1 double, 1 bunk bed; 1 bath/shower room): £395-£795. Dogs £20 per stay. May be left alone in the utility/boot room. 1 dog-friendly bedroom.
Meals	Self-catering.
Closed	Never.

Dog bed and a doggie treat, plus advice on beautiful walks over Shropshire Hills – all from the door!

Victoria Orchard
Lakeside Retreat
Old Hall Farm, Milson,
Cleobury Mortimer DY14 0BH

Tel	+44 (0)1299 270780
Email	info@ludlowholidaylet.co.uk
Web	www.ludlowholidaylet.co.uk

Entry 138 Map 2

Millstream Camp

The charmingly ramshackle Millstream Camp is made up of two different spaces for a self-contained escape – and a dog's kennel replete with bed (though not bedding). The shepherd's hut, beautifully decorated with vintage items from the house, feather down pillows and a huge duvet filled with Welsh sheep's wool, serves as the dog-free sleeping space. The tipi, decked out with old Indian saris, campaign trunks and a lacquered table, is your sitting room. The millstream meanders past – dammed at the mill, on some hot days, to create a bathing pool. Bathing can also take place in a wood-fired tin bath, or under the gas-powered shower, and a private compost loo is just steps away. Food and cooking are an essential part of a Lower Buckton holiday. Carolyn runs cookery courses on site and 'food safaris': tours of local producers with ample opportunity for snacking. Back at the camp, you can use the barbecue, the wood-burner or the campfire to hone your skills. For the less patient, there's a gas hob for a quickly boiled kettle! *Minimum stay two nights. Book through Sawday's Canopy & Stars online or by phone.*

Rooms	Shepherd's hut for 2 (1 double): from £90 per night. Max. 2 dogs. Kennel provided.
Meals	Self-catering.
Closed	October–March.

A juicy bone direct from the village butcher's shop

Sawday's Canopy & Stars
Millstream Camp
Lower Buckton Country House,
Buckton, Leintwardine SY7 0JU

Tel	+44 (0)117 204 7830
Email	enquiries@canopyandstars.co.uk
Web	www.canopyandstars.co.uk/millstreamcamp

Entry 139 Map 2

Shropshire

Lower Buckton Country House

You are spoiled here in house-party style; Carolyn – passionate about Slow Food – and Henry, are born entertainers. Kick off with homemade cake in the drawing room with its oil paintings, antique furniture and old rugs; return for delicious nibbles when the lamps and wood-burner are flickering. Dine well at a huge oak table (home-reared pork, local cheeses, dreamy puddings), then nestle into the best linen and the softest pillows; bedrooms feel wonderfully restful. This is laid-back B&B: paddle in the stream, admire the stunning views, find a quiet spot with a good book. Great fun! *Three-acre field. Stream to play in. Network of footpaths from the door. Wonderful riverside walks and dog-friendly pubs.*

Shropshire

Hopton House

Karen looks after her guests wonderfully and even runs courses on how to do B&B! Unwind in this fresh and uplifting converted granary with old beams, high ceilings and a sun-filled dining/sitting room overlooking the hills. The bedroom above has its own balcony; those in the barn, one up, one down, each with its own entrance, are as enticing: beautifully dressed beds, silent fridges, good lighting, homemade cakes. Bathrooms have deep baths (and showers) – from one you can lie back and gaze at the stars. Karen's breakfasts promise Ludlow sausages, home-laid eggs, fine jams and homemade marmalade. *Long walks – with no stiles involved!*

Rooms	2 doubles; 1 twin/double with separate bath: £100. Dogs £10 per dog per night. Max. 2 per room. May only be left alone in bedrooms, if in cage & no barking!
Meals	Dinner, 4 courses, £35. BYO wine. Pub/restaurant 4 miles.
Closed	Rarely.

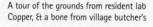 A tour of the grounds from resident lab Copper, & a bone from village butcher's

Rooms	3 doubles: £110–£120. 1 dog-friendly bedroom.
Meals	Restaurant 3 miles.
Closed	19-27 December.

 A jar of biscuits for every dog & details of local dog-friendly pubs & places to visit

Henry & Carolyn Chesshire
Lower Buckton Country House
Buckton, Leintwardine SY7 0JU
Tel   +44 (0)1547 540532
Mobile   +44 (0)7960 273865
Email   carolyn@lowerbuckton.co.uk
Web   www.lowerbuckton.co.uk

Entry 140 Map 2

Karen Thorne
Hopton House
Hopton Heath,
Craven Arms SY7 0QD
Tel   +44 (0)1547 530885
Email   info@shropshirebreakfast.co.uk
Web   www.shropshirebreakfast.co.uk

Entry 141 Map 2

Somerset

Stonebridge

A country house with scrumptious food, a friendly black labrador and croquet on the lawn. When their daughters flew the nest, Liz and Richard opened an independent wing of their listed house: perfect for families and couples. You have two pretty bedrooms (one up, one down) with country furniture and super bathrooms. In winter, a wood-burner keeps your little sitting room cosy; in summer, laze in a sea of flowers. You feast on local eggs, homemade bread and delicious dinners with garden veg. Just off the village road, it's close to Bristol airport, the M5 and Wells. And with hosts this friendly you can't go wrong. *Garden, and field walks.*

Somerset

Tarr Farm Inn

No traffic lights, no mobile signals, peace for miles. Tucked into the Barle valley, a hop from the clapper bridge at Tarr Steps, this well-established 16th-century inn is surrounded by woodland above the hauntingly high spaces of Exmoor. The garden views are sublime – where better to test the best West Country cheeses followed by perfect coffee? Inside, the blue-carpeted, low-beamed main bar has comfy window seats and gleaming black leather sofas, and Exmoor Ale and Magner's cider flow as easily as the conversation. To fill the gap after a bracing walk the menu draws on local game (hunting and shooting are big here) so tuck into venison and rabbit casserole or pan-roasted partridge – partnered by a hundred French and New World wines. *National Park on the doorstep. No limit to number of dogs – providing it's not a pack!*

Rooms	1 double; 1 twin/double: £75–£80. Singles £45–£50. Max. 2 dogs.
Meals	Dinner, 2-3 courses, £19–£24. Pub 2 miles.
Closed	Christmas.
	Garden for dogs to roam, and direct access to a public walkway through fields

Meals	Lunch from £8. Bar meals from £6. Dinner from £13. Sunday lunch, 3 courses, £17.50.
Closed	Open all day.
	Miles & miles of river, woodland and moorland to roam right from the door

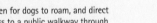

Richard & Liz Annesley
Stonebridge
Wolvershill Road,
Banwell BS29 6DR
Tel   +44 (0)1934 823518
Email liz.annesley@talktalk.net
Web   www.stonebridgebandb.co.uk

Entry 142 Map 2

Judy Carless & Richard Benn
Tarr Farm Inn
Tarr Steps,
Dulverton TA22 9PY
Tel   +44 (0)1643 851507
Email enquiries@tarrfarm.co.uk
Web   www.tarrfarm.co.uk

Entry 143 Map 2

Grove Cottages, The Grove

It's impossible to do justice to the 'nests' that make up Grove Cottages, so here's a taster. Open fires in many, handmade kitchens in all, kilim rugs and characterful throws, charmingly reclaimed doors and floors, all lovingly cared for, all spotless. You're treated to Lavenham bread, real coffee, bacon from the butcher, and butter and eggs in your welcome pack. A lovely big grassy garden laps to the edge of the field; ducks waddle along the lane. Mark, delightful film director and generous host, describes the feel of these rustically romantic outbuildings as 'Suffolk meets New York loft'. All the cottages feel private, especially the self-contained 'Bakery' (perfect for honeymooners) and 'Gun Cottage' at the far end. You'll find deckchairs, washing machine and driers in the 'walk-thru', and an invaluable 'insider's guide' to the area. Set in three river valleys – Box, Brett and Stour – this is the countryside that Constable made famous. Take one of the bikes that are freely available, hire a canoe, follow a footpath across the fields; one leads to a pub. One of our favourite places to unwind! *One acre dog exercise orchard area. Countryside footpaths leading directly from the cottage. Streams, woods and dog-friendly pubs.*

Rooms	3 cottages for 2 (1 double); 1 cottage for 4 (1 double, 1 bunk room; 1 shower room); 1 cottage for 5 (1 double, 1 family room for 3, extra bed; 1 shower room): £351-£791. Dogs £15-£25 per stay. Max. 2. In living areas only, not in bedrooms.
Meals	Self-catering.
Closed	Never.

Dog biscuits. detailed dog walks on OS maps, towels and local vet information

Mark Scott
Grove Cottages, The Grove
Edwardstone,
Lavenham CO10 5PP
Tel   +44 (0)1787 211115
Email   mark@grove-cottages.co.uk
Web   www.grove-cottages.co.uk

Kesgrave Hall

This Georgian mansion sits in 38 acres of woodland and was built for an MP in 1812. It served as home to US airmen during WWII, becoming a prep school shortly after. Refurbished in 2008, it was an instant hit with locals, who love the style, the food and the informal vibe, and despite its country-house good looks, it is almost a restaurant with rooms, the emphasis firmly on the food. Inside, you find wellington boots in the entrance hall, high ceilings in the huge sitting room, stripped boards in the humming bistro and doors that open onto a terrace in summer. Excellent bedrooms have lots of style. One is huge and comes with a faux leopard-skin sofa and free-standing bath. The others might not be quite as wild, but they're lovely nonetheless, some in the eaves, others in beautifully refurbished outbuildings. Expect warm colours, crisp linen, good lighting and fancy bathrooms. Back downstairs tasty bistro food flies from the kitchen, perhaps goats' cheese panna cotta, cottage pie with red cabbage, pear tart with rosemary and vanilla ice cream. Suffolk's magical coast waits. *Eight acres of woodland, Suffolk coast 20 minutes away, forest walks close.*

Rooms	10 doubles; 7 twin/doubles: £125–£230. 6 suites for 2: £275–£300. Dogs £10 per night. Max. 3. 7 dog-friendly bedrooms.
Meals	Breakfast £10–£16. Lunch & dinner, 3 courses, £25–£30.
Closed	Never.
	Good advice about more than 15 local dog-friendly walks, dog bowls and towels

Oliver Richards
Kesgrave Hall
Hall Road, Kesgrave,
Ipswich IP5 2PU

Tel	+44 (0)1473 333741
Email	reception@kesgravehall.com
Web	www.milsomhotels.com

Entry 145 Map 4

Twee Gebroeders

Twee Gebroeders is a fabulous 1897 Dutch Skûtsje type sailing barge, now enjoying a pampered retirement in a quiet corner of Suffolk. In the hands of Gill and Tim Allen, she has undergone an extensive yet subtle modernisation. The original feel of the boat has been maintained in the glowing Iroko panelling and the colouring in the fabrics. Modern touches, such as the shining red Aga at the heart of the boat, the hot shower, flushing loo and entertainment systems, simply enhance the experience of floating in a piece of classic maritime splendour. The boat is normally stationary, but river day trips can be arranged, and Gill and Tim will throw one in if you stay for a week. Crab fishing equipment is provided – if you find you aren't catching, keep the barking to a minimum and the seals and cormorants will appear to show you how it's done. Should you decide to send a landing party ashore, there are villages aplenty to raid for provisions, the Minsmere RSPB reserve to visit, and many miles of the Stour/Orwell path for you and your dog to tread. *Minimum stay two nights, three nights only in peak season. Book through Sawday's Canopy & Stars online or by phone.*

Rooms	Houseboat for 4 (1 double, 2 singles): from £110 per night. Max. 1 large or 2 small dogs.
Meals	Self-catering.
Closed	Rarely.

Dog biscuits provided for hungry dogs

Sawday's Canopy & Stars
Twee Gebroeders
Pin Mill,
Ipswich IP13 0RD

Tel	+44 (0)117 204 7830
Email	enquiries@canopyandstars.co.uk
Web	www.canopyandstars.co.uk/tweegebroeders

Entry 146 Map 4

The Westleton Crown

This is one of England's oldest coaching inns, with 800 years of continuous service under its belt. It stands in a village two miles inland from the sea at Dunwich, with Westleton Heath running east towards Minsmere Bird Sanctuary. Inside, you find the best of old and new. A recent refurbishment has introduced Farrow & Ball colours, leather sofas and a tongue-and-groove bar, and they mix harmoniously with panelled walls, stripped floors and ancient beams. Weave around and find nooks and crannies in which to hide, flames flickering in an open fire, a huge map on the wall for walkers. You can eat wherever you want, and a conservatory/breakfast room opens onto a terraced garden for summer barbecues. Fish comes straight off the boats at Lowestoft, local butchers provide local meat. Bedrooms are scattered about – between the inn and the annexe – and come in cool lime white with comfy beds, crisp linen, flat-screen TVs. Super bathrooms are fitted out in Fired Earth, and some have claw-foot baths. Aldeburgh and Southwold are close by. *Min. two nights at weekends. Year-round dog-friendly beach, big terraced garden, walks in heaths and woodland. Inn to inn map available with fabulous circular walks between The Westleton Crown and The Ship at Dunwich.*

Rooms	26 doubles; 2 twins: £95–£180.
	3 suites for 2: £185–£215.
	2 family rooms for 4: £160–£180.
	1 single: £90–£100.
	Dogs £7.50 per night.
Meals	Lunch & bar meals from £5.50.
	Dinner from £11.95. Sunday lunch £26.
Closed	Never.

Biscuits, bowls, blankets & brilliant walks on the doorstep

Gareth Clarke
The Westleton Crown
The Street, Westleton,
Saxmundham IP17 3AD
Tel   +44 (0)1728 648777
Email   info@westletoncrown.co.uk
Web   www.westletoncrown.co.uk

The Ship

Once a great port, Dunwich is now a tiny (but famous) village, gradually sinking into the sea. Its well-loved smugglers' inn, almost on the beach, overlooks the salt marsh and sea and pulls in wind-blown walkers and birdwatchers from the Minsmere Reserve. In the old-fashioned bar – nautical bric-a-brac, flagged floors, simple furnishings and a stove that belts out the heat – you can tuck into legendary hake and chips washed down with a pint of Adnams. There's also a more modern dining room where hearty food combines with traditional dishes: glorious big platefuls of ham, egg and chips, Blythburgh pork belly and ham hock terrine, and lamb cutlets served with an individual shepherd's pie. Up the fine Victorian staircase are spruced up bedrooms – simple, uncluttered – with period features, cord carpets, brass beds, old pine, little shower rooms. Rooms at the front have glorious salt marsh views, two new rooms overlook the garden, courtyard rooms are cosy with pine, and the family room under the eaves is fabulous: single beds, a big futon-style bean bag, and a flat-screen for the kids. *All year round dog-friendly beach; maps of circular walks.*

Rooms	11 doubles; 1 twin: £95–£125.
	3 family rooms for 4: £95–£135.
	Special mid-week rates off season.
	Dogs £5 per night.
Meals	Lunch from £6.95. Bar meals from £9.75.
	Dinner from £9.95. Sunday lunch £11.95.
Closed	Rarely.
	Fabulous walks on beaches, heaths & forest

Matt Goodwin
The Ship
St James's Street, Dunwich,
Saxmundham IP17 3DT

Tel	+44 (0)1728 648219
Email	info@shipatdunwich.co.uk
Web	www.shipatdunwich.co.uk

Entry 148 Map 4

The Crown & Castle

Orford is unbeatable, a sleepy Suffolk village blissfully marooned at the end of the road. River, beach and forest wait, as does the Crown & Castle, a fabulous English hostelry where the art of hospitality is practised with great flair. The inn stands in the shadow of Orford's 12th-century castle. The feel is warm and airy with stripped floorboards, open fires, eclectic art and candles at night. Rooms come with Vi-Spring beds, super bathrooms, lovely fabrics, the odd armchair. Four in the main house have watery views, the suite is stunning, the garden rooms big and light, the courtyard rooms (the latest addition) utterly sublime. All have crisp white linen, TVs, DVDs and digital radios. Wellington boots wait at the back door, so pull on a pair and explore Rendlesham Forest or hop on a boat and chug over to Orfordness. Ambrosial food awaits your return, perhaps seared squid with coriander and garlic, slow-cooked pork belly with a shellfish broth, crushed pistachio meringue with a chocolate ice cream sundae. A great place to wash up for a few lazy days. Sutton Hoo is close. Very dog-friendly. *Minimum stay two nights. Dinner, B&B at weekends. Exciting riverbank and woodland walks; maps provided.*

Rooms	18 doubles; 2 twins: £130–£190. 1 suite for 2: £245. Dinner, B&B from £99.50 p.p. Dogs £6 per dog per night. Max. 2 per garden room. 5 dog-friendly garden rooms.
Meals	Lunch from £8.50. À la carte dinner around £35.
Closed	Never.
	Homemade biscuits, towels, tap, poop bags & bin; secured long leash outside each room. Special doggie table: bring your dog while you eat

David & Ruth Watson
The Crown & Castle
Orford,
Woodbridge IP12 2LJ

Tel   +44 (0)1394 450205
Email   info@crownandcastle.co.uk
Web   www.crownandcastle.co.uk

Entry 149 Map 4

Suffolk

The Old Rectory

Through the front door to a generously proportioned and flagstoned hall and a smiling welcome from Christopher. Archways lead down the corridor to the library (cosy with maps, books and open fire) and a tall elegant staircase leads to spacious bedrooms, one with delightful bow windows and a view of the sea. There are sash windows and shutters, pelmets and antiques, heaps of good books. Outside: 20 acres of woodlands, meadows, paddocks, croquet lawn and vegetable garden (walled and wonderful). Walks galore on the Deben Peninsula, music at Snape Maltings; it's Suffolk at its best and peace reigns supreme. *Good morning walk from the house. Woodland, coast and water to swim in. No limit on max number of dogs – but not a pack!*

Rooms	2 doubles; 1 twin: £85–£115. Singles from £60. Dogs may be left alone in bedroom for a short time, if well behaved.
Meals	Dinner, 3 courses, £30. Pub 5-min walk.
Closed	Occasionally.

Always the odd treat for doggie visitors; drying towels and blankets available. Advice on walks, dog-friendly pubs and other places

	Christopher Langley
	The Old Rectory
	Alderton,
	Woodbridge IP12 3DE
Tel	+44 (0)1394 410003
Email	clangley@keme.co.uk
Web	www.oldrectoryaldertonbandb.co.uk

Entry 150 Map 4

Suffolk

Pavilion House

A conservation village surrounded by chalk grassland – famous for its flora, fauna and butterflies; marked walks are straight from this 16-year-old red-brick house. Friendly Gretta teaches cooking and you are in for a treat: homemade cake, enormous breakfasts with her own bread and jams, proper dinners or simple suppers. Sleep peacefully in traditional, comfortable bedrooms (one up, two down) with crisp linen and TVs. There's a guest sitting room too: English comfort with an oriental feel, parquet floors, antiques, original drawings, a cosy log-burner. Wander the superb garden. Newmarket and Cambridge are close. *Secure garden, unless dog very small. Good walks locally.*

Rooms	1 double & 1 twin/double with separate bath/shower; 1 twin/double: £85–£105. Singles £55–£60. Child bed available. Dogs £5 per night. Max. 2. Double is dog-friendly.
Meals	Lunch from £10. Dinner from £25. Supper from £15. BYOB. Pub 1.5 miles.
Closed	Christmas.

Towels for drying, advice on walks

	Gretta & David Bredin
	Pavilion House, 133 Station Road,
	Dullingham, Newmarket CB8 9UT
Tel	+44 (0)1638 508005
Mobile	+44 (0)7776 197709
Email	gretta@thereliablesauce.co.uk
Web	www.pavilionhousebandb.co.uk

Entry 151 Map 4

Hambledon House

Through an old ornate iron gate, up a sweeping drive in rolling parkland and… enter another world. With an Elizabethan core and Victorian additions, Vanessa's house is a unique celebration of the Arts and Crafts movement. It's been in her family for generations and the restoration, with a marvellous Italian slant, is well underway. Find rooms of pure opulence with regal beds and bags of character, fabulous bathrooms, art, antiques, vast fireplaces, stunning stained glass, an orangery for breakfasts and a wonderful garden with a long reflecting pond. Vanessa is great fun and you're free to wander everywhere. Magical. *Rivers, lakes and ponds to swim in, balls to chase, acres of parkland and woodland to get lost in.*

Badger's ecstasy is a long sandy beach like Bamburgh, but then, he is always happy! Here, he conquers Polperro Harbour as a giant hound.

Tufty just loves racing through the woods, past the badger sets and lime kilns of Churston Woods and out onto the pebbles of Churston Cove.

Rooms	3 doubles: £110–£130. Singles £75. Extra beds available for children £40 per night.
Meals	Dinner, 3 courses, £30. Catering for house parties. Pubs/restaurants 10-minute walk.
Closed	Rarely.

Biscuits on arrival, towels for wet muddy dogs, a hose, shampoo and doggie blankets

Vanessa Rhode
Hambledon House, Vann Lane,
Hambledon, Godalming GU8 4HW
Tel   +44 (0)1428 683815
Mobile   +44 (0)7768 645500
Email   vanessaswarbreck@yahoo.co.uk
Web   www.hambledonhouse.com

Entry 152 Map 3

The Cat

Owner Andrew swapped grand Gravetye Manor for the buzzy, pubby atmosphere of The Cat in 2009; he hasn't looked back. The 16th-century building, a fine medieval hall house with a Victorian extension, has been comfortably modernised without losing its character. Inside are beamed ceilings and panelling, planked floors, splendid inglenooks, and an airy room that leads to a garden at the back, furnished with teak and posh brollies. Harvey's Ale and some top-notch pub food, passionately put together from fresh local ingredients by chef Max Leonard, attract a solid, old-fashioned crowd: retired locals, foodies and walkers. Tuck into rare roast beef and horseradish sandwiches, Rye Bay sea bass with brown shrimp and caper butter, South Downs lamb chops with dauphinoise (and leave room for treacle tart!). The setting is idyllic, in a pretty village opposite a 12th-century church – best viewed from two of four bright and comfortable bedrooms. Crisp linen on big beds, rich fabrics, fawn carpets, fresh bathrooms and antique touches illustrate the style. A sweet retreat in a charming village backwater. *Lots of ideas for places to walk, along with local Ordnance Survey maps.*

Rooms	4 doubles: £110–£150.
	Max. 2 dogs per room.
Meals	Lunch from £6. Dinner from £13.50.
Closed	Rarely.

Treats are plentiful as are old towels for cleaning down

Andrew Russell
The Cat
Queen's Square, West Hoathly,
East Grinstead RH19 4PP
Tel   +44 (0)1342 810369
Email   thecatinn@googlemail.com
Web   www.catinn.co.uk

Entry 153 Map 4

Withyfield Cottage

Local and sustainable are the two principles at the heart of Withyfield. Half rustic log cabin, half comfortable cottage, this incredible strawbale structure was designed by Ben Law, builder and permaculture expert whose project was voted the most popular ever to feature on Channel 4's Grand Designs. It's a graceful work of art: exposed timber beams sweep down from the high, arched ceiling and sink into the worktops and floor, framing the open-plan kitchen and living room. One of the bedrooms has its own bathroom, two are on the ground floor; all are simply decorated, letting the breathtaking quality of the workmanship shine through. From the veranda, you can see the very woodlands where the timber to clad the exterior was cut and then replenished. Step off the decking and, beyond your enclosed garden, find a pastoral paradise. The local Sussex landscape is criss-crossed with walking trails taking in places of history and beauty. Owner Janice will make sure you have all you need – even a list of dog-friendly pubs. *Bookings begin on Monday or Friday. Book through Sawday's Canopy & Stars online or by phone.*

Rooms	Cottage for 6 (1 twin/double en suite, 1 double, 1 twin/double): from £92 per night. Max. 2. Kennel provided with a run, and dog-sitting sometimes available.
Meals	Self-catering.
Closed	Never.
	Towels for drying, and advice on walks

Sawday's Canopy & Stars
Withyfield Cottage
Merrion Farm, Partridge Green,
Horsham RH13 8EH

Tel	+44 (0)117 204 7830
Email	enquiries@canopyandstars.co.uk
Web	www.canopyandstars.co.uk/withyfield

Entry 154 Map 4

Strand House

Strand House was built in 1425 and originally stood on Winchelsea harbour, though the sea was reclaimed long ago and marshland now runs off to the coast. You can walk down after breakfast, a great way to atone for your bacon and eggs. Back at the house, cosy interiors come with low ceilings, timber frames and ancient beams, all of which give an intimate feel. You'll find warm reds and yellows, sofas galore, a wood-burner in the sitting room and an honesty bar where you help yourself. It's a homespun affair: Hugh cooks breakfast, Mary conjures up delicious dinners: grilled goats' cheese with red onion marmalade, Dover sole with a lemon butter, rhubarb and ginger crumble. Attractive bedrooms are warm and colourful and a couple are small; one has an ancient four-poster, some have wonky floors, all have beamed ceilings, good linen, comfy beds. Tall people are better off with ground-floor rooms as low ceilings are de rigueur on upper floors; all rooms have compact bathrooms. The house, once a workhouse, was painted by Turner and Millais. A short walk through the woods leads up to the village. *Fields on doorstep, beach one mile: perfect walking for dogs and owners.*

Rooms	8 doubles; 1 twin/double; 1 suite for 4; 3 triples: £70–£180. Singles from £60. Dogs £7.50 (by arrangement). Max. 2. 3 dog-friendly bedrooms.
Meals	Dinner, 3 courses, £34.50.
Closed	Rarely.

Dog treats on arrival

Mary Sullivan & Hugh Davie
Strand House
Tanyards Lane,
Winchelsea, Rye TN36 4JT
Tel   +44 (0)1797 226276
Email   info@thestrandhouse.co.uk
Web   www.thestrandhouse.co.uk

Entry 155 Map 4

The Ship Inn

The 16th-century smuggler's warehouse stands by the quay at the bottom of cobbled Mermaid Street. Climb the church tower for stunning coast and marsh views, then retreat to the laid-back warmth of the Ship's rustic bars. Cosy nooks, ancient timbers, blazing fires and a quirky delicious décor characterise this place; there are battered leather sofas, simple café-style chairs, old pine tables and good paintings and prints. Quaff a pint of Harvey's Sussex or local farm cider, leaf through the daily papers, play one of the board games – there are heaps. Lunch and dinner menus are short and imaginative and make good use of local ingredients, so tuck into confit duck with grilled aubergine and saffron yogurt, roast sea bream with buttered samphire, warm salad of squid, fennel and chorizo, and fresh Rye Bay fish. The relaxed funky feel extends to bright and beachy bedrooms upstairs: find painted wooden floors, jazzy wall coverings, comfortable beds, splashes of colour. Quirky extras include Roberts radios, sticks of rock, and rubber ducks in simple bathrooms. And they love dogs. *Walks on sandy beaches, in woods and by river.*

Rooms	10 doubles: £80–£110.
	Dogs £10 per dog per stay. Max. 2.
Meals	Lunch & dinner £11.75–£18.50.
Closed	Rarely.

Advice and maps for walks, bowls, pigs' ears – and a tasty sausage for breakfast

Karen Northcote
The Ship Inn
The Strand,
Rye TN31 7DB
Tel   +44 (0)1797 222233
Email   mayistay@theshipinnrye.co.uk
Web   www.theshipinnrye.co.uk

Entry 156 Map 4

Poppy on her first camping trip.

Ned's favourite spot is Studland beach – he's allowed here all year long and loves swimming to fetch sticks in the sea.

Appletree Cottage

An enviable position facing south for this 1820s hung-tile farmer's cottage, covered in roses, jasmine and wisteria; views are over farmland towards the coast at Fairlight Glen. Jane will treat you to tea and cake when you arrive – either before a warming fire in the drawing room, or in the garden in summer. Bedrooms are sunny, spacious, quiet and traditional, one with gorgeous garden views. Breakfast well on apple juice from their own apples, homemade jams and marmalade, local bacon and sausages. Perfect for walkers with a footpath at the front gate; birdwatchers will be happy too, and you are near the steam railway at Bodiam. *Min. stay two nights at weekends May-September. Children over eight welcome. Spacious, fenced garden. National footpath runs past.*

Rooms	1 double with separate private bath; 1 twin/double (en suite): £80. 1 single with separate private bath: £50. Dogs £5 per dog per night. Max. 2 well-behaved.
Meals	Pub/restaurant 0.5 miles.
Closed	Rarely.

Woodland with lots of interesting sights and smells: dog heaven! Towel available after a wet walk

🐕 📶 🦴 ♿ 🚂

Jane & Hugh Willing
Appletree Cottage
Beacon Lane, Staplecross, Battle,
Robertsbridge TN32 5QP

Tel	+44 (0)1580 831724
Email	appletree.cottage@hotmail.co.uk
Web	www.appletreecottage.co

Entry 157 Map 4

The Red Lion

Dogs are welcome in this ancient warren of a pub where canine sketches adorn the walls; 'the Landlady' – the pub's own Cocoa – is often around. But that doesn't mean the whiff of wet canine… rather the mouthwatering aroma of imaginative dishes from chef/co-patron Sarah Keightley. Crispy-battered cod and chips with caper berries and mushy peas are served on *The Red Lion Times*, and pork tenderloin comes wrapped in pancetta with apple purée, black pudding and Dijon mustard sauce. A meltingly warm pear and ginger pudding with toffee sauce should round it all off nicely. You can also stay, in five bedrooms that reflect the unfussy approach. With natural colours and crisp ginghams, their comfort and attention to quality make up for their size; in an inn that goes back two centuries, bedrooms are not likely to be huge. Downstairs is space for everyone, from the pool room to the restaurant to the beautiful flagged bar warmed by a fire and a wood-burning stove. A smart but sensitive refurb has not cost this village pub its character, nor its sense of community. *Large garden and walks nearby.*

Rooms	2 doubles; 1 twin; 1 family room for 4: £90–£140. 1 single: £60. Singles £55–£75. Max. 2 small dogs or 1 medium-sized.
Meals	Lunch & dinner £11.95–£18.95.
Closed	Never.

Delicious home-cooked pigs' ears for sale behind the bar

Lisa Phipps & Sarah Keightley
The Red Lion
Main Street, Long Compton,
Shipston-on-Stour CV36 5JS
Tel   +44 (0)1608 684221
Email   info@redlion-longcompton.co.uk
Web   www.redlion-longcompton.co.uk

Entry 158 Map 3

The Fuzzy Duck

Nestled in the rolling folds of the Cotswold countryside, close to Stratford-upon-Avon, is this pretty 18th-century coaching inn, polished to perfection by Tania, Adrian and their team. Beautiful fireplaces and gleaming tables, fine china and big sprays of wildflowers tell a tale of comfort and luxury, while the smiling staff are rightly proud of this gem of a pub. You dine like kings and queens in the sparkling bar, or in the clever conversion at the back, overlooking grounds that are part-orchard, part-walled-garden. Chef Richard, husband to manager Sol Craven, has a love of wild food and all the right connections to bring the best of it to your table; try Scottish grouse with bread sauce and local honey, or a splendid ploughman's with warm scotch quail's egg. Borrow wellies in your size for a bracing walk then back to your beautiful bed above the bar; rooms are sound-proofed and two have double loft beds (up very vertical ladders) for families. Best of all, the generous team has provided indulgent treats: lovely slippers, nightcap tipple — come prepared to be spoiled. Bliss. *Secure garden; miles of woodland, parkland and farmland.*

Rooms	2 doubles: £110–£140.
	2 family rooms for 4: £180–£200.
	4 dog-friendly bedrooms. Max. 2-4 dogs
	(doubles more suited to small dogs).
Meals	Breakfast from £14.50. Lunch from £14.50.
	Dinner from £14.
Closed	Never.

Pigs' ears, dog biscuits and blankets

Sol Craven
The Fuzzy Duck
Ilmington Road, Armscote,
Stratford-upon-Avon CV37 8DD

Tel	+44 (0)1608 682 635
Email	info@fuzzyduckarmscote.com
Web	www.fuzzyduckarmscote.com

The Chequers Inn

New life has been breathed into this north Cotswold pub by Kirstin and James – and how! A bold style of classic British meets country French thanks to rich tapestries, gilt mirrors, padded chairs, round tables and aged wooden flooring throughout. There is a proper glowing wood bar with St Austell Tribute and London Pride on tap; plus Stowford Press cider, an impressive wine selection and several varieties of fizz for special occasions. The calm, elegant Provençal dining area at the back overlooks a well-planted and sheltered garden which hides the chef's veg patch. Start with honey-glazed crispy duck salad with hoisin dressing and cashew nuts, move on to brill with buttered mash and gremolata. The puds will also tempt, and then there's freshly ground coffee. Different, slightly decadent, and definitely worth a visit. *Dog-friendly fields nearby.*

Marston House

A generous feel pervades this lovely family home; Kim's big friendly kitchen is the hub of the house. She and John are easy-going and kind and there's no standing on ceremony. Feel welcomed on tea on arrival, delicious breakfasts, oodles of interesting facts about what to do in the area. The house, with solar electricity, is big and sunny; old rugs cover parquet floors, soft sofas tumble with cushions, sash windows look onto the smart garden packed with birds and borders. Bedrooms are roomy, traditional and supremely comfortable. A special, peaceful place with a big heart, great walks from the door and Silverstone a short hop. *Good walks all around; loan of Ordnance Survey map & advice on walks.*

Meals	Lunch & bar meals from £4.50. Dinner £9.50–£16.95. Sunday lunch, 3 courses, £23.45.
Closed	3pm–5pm. Sunday evenings & Monday.

 Dog chews, water & plenty of fuss provided

Rooms	1 twin/double with separate bath; 1 twin/double with separate shower: £95–£110. Singles £75. Dogs may be left unattended in bedroom, but prefer them to stay in kitchen.
Meals	Supper, 3 courses, £29.50. Dinner £35 (min. 4). Pub 5-minute walk.
Closed	Occasionally in winter.

 Edible treats and lots of spoiling

James & Kirstin Viggers
The Chequers Inn
91 Banbury Road, Ettington,
Stratford-upon-Avon CV37 7SR
Tel   +44 (0)1789 740387
Email   hello@the-chequers-ettington.co.uk
Web   www.the-chequers-ettington.co.uk

Entry 160 Map 3

Kim & John Mahon
Marston House, Byfield Road,
Priors Marston, Southam CV47 7RP
Tel   +44 (0)1327 260297
Mobile   +44 (0)7813 831028
Email   kim@mahonand.co.uk
Web   www.ivabestbandb.co.uk

Entry 161 Map 3

Fox & Hounds

Beech trees and high ridges: make time for a walk with views over the vale, then land at the 17th-century thatched pub on the green. Inside are two areas: one bright and conservatory-like, with a great view, the other older and cosier, its fireplace flanked by small red leather sofas. There are warming ales from Palmers and Butcombe, and Hop Back's inimitable Summer Lightning, and a well-presented wine card that tells you exactly what you'll get. No-nonsense New Zealander Murray cooks in an eclectic, untypical gastro style. Tuck into a chorizo, bean and red pepper casserole in red wine with belly pork, or a sweet onion, ricotta and parmesan tart, and follow with melting chocolate fondant and mascarpone cream; no need to feel sinful. Then stay till the pub closes. *Walks in the village and on village green in front of pub.*

This is Prince, a Vizsla/Labrador (Vizslador), posing above Devil's Kitchen in Snowdonia!

Meals	Lunch & dinner £9–£17.
Closed	3pm–5.30pm.

 A pub is man's best friend – & man's other best friend is always welcome here. Dog bowl and dog treats at the bar

Murray Seator
Fox & Hounds
The Green, East Knoyle,
Salisbury SP3 6BN

Tel	+44 (0)1747 830573
Email	fox.hounds@virgin.net
Web	www.foxandhounds-eastknoyle.co.uk

Entry 162 Map 3

Tess, the English Springer Spaniel, on a day out in the Cotswolds. She keeps warm with her tweed cap and really looks the part.

Long Cover Cottage

Stealing its name from the backdrop of ancient undisturbed woodland, the cottage and its surrounds make a natural family home – for both frazzled humans and local badgers. Winding your way up the long peaceful track to this converted stable, you catch glorious glimpses of the Teme and Kyre valleys; the setting is spectacular. On arrival, you're greeted by the delightful Ellie, whose grounds and beautifully tended English country garden you share. Generous windows flood rooms with light that bounces off polished elm floorboards; a wood-burner and Aga keep things cosy, the kitchen is handcrafted, the views are long and bucolic. Upstairs, bedrooms are brass-bedded and floral, tucked under the eaves in that cottagey way. You get a handy loo and basin up here, and a sparkling bathroom with a roll top tub downstairs. Lucky children have seven acres to romp in, a secret treehouse with hammocks and a barbecue for midnight feasts. Resting on the borders of three counties, this is prime walking country. Bustling Ledbury and Ludlow, England's Slow Food capital, are just a drive away. *Seven acres of specially fenced land for carefree scampers & no roads for miles.*

Rooms	1 cottage for 6 (2 doubles, 1 twin; 1 bath & shower room, 1 separate wc): £900.
Meals	Self-catering.
Closed	Never.

 Towels, dog bowl & doggie treats

Ellie Van Straaten
Long Cover Cottage
Vine Lane, Kyre,
Tenbury Wells WR15 8RL
Tel   +44 (0)1885 410208
Email   ellie_vanstraaten@yahoo.co.uk
Web   www.a-country-break.co.uk

Entry 163 Map 2

The Coach House

Head for the hills… and the dancing daffodils. In the grounds of a 16th-century timber-framed house, the perfect retreat à deux. Way up a simple track, your stone-walled, stone-tiled hideaway was built almost entirely from reclaimed materials. Inside is open-plan and easy. Recline on your leather chesterfield, toes directed at a wood-burner stacked with logs from the woods. The kitchen, of hand-crafted oak, has a double Belfast sink and a sweep of wood floor, the well-dressed bed is to the side, and the shower room is a step away. Follow the brook through this ancient orchid-dotted woodland, rest awhile at the owner's little treehouse (with hammocks), then come home to your own little patch and magnificent views across open pastures to the Teme and Kyre valleys. Venture further to foodie Ludlow, book-lined Hay-on-Wye and the grand industrial heritage that is Ironbridge. Take to the slow life on the steam railway, stride out on the Mortimer Trail, meander through Herefordshire villages. Buzzards soar overhead, rabbits scamper in the fields that surround you. *Seven acres of fenced land.*

Rooms	1 house for 2 (1 double; 1 shower room): £700.
Meals	Self-catering.
Closed	Never.

Towels, water bowls & doggie treats

Ellie Van Straaten
The Coach House
Vine Lane, Kyre,
Tenbury Wells WR15 8RL

Tel	+44 (0)1885 410208
Email	ellie_vanstraaten@yahoo.co.uk
Web	www.a-country-break.co.uk

Entry 164 Map 2

The Traddock

A northern outpost of country-house charm, beautiful inside and out. It's a family affair and those looking for a friendly base from which to explore the Dales will find it here. You enter through a wonderful drawing room – crackling fire, pretty art, the daily papers, cavernous sofas. Follow your nose and find polished wood in the dining room, panelled walls in the breakfast room, then William Morris wallpaper in the sitting room bar, where you can sip a pint of Skipton ale while playing a game of Scrabble. Bedrooms are just the ticket, some coolly contemporary, others deliciously traditional with family antiques and the odd claw-foot bath. Those on the second floor are cosy in the eaves, all have fresh fruit, homemade shortbread and Dales views. Elsewhere, a white-washed sitting room that opens onto the garden and a rug-strewn restaurant for fabulous local food, perhaps Whitby crab, slow-roasted pork, raspberry and white chocolate soufflé. Spectacular walks start at the front door, there are cycle tracks and some extraordinary caves – one is bigger than St Paul's. Brilliant. *Min. two nights at weekends Mar-Nov. National Park with miles of walking; caves and forests on doorstep.*

Rooms	7 doubles; 1 twin/double: £95–£195.
	2 family rooms for 4: £95–£165.
	1 single: £85–£95.
	Dinner, B&B £78–£128 p.p.
	Extra bed/sofabed £15 p.p per night.
	Dogs £5 per dog per stay. Max. 2.
	Allowed to stay in bedroom at supper
	time if well behaved,
Meals	Lunch from £9.50.
	Dinner, 3 courses, around £30.
Closed	Never.

Dog washing facilities and towels

Paul Reynolds
The Traddock
Austwick,
Settle LA2 8BY

Tel	+44 (0)1524 251224
Email	info@thetraddock.co.uk
Web	www.thetraddock.co.uk

Entry 165 Map 6

The Lion at Settle

Generations of travellers have enjoyed the welcome at this grand 17th-century coaching inn; following a recent renovation its doors are open to all. Original features have been saved, including smooth oak floors, a fabulous inglenook fireplace in the grand entrance hall and the graceful sweeping staircase; comfortable sofas and chairs are upholstered in tartan wool. Locally sourced ingredients dominate a menu which places its emphasis on comfort: try Settle Pudding (tender braised beef with a suet lid) and homemade Scotch egg with thick-cut chips, and, if you can find room, Phillipa's sticky toffee pudding is a must. The elegant but cosy dining room with its pleasingly mismatched furniture, panelled walls and old photos buzzes with friendly chat. If you're a Three Peaks bagger, a devotee of the stunning Settle to Carlisle railway or simply want to get away from it all you can stay in characterful bedrooms with five-star mattresses, white cotton bed linen, immaculate bathrooms, plasma screens and fresh milk for your morning cuppa. The historic town is worth exploring: lose yourself in its cobbled alleyways. *Good walks.*

Rooms	14 twin/doubles: £75–£130. Larger family rooms available. Dogs £15 per night. 2 dog-friendly rooms.
Meals	Lunch from £6.95. Bar meals from £5.95. Dinner from £8.95.
Closed	Rarely.

Recommendations for dog-friendly walks. 10% of the overnight charge is donated to Teckels Animal Sanctuaries

Louise Van Delft
The Lion at Settle
Duke Street,
Settle BD24 9DU

Tel   +44 (0)1729 822203
Email   relax@thelionsettle.co.uk
Web   www.thelionsettle.co.uk

The Lister Arms at Malham

You'll be hard pushed to find a better looking pub in a more gorgeous village. The National Trust's Malham is a favourite with potholers – this part of Yorkshire is riddled with caverns – but there are many surface pleasures to be had. Sitting on the edge of the village green, the 17th-century coaching inn was once home to the first Lord of Ribblesdale; very grand it looks too. But don't stand on ceremony; inside are flagged floors, wood-burning stoves and well-kept local ales. Andrew and Tracey have also put an interesting menu together using mostly local produce. Start with potted Malham pork with sticky apples, herbs and crackling... push the boat out and order slow-cooked shoulder of lamb served with pan juice gravy and pumpkin purée; then, if you still have room, finish off with rhubarb and ginger crème brûlée. Upstairs are comfortable bedrooms with calm colours, lovely linen and immaculate bathrooms; most have views over the village green to the lush hills beyond. A perfect place to park yourself for a few days above ground. *Large National Park to roam.*

Rooms	5 doubles; 1 twin; 3 family rooms for 4: £80–£130. Singles £59–£79. Dogs £15 per night. 2 dog-friendly bedrooms.
Meals	Lunch & dinner from £10.50. Bar meals from £6.95. Sunday lunch, 3 courses, £15.50.
Closed	Never.
	Recommendations for dog-friendly walks. 10% of the overnight charge is donated to Teckels Animal Sanctuaries

Andrew McGeorge
The Lister Arms at Malham
Malham,
Skipton BD23 4DB

Tel   +44 (0)1729 830330
Email   relax@listerarms.co.uk
Web   www.listerarms.co.uk

Entry 167 Map 6

Bewerley Hall Cottage

Pretty pretty pretty! Once the home of Bewerley Hall's head gardener, this couple's hideaway is comfy, cute and at the tail of a terrace of stone cottages. Step in to a sitting room that envelops you in cheering warmth: a wood-burner in the inglenook; two squishy red sofas dotted with cushions; a bookcase brimming with books, an iPod dock, guides and maps. For muddy wellies there's a boot room, and next to this, a cottagey kitchen. Upstairs is a double with excellent linen and lovely views over cherry trees and the village green, and a bathroom with slipper bath and local lotions. On sunny days, follow the sun front or back, dine out and soak up the views over Bewerley Park, the river and town beyond. Walk from the door, along the river Nidd or to How Stean limestone gorge; you're in beautiful Nidderdale and the Yorkshire Dales are a few miles away. Explore by foot, bike or horse – a mountain bike centre and stables are nearby – and well-behaved dogs are welcome (downstairs). For a more sedate ramble, stroll to charming Pateley Bridge (five minutes) and pick up your dinner – there's a deli, butchers and a good pub. Perfect. *Min. four nights on weekdays; three at weekends. Enclosed garden; good woodland and river walks nearby.*

Rooms	1 cottage for 2: £495-£595.
	Short breaks available.
	Max. 2 dogs. To be kept downstairs.
Meals	Self-catering.
Closed	Never.

Bowl, doggie treats in the fridge, and the best local info on where to walk – and where to enjoy a friendly pub or two!

Sarah Bray
Bewerley Hall Cottage
9 The Green, Bewerley,
Pateley Bridge HG3 5HU
Tel   +44 (0)1765 688210
Email   info@yorkshireboltholes.com
Web   www.cottageinbewerley.com

Entry 168 Map 6

The Hayloft at Flamborough Rigg

On and on the road goes, deeper into the woods until the single track stops at an 1820s farmhouse surrounded by open fields. The gravelled drive crunches nicely under the tyres and the kitchen sports a hamper of local goodies (and, on occasion, home-brewed elderflower champagne!). Philip and Caroline love making guests feel at home and you may freely roam their super big garden with orchard, vegetable patch, loungers and barbecue. You can head off for a long walk over the rolling North Yorkshire Moors and come back to deep comfort. Snuggle up with a book in front of the wood-burner, watch a DVD, play a round of cards at the chunky table. There are quirky touches like old Singer sewing machines as table bases, a shelf of vintage china in the well-thought out kitchen/diner, and modern art on the walls. The bedrooms feel light and fresh with local oak furniture and cheerful cushions. Jump in the car for a trip to the coast or wander round the charming market town of Helmsley. The Hayloft feels as though it's in the middle of nowhere and yet moors, dales and the sea are wonderfully close. *Short breaks available. Large fully enclosed garden, great forest walks, dog-friendly beaches nearby. Dogs are welcome in many local pubs.*

Rooms	1 barn for 4 (1 double with en suite shower, 1 twin; 1 bathroom): £295-£650. Short breaks available. Max. 2 dogs. May not be left alone in bedroom unless in a cage.
Meals	Self-catering.
Closed	Rarely.
	Every dog receives a guide to local dog-friendly pubs & beaches

Philip & Caroline Jackson
The Hayloft at Flamborough Rigg
Middlehead Road,
Stape, Pickering YO18 8HR

Tel	+44 (0)1751 475263
Email	enquiries@flamboroughriggcottage.co.uk
Web	www.thehayloftatflamboroughrigg.co.uk

Entry 169 Map 6

Skipwith Station, Derwent Flyer

Families would love this – so might honeymooners! In stunning contrast to the carriages of old, these three are sleek and luxurious. Find wooden floors, Venetian blinds, snazzy cushions, snowy linen and, in the latest, a central work station at the kitchen end and a super-contemporary, almost Scandinavian feel. Kitchens are well-equipped, showers are fabulous and there's a vintage rocking chair in shabby-chic fashion. The spaces are cosy but not cramped, well-designed but homely – the owners (she a garden designer), who live in the old ticket office, have done a superlative job. The setting is lush, and Skipwith Common is the largest wetland heath in the north of England: there are cycle tracks, bridle routes and wildlife galore, and the lane leading to the tiny village is utterly rural. Lizanne's creativity has extended to two landscaped acres. Add several hens and two wagging dogs (you're welcome to walk them) and you'll soon feel at home. Books, games, DVDs, storage and air con – they're all here, and if you stay for four nights there's a hamper as well. *Dogs welcome in Derwent Flyer and Derwent Mail.*

Rooms	1 train carriage for 4 (1 double, 1 bunk room; 1 shower room); 1 train carriage for 4 (1 double, 1 bunk room & futon; 1 shower room); 1 train carriage for 4; (1 double, 1 twin, both en suite): £290–£650. Max. 2 dogs per unit.
Meals	Self-catering.
Closed	Rarely.

Leaf through the dog-walk guide & pick a route, then step out of your carriage into the country

Lizanne Southworth
Skipwith Station,
Derwent Flyer
North Duffield YO8 5DE
Tel   +44 (0)1757 282288
Email   lizanne@skipwithstation.com
Web   www.skipwithstation.com

The Mollycroft

The Mollycroft is a 1940s showman's living van, restored to gleaming glory and as eccentric as the people who once toured in it. Inside, a combination of dark wood and bright yellow and green décor creates a lively but homely feel. There are sofas in both the living room and the bunk room, which doubles as the kitchen, so you have plenty of space for lazy loafing in this tumbling, spacious wagon. You're far from the '40s in comforts: gas hobs and fridge in the kitchen, mains power and WiFi bring things up-to-date. Next to the Mollycroft is a fire pit complete with cooking gear, and the compost loo and outdoor shower are both a walk away (you're still camping, after all). With no other guests around, it's ideal for a family or those looking for peace, though the 3ft high deck makes it unsuitable for toddlers. The grounds hold rare bamboo gardens, a lake, and your host Greville's converted chapel; the Yorkshire Dales are stunning and close. Don't miss the enormous Sunday market at Catterick racecourse – or the races, of course. *Minimum stay two nights. Book through Sawday's Canopy & Stars online or by phone.*

Rooms	Showman's wagon for 4 (1 double, 2 bunks): from £75 per night. Dogs to be kept on leads.
Meals	Self-catering.
Closed	Rarely.

 A swim in the lake from the jetty

Sawday's Canopy & Stars
The Mollycroft
Saint Paulinus, Brough Park,
Richmond DL10 7PJ
Tel   +44 (0)117 204 7830
Email   enquiries@canopyandstars.co.uk
Web   www.canopyandstars.co.uk/mollycroft

Entry 171 Map 6

The Garden Cottage

Enter a stone-flagged passage at the end of which is a grand old door to the garden beyond: intriguing is the higgledy-piggledy approach to the pretty house on the hill. To the right is the cottage entrance. Garden Cottage, listed and delightful, was once cottage to the main house (demolished in 1824), and one of its many charms is its garden, large, sloping and full of shrubs, apple trees, herbs, borders and magnificent monkey puzzle tree; a mellow old brick wall runs down one side. You are halfway up steep Cravengate and the lofty setting is stunning; convenient too, a five-minute walk from town, woodland and river. There's lots of space inside too, and plenty of original features. Paintwork is perfect, walls nicely patterned, curtains well-hung, and the traditional striped sofas are pristine. The main bedroom is gorgeous with double bed and rafters; another has a suede headboard; windows have long views over the Norman castle and the atmospheric old town. For cosy nights in: books, games, DVDs, a wood-burner and a piano. For nights out: two cinemas, the Georgian Theatre Royal and several enjoyable places to dine. *Female dogs preferred; call to discuss with owner. Secure garden; woodland, fields and river all within five-minute walk.*

Rooms	1 cottage for 6 (1 double en suite, 1 double, 1 twin; 1 bath/shower room): £545–£895. Max. 2 dogs.
Meals	Self-catering.
Closed	Never.

Every pooch gets a Lucky Dog Surprise Bag, & a folder filled with local trails – owners bring your walking boots!

Dennis & Marcia McLuckie
The Garden Cottage
Richmond DL10 4RG

Tel	+44 (0)1748 825525
Email	marcia.scorton@btconnect.com
Web	www.yorkshirecountryholidays.co.uk

Old Cello Workshop

The stringed instrument workshop – originally a farm byre – has become a delicious home for six. Its setting is off Richmond's pretty green, flanked with Georgian houses. Views sail over Marcia's garden (she, smiley and hospitable, lives just across the road) and up to Culloden Tower. A black wrought-iron gate opens to a paved front patio and a white front door. Step in to find three storeys of comfort and charm: a kitchen/breakfast room and a bathroom on the ground floor, a short flight of stairs to the living area above, then steps down to two doubles. A separate stair leads to the twin room in the attic – sweet, secluded and perfect for older children. The fresh and contemporary double (and double-glazed) bedrooms face the road, with feature wallpapers and super new beds. The living room, lofty but cosy, has matching sofas and armchairs, a gas-fired 'wood' stove, a bookcase stuffed with novels and guides, and plenty of night-time diversions, from jigsaws to DVDs. The river Swale lies just below and there's a wonderful walk alongside it to Easby Abbey. Bring the dog. *Short breaks available. Enclosed courtyard; woodland, fields and river all within five-minute walk.*

Rooms	1 house for 6 (2 doubles, 1 twin; 1 bath/shower room, separate wc): £545–£895. Max. 3 dogs.
Meals	Self-catering.
Closed	Never.

Every pooch gets a Lucky Dog Surprise Bag & a folder filled with local trails – owners bring your walking boots!

Dennis & Marcia McLuckie
Old Cello Workshop
28 The Green,
Richmond DL10 4RG

Tel	+44 (0)1748 825525
Email	marcia.scorton@btconnect.com
Web	www.yorkshirecountryholidays.co.uk

Entry 173 Map 6

Millgate House

Prepare to be amazed. In every room of the house and in every corner of the garden, the marriage of natural beauty and sophistication exists in a state of bliss. Beds from Heals, period furniture, cast-iron baths, myriad prints and paintings and one double bed so high you wonder how to get onto it. Tim and Austin, both ex-English teachers, have created something special, and the breakfasts are superb. A stay at Millgate House without exploring the prize-winning walled town garden would be an unforgivable omission; it deserves every bouquet and adulatory article it has received. A narrow lane adorned with immaculate hostas, introduces the main garden. The long terraced grounds, sloping steeply down towards the river, are divided into a rhythmic series of lush compartments. If you just want to explore the garden you can arrange a visit. *Good walks: river and open spaces.*

Rooms	2 doubles, 1 with separate bath/shower; 1 twin: £110–£145. Singles £95. Children over 10 welcome. Max. 2 dogs. No dogs in garden please!
Meals	Restaurant 250 yds.
Closed	Rarely.

 Advice on walks; towels, water and three resident whippets

Austin Lynch & Tim Culkin
Millgate House
Richmond DL10 4JN
Tel   +44 (0)1748 823571
Mobile   +44 (0)7738 298721
Email   oztim@millgatehouse.demon.co.uk
Web   www.millgatehouse.com

Entry 174 Map 6

The Postgate Inn

This neck of the woods is best known for its *Heartbeat* celebrity. Indeed, the Victorian stone pub sitting so handsomely at the bottom of the leafy Esk Valley – right by the historic train line – is *Heartbeat's* 'Black Dog'. Every reason to take the trip inland from Whitby: the big welcome, the homely feel (stone floors, beams, open fires) and the ever-changing menus of local ingredients brought together with such skill. Lamb noisettes with minted pea mash and a redcurrant and heather honey sauce are dense and toothsome; Whitby haddock and crab with gin crème sauce and white asparagus make the very best of the local catch. A terraced garden takes advantage of the views, making this a brilliant spot for lunch before stepping onto the steam train and rolling across the famous moors to Pickering. *Footpaths across the North Yorkshire moors, one 50 yards from door, beach walks in winter.*

| Meals | Lunch & dinner £10.95–£18.95. |
| Closed | 3.30pm–6.30pm (5.30pm in summer). |

 River walks & snoozes in front of an open fire

Mark & Shelley Powell
The Postgate Inn
Egton Bridge,
Whitby YO21 1UX
Tel   +44 (0)1947 895241
Email   info@postgateinn.com
Web   www.postgateinn.com

Entry 175 Map 6

Field House

You drive over bridge and beck to this listed, 1713 farmhouse — expect comfort, homeliness and open fires. Pat and Geoff love showing guests their hens, horses, goats and lambs, and will tell you about the 14 circular walks or lend you a torch so you can find the pub across the fields! Ramblers and dog walkers will be in heaven — step out of the front door, past the lovely walled garden and you're in rolling, Brontë countryside. Good big bedrooms are in farmhouse style, one bathroom has a roll top bath. Geoff's breakfasts are generous in the finest Yorkshire manner. Cot & highchair available. *Dog-friendly walks galore.*

His lordship Buster relaxes in the sun when he's not on his spot on the couch.

Rooms	1 double (extra single bed); 1 twin/double: £70-£78. 1 family room for 4 (separate bath/shower): £68-£74. Singles £45. Children £20. Dogs £5 in bedroom; £4 in stables (if cage brought). Prices per dog per night. Max. 2 per room.
Meals	Packed lunch. Pub/restaurant 200 yds
Closed	Rarely.

 Bronte and owner lead a guided walk from the house – 14 to choose from!

Pat & Geoff Horrocks-Taylor
Field House, Staups Lane,
Stump Cross, Halifax HX3 6XX

Tel	+44 (0)1422 355457
Mobile	+44 (0)7729 996482
Email	stayatfieldhouse@yahoo.co.uk
Web	www.fieldhouse-bb.co.uk

Entry 176 Map 6

Toastie the Airedale Terrier is a healthy, happy and obedient dog who responds well to being directed at photoshoots.

Wales

Photo: The Hand at
Llanarmon, entry 182

The Black Lion Inn

The lion roars again thanks to the hard work of owners Mari and Leigh who have transformed this once derelict late 18th-century country inn into an award-winning local champion. Contemporary slate tiles wrap round a modern bar, lime rendered walls host modern pictures – one a fabulous collage of the menu's provenance. French windows open to a paved patio with views across the car park to fields, one of which will soon grow vegetables and herbs for the kitchen. Ales from Marstons and local Welsh breweries and interesting wines set you up for modern British dishes. Try fresh-as-can-be local pan-fried scallops with black pudding on a bed of wilted lettuce topped with butter sauce, or beef from Mari's father's own Hereford herd. Upstairs are two hugely comfortable rooms with open rafters, thick carpets and handmade oak furniture: the mattresses are top of the range, the bathrooms gleam with white tiles, mosaic inlay and sleek chrome. You are beside a road but thick walls and small windows ensure blissful calm, while eco-energy keeps you snug. Glorious Anglesey awaits. *Beaches, woodland, quiet country lanes.*

Rooms	1 double: £115. 1 family room for 4: £140. Singles £90. Max. 2 per stay. 1 dog-friendly room.
Meals	Lunch & dinner £6–£19.
Closed	3-6pm Mon-Fri. Open all day Saturday & Sunday. November to Easter, closed Monday & Tuesday.
	Dog biscuits, towels for drying, advice on walks and dog-friendly beaches and venues

Leigh & Mari Faulkner
The Black Lion Inn
Llanfaethlu,
Holyhead LL65 4NL

Tel	+44 (0)1407 730718
Email	info@blacklionanglesey.co.uk
Web	www.blacklionanglesey.com

Entry 177 Map 5

Ty Mawr Country Hotel

Pretty rooms, attractive prices and delicious food make this super country house hard to resist. It's a very peaceful, tucked-away spot. You drive over the hills, drop into the village and wash up at this 16th-century stone house that glows in yellow. Outside, a sun-trapping terrace laps against a trim lawn, which in turn drops into a passing river. Gentle eccentricities abound: croquet hoops take the odd diversion, logs are piled high like giant beehives, a seat has been chiselled into a tree trunk. Inside, exposed stone walls, terracotta-tiled floors and low beamed ceilings give a warm country feel. There are fires everywhere – one in the sitting room, which overlooks the garden, another in the dining room that burns on both sides. Excellent bedrooms are all big. You get warm colours, big beds, crisp linen, good bathrooms. Some have sofas, all are dog-friendly, three overlook the garden. Back downstairs, the bar doubles as reception, and there's Welsh art on sale. Steve's cooking is the final treat: Cardigan Bay scallops, organic Welsh beef, calvados and cinnamon rice pudding. First class. *Children over ten welcome. Stream at the edge of the garden and miles of walks in the Brechfa Forest.*

Rooms	4 doubles; 2 twin/doubles: £115-£130.
	Singles from £70.
	Dinner, B&B from £80 p.p.
	Dogs to be kept on lead in bar & sitting room.
Meals	Dinner £24-£29.
Closed	Rarely.

🐾 Details of dog-friendly walks, poop bags and towels for drying

Annabel & Steve Thomas
Ty Mawr Country Hotel
Brechfa SA32 7RA
Tel   +44 (0)1267 202332
Email   info@wales-country-hotel.co.uk
Web   www.wales-country-hotel.co.uk

Y Talbot

In the centre of tiny Tregaron, the crisply Georgian frontage of Y Talbot makes a big impression, part modern-rustic drovers inn and part old-fashioned hotel. Inside the inn: an enormous inglenook with bread oven, slate floors, thick walls gleaming with hanging brass and copper. You dine in what was once the stable, with oak furniture and soapstone sculptures, where everything is light and bright. The hotel is all white corridors and glass doors, its curved wooden staircase leading to rooms which are cool and white and comfortable, with big smart bathrooms. The rooms on the top floor are cosiest, with low windows to views over the square. Two new airy suites at the rear of the pub are big enough for families. Friendly Mick and Nia will point you towards the best walks or rambles while head chef Dafydd Watkin (who worked under Marco Pierre White) does a mean Cambrian lamb shoulder, and works wonders with the day's fresh fish catch. All this and local tipples such as Purple Moose, Gwynt y Ddraig cider and Mantle from the latest micro brewery on the block. *Masses of walks, including flat ones, rivers, mountains, and a big bog.*

Rooms	13 twin/doubles: £70–£160.
	Singles £50–£70.
	Dogs £15 per dog per night. Max. 2.
	2 dog-friendly bedrooms.
Meals	Starters from £4.75. Mains £9–£18.
Closed	Christmas Day.
	Dog bowls. Mick will tell you the best walks

Mick Taylor
Y Talbot
Tregaron SY25 6JL
Tel   +44 (0)1974 298208
Email   info@ytalbot.com
Web   www.ytalbot.com

Troedyrhiw Holiday Cottages

Come for the wide wooded valley, the Preseli hills on show in the distance, and plenty of animals for children to befriend. You're down a rural track with other holiday makers; pygmy goats, Shetland ponies, kune kune pigs and chickens litter the fields around you and the owners (who will greet you) live on site should you need them. All the sitting rooms have wood-burners (logs are on the house), local art on the walls and comfy sofas and chairs; kitchens and bathrooms are modern (if slightly small) but fine for holiday needs. Bedrooms are spotless and bright – you'll sleep well, away from traffic noise. Each cottage has its own small garden or tranche of decking, plus barbecue and furniture so you can spill out for summertime meals and games. Fields lead down to the wide stream, perfect for welly (or barefoot in summer) splashing, and woodland walks. You're just a mile away from the nearest pub and shops and there are wide safe beaches for picnics and swimming; also walking, birdwatching, rugged mountain biking. Shopaholics will enjoy Cardigan, an appealing Welsh estuary town. *Short breaks available, please contact the owner. Woodland walks and stream on site; beaches and many great walks just a bark and a woof away!*

Rooms	1 cottage for 2; 2 cottages for 4; 1 cottage for 6; 1 cottage for 8: £235–£1,250. Dogs £20 per stay. Max. 2. Dogs can only be left unattended in the bedrooms if in a cage.
Meals	Self-catering.
Closed	Never.

 Dog treat included in welcome pack

Rob & Michelle Silcox
Troedyrhiw Holiday Cottages
Penparc, Cardigan SA43 2AE
Tel   +44 (0)1239 811564
Email   info@troedyrhiw.com
Web   www.troedyrhiw.com

Entry 180 Map 1

Penbontbren

You're lost in lovely hills, yet only three miles from the sea. Not that you're going to stray far. These gorgeous suites don't just have wonderful prices, they're also addictive – this is a great spot to come and do nothing at all. Richard and Huw have thought it all through. You get crockery and cutlery, kettles and fridges, you're also encouraged to bring your own wine and to nip up to the farm shop for provisions for lunch. As for the suites, they have big beds, super bathrooms, sofas and armchairs in cosy sitting areas, and doors onto semi-private terraces – perfect for lunches in summer. Potter about and find iPod docks, flat-screen TVs, robes and White Company lotions. Breakfast is served in the big house – the full Welsh works. Beaches, hills, Cardigan and magical St Davids all wait. Good local restaurants are on hand: lobster from the sea, lamb from the hills. A great place to unwind. *Min. two nights in high season. Large garden, long walks and close to beaches.*

Rooms	5 suites for 2: £99–£120.
	1 cottage for 7: £700–£995.
	Max. 2 dogs per room. May be left in room alone if trusted!
Meals	Restaurants within 3 miles.
Closed	Christmas.

Lots of advice on walks; no dog fee for Sawday's guests; Edward & William, the resident spaniels, are ultra-friendly

Richard Morgan-Price & Huw Thomas
Penbontbren
Glynarthen,
Llandysul SA44 6PE

Tel	+44 (0)1239 810248
Email	contact@penbontbren.com
Web	www.penbontbren.com

Entry 181 Map 2

The Hand at Llanarmon

Single-track lanes plunge you into the middle of nowhere. All around, lush valleys rise and fall, so pull on your boots and scale a mountain or find a river and jump into a canoe. Back at The Hand, a 16th-century drovers' inn, the pleasures of a traditional country local are hard to miss. A coal fire burns on the range in reception, a wood fire crackles under brass in the front bar and a wood-burner warms the lofty dining room. Expect exposed stone walls, low beamed ceilings, old pine settles and candles on the mantelpiece. There's a games room for darts and pool, a quiet sitting room for maps and books. Delicious food is popular with locals, so grab a table and enjoy seasonal menus – perhaps game broth, lamb casserole, then sticky toffee pudding. Bedrooms are just as they should be: not too fancy, cosy and warm, spotlessly clean with crisp white linen and good bathrooms. A very friendly place. Martin and Gaynor are full of quiet enthusiasm and have made their home warmly welcoming. John Ceiriog Hughes, who wrote *Bread of Heaven*, lived in this valley. Special indeed. *Great walks: keep dogs on lead because of sheep; pheasant shooting area too.*

Rooms	8 doubles; 4 twins: £90–£127. 1 suite for 2: £90–£127. Singles from £52.50. Dogs £5 per night. Max. 2. Dogs restricted to downstairs, own entrance.
Meals	Lunch from £6.50. Sunday lunch £21. Dinner £12–£20.
Closed	Rarely.

 Gravy bones in the bar, dog towels, & their own book for the very best walks

Gaynor & Martin De Luchi
The Hand at Llanarmon
Llanarmon Dyffryn Ceiriog,
Llangollen LL20 7LD

Tel	+44 (0)1691 600666
Email	reception@thehandhotel.co.uk
Web	www.thehandhotel.co.uk

Entry 182 Map 5

Pentre Mawr Country House

The setting is beautiful, 190 acres of deep country at the end of a lane. The house isn't bad either. This is an old estate, which fell into ruin 80 years ago. It has been in Graham's family for 400 years and he and Bre have done a fine job renovating the place. Outside, a lawn runs down to fields, Doric columns flank the front door. Inside is half B&B (informal, personal, very welcoming), half hotel (smart rooms, attentive service, a menu in the restaurant). Wander about and find a couple of sitting rooms, open fires, vast flagstones, a bust of Robert Napier. Bedrooms are scattered about. Big rooms in the main house have a country-house feel and spa baths for two; stylish suites in the gardener's cottage have hot tubs on private terraces; super-cool safari lodges in the garden flaunt faux leopard-skin throws and fabulous bathrooms. There's a sun-trapping courtyard with a small pool, tennis on the grass, a kitchen garden that's being teased back to life. And Bre cooks a fine dinner, perhaps smoked salmon, rack of lamb, bread and butter pudding. *Min. stay two nights in hot-tub suites & at weekends. Two hundred acres of parkland, meadows, and woodland: doggie heaven.*

Rooms	3 doubles & 6 doubles (6 Canvas Lodges): £150–£210. 2 suites for 2 (Gardener's Cottage suites): £180–£230. Dinner, B&B £100–£140 p.p. (obligatory Friday & Saturday). Dogs may be left alone in bedroom if well behaved.
Meals	Dinner, 5 courses, £35.
Closed	Christmas.
	Treats, towels and snug blankets

Graham & Bre Carrington-Sykes
Pentre Mawr Country House
Llandyrnog,
Denbigh LL16 4LA

Tel	+44 (0)1824 790732
Email	info@pentremawrcountryhouse.co.uk
Web	www.pentremawrcountryhouse.co.uk

Entry 183 Map 5

Monty has not been to many beaches, but he does love Woolacombe Beach in Devon, where he gets a sandy nose from all the investigating.

Plas Penucha

Swing back in time with polished parquet, tidy beams, a huge Elizabethan panelled lounge with books, leather sofas and open fire – a cosy spot for Nest's dogs and for tea in winter. Plas Penucha – 'the big house on the highest point in the parish' – has been in the family for 500 years. Airy, old-fashioned bedrooms have long views across the garden to Offa's Dyke and one has a shower in the corner. The L-shaped dining room has a genuine Arts & Crafts interior; outside, rhododendrons and a rock garden flourish. There are views to the Clywdian Hills and beyond is St Asaph, with the smallest medieval cathedral in the country. *Secure garden, river to jump in, good woodland and coastal walks.*

Oska's favourite place is the North Yorkshire Moors. Long winter walks down to the beach and back, and a warm fire in the evening.

Rooms	1 double; 1 twin: £72. Singles from £36.
Meals	Dinner £19. Packed lunch £5. Pub/restaurant 2-3 miles.
Closed	Rarely.

Cosy dog blankets, dog biscuits and a roaring open fire for evening naps

Nest Price
Plas Penucha
Pen y Cefn Road,
Caerwys, Mold CH7 5BH
Tel   +44 (0)1352 720210
Email   nest@plaspenucha.co.uk
Web   www.plaspenucha.co.uk

Entry 184 Map 5

Bryn Adda

High up on private land, down the driveway, through the natural garden, and there it is, Bryn Adda – a rambling L-shaped stone building that dates from the 16th century. It's a fine house in anyone's book. Landscaped gardens drop away in all directions and you can walk to Dolgellau. Find a warren of little stairways and landings in the old part, larger rooms in the new and a low-ceilinged farmhouse kitchen right in the middle, with Belfast sinks and a big old Aga, and a stunning welcome hamper. You get a dining room for 18, two sitting rooms opening to terraces – one big and sunny, with a dog-dozy fire and an old-fashioned charm, the other with nut-brown sofas and gleaming parquet floor. There's a bedroom on the ground floor and seven more above, all comfy, all delightful, with various modern takes on traditional design. Bathrooms are new with a retro feel; antiques, pictures and books abound. Play hide-and-seek in the rhododendrons, table tennis in the barns, surf at Barmouth, hike in the forest, fish on their own stretch of river. Return to a blissful sauna – and toast your good fortune! *Huge secure garden with stream. Within walking distance of Mawddach Trail and Cader Idris mountain; easy driving to beaches.*

Rooms	1 house for 16 (4 doubles, 3 twins/doubles, 1 bunk room; 4 shower rooms, 2 bathrooms): £550–£2,400. Short breaks & discounts for reduced occupancy available. £20 per dog per stay (up to max. £40). Dogs welcome in 3 uncarpeted rooms.
Meals	Self-catering.
Closed	Rarely.

Advice on walks & maps in Welcome Pack, special towel, biscuits in Welcome Hamper; Facebook page for uploading your dog photos & anecdotes too!

Ruth Tudor
Bryn Adda
Dolgellau LL40 1YA

Mobile	+44 (0)7530 528600
Email	ruth.trealy@btinternet.com

Entry 185 Map 5

Y Felin

Such a stunning drive through the Snowdonia National Park, down a long track to this remote water mill with the Dysynni river babbling past the front door. Inside is a symphony of local oak, slate and stone in a modern hi-tech interior with white walls and plenty of games and books; heat comes from an air-source pump and wood for the burner from the farm: you'll be cosy on the chilliest days. Cooks will be thrilled with the river view from the kitchen window – and the breadmaker. All has been beautifully considered. The three bedrooms are on the ground floor, the master with its own wood-burner and windows on three sides, the smaller double bright and sweet. The bunk room is suitable for children and teenagers; the big bathrooms are fabulous. An honesty freezer is filled with local produce if you can't be bothered to shop, and there's a fire pit outside with wooden seats for flame-gazers. The owners can point you towards rugged mountain walking and bike rides, farm tours, fell running and sheep dog trials. Long sandy beaches are near, and the air is superb. *Secure garden: 1,450 acre farm with river. Within walking distance of Tal-y-llyn Lake, Cader Idris; easy drive to beaches.*

Rooms	1 cottage for 8 (1 double, 1 twin/double, 1 bunkroom for 4; 1 bath, 1 shower): £590–£860. Short breaks 3-4 nights £320–£460. £20 per dog per stay (up to max. of £40).
Meals	Self-catering.
Closed	Rarely.

Advice on walks & maps in Welcome Pack, special towel, biscuits in Welcome Hamper. Facebook page for uploading your dog photos & anecdotes too!

Ruth Tudor
Y Felin
Maes y Pandy Farm,
Tal y Llyn LL36 9AQ

Mobile	+44 (0)7530 528600
Email	ruth.trealy@btinternet.com
Web	www.distinctlywales.com

Entry 186 Map 5

Hafod Cae Maen

You approach from the back, down the bumpy track, over the cattle grid... but the glory of the house is the front and the view. Overlooking estuary and hills, this handsome villa sits above the Italianate fantasy village Portmeirion. Hafod Cae Maen was built in 1919 for the botanist who planted the estate's subtropical woodlands, and it is within easy reach of the village (restaurants, cafés, a deserted beach). The house's terraced gardens, part-overrun, are heaven for children to hide in, while adults have long lawns and a barbecue for dining. Inside, all is as luxurious as it is possible to be. Edwardian windows and polished oak floors, wood-burners in fireplaces, local art on white walls. Toys, games and DVDs invite children to settle in, there's a panelled library with an open fire, a hamper waits on the slate worktop, warm towel rails gleam, and bedrooms — heritage colours, seagrass floors — are enticing. The master room flourishes a balcony for sunsets and champagne, and well-behaved pets will be happy to sleep downstairs. Best of all, you could spend two weeks here and leave the car untouched. *Short breaks available. Secure garden. Fabulous farmland and beach walks. Please note that dogs are not allowed into Portmeirion Village.*

Rooms	1 house for 8 (2 doubles, 2 twins; 1 bath/shower room, 1 shower room, 1 separate wc): £1,300–£2,450. Max. 2 dogs. Dogs allowed downstairs only.
Meals	Self-catering.
Closed	Rarely.
🐕	2 dog bowls, 2 doggie blankets, hide chews, biscuits, dog ball-launcher, towels, spare lead & advice on the best dog walks in the area

Claire Bookings
Hafod Cae Maen
Minffordd,
Portmeirion LL48 6EP

Mobile	+44 (0)7525 487295
Email	info@historichouseretreats.com
Web	www.historichouseretreats.com

Entry 187 Map 5

Hen Dy, Nanhoron

In the heart of the Llyn peninsula, an immaculate house with gardens people travel to see. The 5,000 acre estate has been in David's family for centuries; open to guests until 6pm, ablaze with rhododendrons and azaleas in spring, it has views down to lake, pastures, woodland and sea. As for Hen Dy, it's the oldest house on the estate and was the gardener's bothy and laundry, with a bell tower that once announced mealtimes. Find a sitting room large, light and serene, with books, games, soft sofas and SkyTV; in winter, estate logs crackle. The kitchen is to star in (superb equipment, gleaming red Aga), the dining room seats eight. Up stairs – or lift – to big bedrooms that feed off a wide landing, three of which overlook the gardens (one with topiary, statues and gazebo). Red fabrics add pizzazz to the master room, whose dressing room is now a charming double (access being via the shared bathroom). For ball games and barbecues you have your own patch. Just the ticket for garden lovers, comfort-seekers and aspiring country landowners... and you are surrounded by the some of most gorgeous countryside in Gwynedd. *Gardens and walks.*

Rooms	1 house for 7 (1 twin, 1 double, 1 twin/double, 1 single; 1 bath/shower room, 1 shower room): £750–£1,350.
Meals	Self-catering.
Closed	Rarely.

The four resident dogs are very welcoming to visitors!

Bettina Harden
Hen Dy,
Nanhoron
Pwllheli LL53 8DL

Tel	+44 (0)1758 730610
Email	bettina.harden@farming.co.uk
Web	www.nanhoronestate.co.uk

Entry 188 Map 5

Little Oasis

Emma and Paul fell for the wooded land where they have created their Little Oasis while in search of an escape from London. They replaced the existing campsite with the two lovely wagons, but kept eccentric former owner Bill's network of streams and mini watermills, adding friendly sheep, and curious chickens who make hide and seek tricky as well as laying fresh eggs. From the moment you arrive, when you gleefully raid your welcome hamper for marshmallows and wine, you'll find Little Oasis an amazing place to unwind. Josie the Blue Wagon sits at the bottom of the meadow, and Rosy the Red Wagon has settled at the top. They both have a 5ft pull-out double bed, as well as space for two roll out mattresses for kids to sleep on the floor. There is ample storage under the main bed, perfect for stashing picnic blankets, spare clothes and for kids to hide in. Each wagon has a private compost loo, camp kitchen and outdoor seating, and there are shared showers about 100 metres away in the barn. *Bookings begin on Monday, Wednesday or Friday. Book through Sawday's Canopy & Stars online or by phone.*

Rooms	2 Gypsy wagons for 2+2 (1 double, 2 child singles): from £65 per night. £10 per dog. Max. 2 per wagon.
Meals	Self-catering.
Closed	October-April.

Advice on local dog-friendly places, drinking bowls and dog blankets

Sawday's Canopy & Stars
Little Oasis
Ty Newydd Farm, Pandy,
Abergavenny NP7 8DW
Tel   +44 (0)117 204 7830
Email enquiries@canopyandstars.co.uk
Web   www.canopyandstars.co.uk/littleoasis

Entry 189 Map 2

The Bell at Skenfrith

The position here is magical: an ancient stone bridge, a magnificent valley, glorious hills rising behind, cows grazing in lush fields. It's a perfect spot, not least because providence has blessed it with this sublime inn, where crisply designed interiors ooze country chic. In summer doors fly open and life spills onto a stone terrace, where views of hill and wood are interrupted only by the odd chef pottering off to a productive and organic kitchen garden. Back inside, airy rooms come with slate floors, open fires and plump-cushioned armchairs in the locals' bar, but the emphasis is firmly on the food, with the kitchen turning out delicious fare, perhaps seared scallops with cauliflower purée, heather-roasted venison with chestnut gnocchi, marmalade soufflé with whisky ice cream. Country-house bedrooms are as good as you'd expect: uncluttered and elegant, brimming with light, some beamed (mind your head!), all with fabulous bathrooms. All have sweet views, either of the kitchen garden or the river. Idyllic circular walks sweep you through blissful country. *Minimum stay two nights at weekends. Six circular walks on the doorstep, in the middle of the countryside.*

Rooms	5 doubles; 3 twin/doubles; 3 four-posters: £110–£220. Singles from £75. Dogs £5 per stay. Max. 3 per bedroom.
Meals	Lunch from £18. Sunday lunch from £22. Dinner, 3 courses, around £35.
Closed	Tues, November to March.
	Dog bowl and hose for muddy paws; lowdown on good walks from two to six miles

William & Janet Hutchings
The Bell at Skenfrith
Skenfrith,
Abergavenny NP7 8UH

Tel	+44 (0)1600 750235
Email	enquiries@skenfrith.co.uk
Web	www.skenfrith.co.uk

Entry 190 Map 2

The Humble Hideaway

Kate Humble and husband Ludo stepped in to save Upper Meend Farm when it was nearly sold off in pieces. They and their team have preserved it carefully, keeping sheep and cattle as well as doing their best to help all the local wildlife flourish. Screened from curious animals with a chunky log fence, you'll find your two huts, firepit and bench seating under the trees in a large wooded area. It's an off-grid, cosy space that suits its woodland haven perfectly. The first hut is the bedroom, containing the big double bed with custom made mattress stuffed with wool from the farm's own sheep. The second was once the property of Great Western Railways, and has been ingeniously converted into your kitchen and shower room. A double compost loo about five metres away from the huts completes your private, hidden camp. Around the farm you'll find plenty to do: join one of the crafty courses and learn anything from woodcraft to sheep shearing, walk in the woods and the Wye Valley, or head down to Kingstone Brewery for a tour and a dark ale. *Minimum stay three nights. Book through Sawday's Canopy & Stars online or by phone.*

Rooms	Shepherd's hut camp for 2 (1 double): from £80 per night. £5 per dog per night. Max. 2. Dogs must be left in the bespoke kennel and not the shepherd's hut
Meals	Self-catering.
Closed	November–March.

A bespoke dog kennel, made by The Hobbit, who has made all of the outdoor furniture at Upper Meend Farm

Sawday's Canopy & Stars
The Humble Hideaway
Upper Meend Farm,
Lydart, Monmouth NP25 4RP

Tel	+44 (0)117 204 7830
Email	enquiries@canopyandstars.co.uk
Web	www.canopyandstars.co.uk/thehumblehideaway

Entry 191 Map 2

The Piggery

A neat-as-a-pin refurbishment of an 18th-century Welsh farmhouse bang in the middle of a proper working farm. You're surrounded by a sweet garden (mostly edible) and sheep, cows, chickens, the most beautiful pigs and inspiring views. If you're keen you can join farmer Tim for a morning and learn the ropes. Or try your hand at bee keeping, orchard planting, smallholding or foraging. This is Wordsworth and Turner country, with delicious landscapes accessible by foot, canoe, car or bike. Return to a perfect home-from-home with slate floors, jolly rugs, good art, a roaring wood-burner (logs on the house), comfy vintage chairs and sofa, books, games, and a cook's dream of a blue-panelled kitchen where local cook Katherine Marland can come and give you a private lesson – but lazy bones can order tasty home-cooked food to be delivered. Sleep peacefully: pristine bedrooms have soft Welsh blankets and thick blinds at the windows with a bit of a hare theme going on; wallow in a deep bath – solace for walk-weary limbs. In summer spill out to the garden for perfect barbecues and long convivial evenings watching the sun slither down. *Plenty of good walking: woodland tracks, river Wye close by. Fenced garden. Dogs must be kept on leads, due to chicken pen & farm dogs.*

Rooms	1 cottage for 4 (1 double, 1 twin; 1 bathroom): £395–£595. Short breaks £100 a night. Min. 3 nights. £5 per dog per night. Max. 2. Dogs downstairs only. Keep on lead while walking through farm fields.	
Meals	Self-catering.	
Closed	Never.	
🏃🐕	Advice on walks	

Ludo Graham
The Piggery
Upper Meend Farm,
Lydart, Monmouth NP25 4RP

Tel +44 (0)1600 714595
Email info@humblebynature.com
Web www.humblebynature.com/accommodation

Entry 192 Map 2

Monmouthshire B&B

Allt-y-bela

It's a rare treat to come here. This beautiful medieval farmhouse sits in its own secret valley and is reached down a narrow lane. Built between 1420 and 1599, Allt-y-bela is now perfectly presented for the 21st century. You'll find conviviality and warmth, soaring beams, period furniture and an enormous log fire. There's a super farmhouse kitchen for delicious and social eating, or the table might be set outside in the sun: homemade everything, beautifully cooked. Bedrooms soothe with limewashed walls, fabulous beds, no TV and stunning art. Peace, privacy and an amazing garden in deep yet accessible countryside. Exceptional. *Deep countryside, no roads, great walking; woodland, pasture, streams, hills all from the doorstep.*

I'm Bear. Here I am in Daymer Bay, contemplating the distant horizon as the sun dries my curls, but ever alert for the next distraction!

Rooms	2 doubles: £125.
	£25 room supplement for 1 night stay.
	More than 1 dog by arrangement.
Meals	Farmhouse supper £30.
	Pubs/restaurants 3 miles.
Closed	Rarely.

 Advice for walks, dog towels available

William Collinson & Arne Maynard
Allt-y-bela
Llangwm Ucha,
Usk NP15 1EZ

Mobile	+44 (0)7892 403103
Email	bb@alltybela.co.uk
Web	www.alltybela.co.uk

Entry 193 Map 2

Whether it's in a pub or a castle, Maggie the mini schnauzer loves to spend her days in the best doggie-friendly places around.

Llys Meddyg

This fabulous restaurant with rooms has a bit of everything: cool rooms that pack a designer punch, super food in a sparkling restaurant, a cellar bar for drinks before dinner, a fabulous garden for summer treats. It's a very friendly place with charming staff on hand to help, and it draws in a local crowd who come for the seriously good food, perhaps mussel and saffron soup, rib of Welsh beef with hand-cut chips, cherry soufflé with pistachio ice cream. You eat in style with a fire burning at one end of the restaurant and good art hanging on the walls. Excellent bedrooms are split between the main house (decidedly funky) and the mews behind (away from the road). All have the same fresh style: Farrow & Ball colours, good art, oak beds, fancy bathrooms with fluffy robes. Best of all is the back garden with a mountain-fed stream pouring past. In summer, a café/bistro opens up out here – coffee and cake or steak and chips – with doors that open onto the garden. Don't miss Pembrokeshire's fabulous coastal path for its windswept cliffs, sandy beaches and secluded coves. *Estuary path from the doorstep: doggie heaven.*

Rooms	4 doubles; 4 twin/doubles; 1 suite for 2: £100-£180. Singles from £85. No charge but dogs must be clean and well behaved! Max. 2 per bedroom. 3 dog-friendly bedrooms.
Meals	Lunch from £7. Dinner from £14.
Closed	Rarely.

 Newport Sands is dog-friendly all year with dunes & miles of sand – & cafés for exhausted owners

Louise & Edward Sykes
Llys Meddyg
East Street,
Newport SA42 0SY
Tel   +44 (0)1239 820008
Email   info@llysmeddyg.com
Web   www.llysmeddyg.com

Entry 194 Map 1

Cwtch Camping

The Welsh camping experience has been given a thoroughly contemporary spin by Beth, creator of the Cwtch (meaning a hug, or a snug place, in Welsh). The three handcrafted timber pods are a short walk through the trees from where you park your car, or a scenic cycle from local stations. Light pours through French doors, chunky brocante finds distinguish the interiors and a real double bed is bliss after a day in the fresh air. The cabins share a kitchen, shower and WC, but are privately sited with their own deck and picnic table. Local eggs, fresh bread and organic milk are among the goodies in your welcome hamper and Beth can supply extras for your private barbecue if you ask in advance. The Cwtch stands firm in all seasons in the midst of Pembrokeshire's natural beauty: follow the riverbank walk to a nature reserve teeming with bird life – and a family of otters – or take a boat trip to the island of Skomer. You're a short drive from the estuary and dog friendly beaches. Camping has never been cosier! *Minimum stay two nights. Book through Sawday's Canopy & Stars online or by phone.*

Rooms	2 cabins for 2 (1 double); 1 cabin for 3 (1 double, 1 single bunk): from £80 per night. Max. 2 dogs per cabin.
Meals	Self-catering.
Closed	November–March.

A jar of dog biscuits will greet your dog on arrival. Water bowls are dotted about the camp, extra towels available for wet dogs; advice on walks, OS maps & guide books too

---

Sawday's Canopy & Stars
Cwtch Camping
Rosemarket SA73 1LH
Tel   +44 (0)117 204 7830
Email   enquiries@canopyandstars.co.uk
Web   www.canopyandstars.co.uk/cwtchcamping

Entry 195 Map 1

Pandy Cottage

No-one is quite sure when Pandy Cottage was built but suffice it to say, where a slate step has been worn down inches by footfall, it's probably ancient. It's pretty too, clinging to the mossy side of the Dulas valley, with sheep fields and pine forests soaring above and a wooden deck the length of the cottage jutting over the river. Katie and Andy's interiors are atmospheric, cottage-cosy, full of personality and touched by trendy but appropriate detail – a metal chest used as a side table, Wee Willie Winkie candleholders, sheep skulls, storm lanterns, and a mish-mash of textiles including piles of Welsh blankets for the beds. Local carpenter Chris made cupboards in keeping with what was there; of particular interest are the kitchen units and the double bunk bed in the second bedroom, ideal for children or a bunch of good mates. The other double has a wood-burner and a skylight, as does the small but sweet bathroom: no darkness or pokiness upstairs. There's a handsome range in the vast inglenook – the perfect place to rustle up some Welsh cakes after a blustery walk! *Sand dunes, beaches, forests, mountains: all on the doorstep.*

Rooms	1 cottage for 4 (1 double, 1 double bunk bed; 1 bath/shower room): £450-£650. Small double sofabed downstairs and travel cot. Dogs £20 per stay. Max. 3. Dogs can be left alone, but kept downstairs only.
Meals	Self-catering.
Closed	Rarely.

  A river for heaps of fun, an outside tap with hose for washing muddy paws, and an open fire or Esse range to snooze by. It's a dog's paradise!

Katie Jones
Pandy Cottage
Corris,
Machynlleth SY20 9RJ

Mobile	+44 (0)7984 463317
Email	pandycottage@gmail.com
Web	www.pandycottagewales.com

Brewers Barn

Walk out of the door into 400 wildlife-rich acres... with distant views of the Begwyn Hills. Any small family in search of rural seclusion (the nearest shop is seven miles) and hill-farm activity (beef cattle and 1,000 black-faced sheep) would love it here. Friendly Kathryn, who meets and greets and lives a mile away, gives you free tours of the farm, homemade cake (delicious) and logs for the wood-burner. A keen cook, she is also more than happy to cater (and lamb and eggs come straight from the farm). Step into a traditional old Welsh granary of slate and stone, at the end of its own driveway and totally happy in its surroundings. You have your bedrooms on the ground floor and your open-plan living space on the first, and a big utility room down from the kitchen ideal for wet boots and togs. All feels simple, comfortable, cheerful, full of light and views. Walk along the banks of the Wye, kayak and canoe, book a pony, visit Hay-on-Wye and Builth Wells. Return to a barbecue on your terrace and a cosy night in; your homely retreat is stocked with puzzles, games and films. *Short breaks available. Walks from house up to hills and common.*

Rooms	1 barn for 4 (1 twin, 1 double, campbed; 1 bathroom, 1 shower room): £395–£650. Dogs £15 per week. Max. 3. May stay in utility room unattended.
Meals	Self-catering.
Closed	Never.
	Bowls and blankets and beds on request

Kathryn Tarr
Brewers Barn
Trowley Farm,
Painscastle,
Builth Wells LD2 3JH

Tel	+44 (0)1497 851665
Email	trowleyfarmhouse@gmail.com

Entry 197 Map 2

The Felin Fach Griffin

It's quirky, homespun, and thrives on a mix of relaxed informality and colourful style. The low-ceilinged, timber-framed bar resembles the sitting room of a small hip country house, with squashy sofas in front of a fire that burns on both sides and backgammon waiting to be played. Painted stone walls throughout come in blocks of colour; on Sundays a musician plays. More informality in the restaurant, where stock pots simmer on an Aga; try cured salmon, shoulder of local lamb, Eve's pudding with cinnamon custard... delicious veggie options too. Bedrooms above are warmly simple with comfy beds wrapped in crisp linen, making this a must for those in search of a lovely billet near the mountains. There are framed photographs on the walls, the odd piece of mahogany furniture, good books, no TVs (unless you ask). Breakfast is served in the dining room; wallow with the papers, make your own toast. A main road passes outside, quietly at night, lanes lead into the hills, and an organic kitchen garden provides much for the table. Walk, ride, cycle, canoe, or head to Hay for books galore. *Black Mountains, Brecon Beacons, forests, rivers — miles of walking for dogs.*

Rooms	2 doubles; 2 twin/doubles; 2 four-posters: £115–£165. 1 family room for 3: £160. Singles from £100. Dinner, B&B from £82.50 p.p.
Meals	Lunch from £18.50. Dinner £27.50. Sunday lunch, 3 courses, £23.50.
Closed	Christmas Eve (evening only) & Christmas Day. 4 days in January.

A whole cabinet dedicated to dogs, various size dog treats for various size dogs, gravy bones, marrow bones, dog towels, sheets, bowls and poop bags

Charles & Edmund Inkin
The Felin Fach Griffin
Felin Fach,
Brecon LD3 0UB

Tel	+44 (0)1874 620111
Email	enquiries@felinfachgriffin.co.uk
Web	www.felinfachgriffin.co.uk

Entry 198 Map 2

Powys

Self-catering

Danyfan

Squeeze down wildflower-strewn lanes with extra large hedges to this Edwardian villa at the foot of Pen-y-Fan, the highest peak in South Wales. Step into a generous, cheerful hallway to find a house full of comfort and colour. You can settle around the log fire in the soft-painted sitting room, or relax in the sunny conservatory with garden and panoramic mountain views. Boutique bedrooms are light and lovely with art, antiques, books, pretty fabrics and flat-screen TVs; sleep peacefully on perfectly ironed white cotton. Bathrooms are swish and slate-floored, and one has a vast free-standing bath. You're in the middle of the Brecon Beacons so there are spectacular walks to discover, food and literary festivals, bike rides and good pubs galore. Smiling Emma, who lives next door, will let you feed the hens in the pretty tree-filled garden, lend you binoculars to peek at the woodpeckers (shy nuthatches, too) and help plan outings. There's a telescope too; the Brecon Beacons have been granted International Dark Sky Reserve status. Find a welcome hamper of homemade bread, jam and garden produce. You will not want to leave. *Short breaks available. Big garden, wonderful open hillside, fantastic walks, rivers, streams.*

Rooms	1 cottage for 10 (4 doubles, 1 twin/double; 4 bathrooms): £874–£1,359. Max. 2 dogs (unless agreed by owner).
Meals	Self-catering.
Closed	Never.

Spare collars, leads and dog bowls and two toasty log-burners to lounge by

Emma Bald
Danyfan
Cwmgwdi, Brecon LD3 8LG
Tel   +44 (0)1874 610522
Mobile   +44 (0)7894 473907
Email   hello@danyfan-brecon.co.uk
Web   www.danyfan-brecon.co.uk

Entry 199 Map 2

Danyfan Carriage

Danyfan Carriage is the latest project of Emma & Stevie, who fled London for the country life a few years ago. They found a perfect spot to make their home, and also the perfect place for a little glamping. The railway wagon, as far as they know, is an early 20th-century artefact. In converting it they have kept as much of the original work as possible, adding only what will complement the period feel, with a grand wicker-headboarded bed and a burnished walnut wardrobe. The whole site is completely off-grid, with a cleverly designed (piping hot!) shower and washing up area, plus a separate compost loo, just steps from the carriage. Being off-grid doesn't have to mean hardship: the wood-burner keeps you beautifully warm, the bed is a wonder of mountainous soft pillows. Lanterns and torches give a soft light, and the gas hobs make cooking easy. Your corner of the garden is sheltered, with mountain views and a rushing stream. Walks through the Brecon Beacons National Park stretch out from the door and wildlife and nature surround you. *Minimum stay two nights. Book through Sawday's Canopy & Stars online or by phone.*

Rooms	Railway wagon for 2 (1 double): from £65 per night. Max. 1 dog. Well-behaved dogs can be left in the carriage.
Meals	Self-catering
Closed	Never.
	Advice on walks

Sawday's Canopy & Stars
Danyfan Carriage
Danyfan,
Cwmgwdi, Brecon LD3 8LG
Tel   +44 (0)117 204 7830
Email   enquiries@canopyandstars.co.uk
Web   www.canopyandstars.co.uk/danyfan

Pen Yr Heol, Pentwyn

Pen Yr Heol means 'head of the road': from here on up you're on foot. High on the hillside is a craftsman restoration of a 200-year-old shearing shed. All is warm, bright and open-plan inside, with room aplenty for ten. This is simple, solid barn living; white walls, oak beams, wide floorboards, raftered ceilings. Everything has been thoughtfully worked out: underfloor heating and a wood-burner stocked with logs, home entertainment that includes BT Vision, a play area – even a toy box! – and a fabulous drying room for wet gear. You have two shower rooms and two bedrooms downstairs – one with a bath where you can soak to valley views – and two further bedrooms upstairs. Outside are views, inspirational and reaching to the Black Mountains; seating areas at the front and back make the most of them. Whatever the weather, the walking is spectacular. Take the footpath behind the barn: it leads directly onto the Brecon Beacons and ultimately to Pen-y-Fan, while a half hour trek across fields delivers you to the village pub. *Short breaks available. Secure garden, river to jump in, good walks, woodland.*

Rooms	1 barn for 10 (1 double en suite, 2 twins/doubles, 1 quadruple; 2 shower rooms, 2 separate wcs): £810-£1,368. 3 nights £748. Dogs £15 per stay.
Meals	Self-catering.
Closed	Never.

Towels for drying wet dogs

Thomas Jones
Pen Yr Heol, Pentwyn
Llanfrynach, Brecon LD3 7BQ

Tel	+44 (0)1874 665271
Mobile	+44 (0)7814 189810
Email	enquiries@penyrheol-barn.co.uk
Web	www.penyrheol-barn.co.uk

Entry 201 Map 2

The Old Store House

Unbend here with agreeable books, chattering birds, and Peter, who asks only that you feel at home. Downstairs are a range-warmed kitchen, a sunny conservatory overlooking garden, chickens, ducks and canal, and a charmingly ramshackle sitting room with a wood-burner, sofas and a piano – no babbling TV. Bedrooms are large, light and spotless, with more books, soft goose down, armchairs and bathrooms with views. Breakfast, without haste, on scrambled eggs, local bacon and sausages, blistering coffee. Bliss – but as far from tickety boo as possible. Walk into the hills from the back door. *Children over six welcome. Thirty miles of dog-proof towpath for lovely walks.*

Rooms	3 doubles; 1 twin: £80.
	Singles £40.
Meals	Packed lunch £4. Pub/restaurant
	0.75 miles.
Closed	Rarely.

 Free dog-sitting for owners who fancy a night out on the town – or a supper down the pub

Peter Evans
The Old Store House
Llanfrynach,
Brecon LD3 7LJ
Tel   +44 (0)1874 665499
Email   oldstorehouse@btconnect.com
Web   www.theoldstorehouse.co.uk

Entry 202 Map 2

Ty'r Chanter

Warmth, colour, children and activity: this house is fun. Tiggy welcomes you like family; help collect eggs, feed the lambs or the pony, drop your shoes by the fire. The farmhouse and barn are stylishly relaxed; deep sofas, tartan throws, heaps of books, views to the Brecon Beacons and Black Mountains. Bedrooms are soft, simple sanctuaries with Jo Malone bathroom treats. The two children's rooms zing with murals; toys, kids' sitting room, sandpit – child heaven. Walk, fish, canoe, book-browse in Hay or stroll the estate. Homemade cakes, whisky to help yourself to: fine hospitality. *Hills and river walks from the door; mind the sheep! Black Mountains and Brecon Beacons within four miles.*

Rooms	2 doubles; 2 children's rooms,
	1 with separate bath/shower: £95.
	Singles £55. Children £20.
Meals	Packed lunch £8. Pub 1 mile.
Closed	Christmas.

 A banger for brekkie! Dogs can snooze on the heated floor & enjoy a marshmallow in front of the fire

Tiggy Pettifer
Ty'r Chanter
Gliffaes, Crickhowell NP8 1RL
Tel   +44 (0)1874 731144
Mobile +44 (0)7802 387004
Email   tiggy@tyrchanter.com
Web   www.tyrchanter.com

Entry 203 Map 2

Bear Hotel

Viewed from the square of this small market town, the 15th-century frontage of the old coaching inn is modest. Behind the cobbles and the summer flowers, it is a warren of surprises and mild eccentricity – bars and brasserie at the front, nooks and crannies at the back – behind which is the family- and dog-friendly garden. The beamy lounge has parquet, plush seating and a mighty fire; settle in and savour wines, whiskies, ports and good beers. There are two dining areas where at night you feast on Welsh Black beef, Usk salmon, Brecon venison, and local cheeses and vegetables. Homemade ice creams, mousses and puddings are sumptuous and we've never seen the place empty. Mrs Hindmarsh is still firmly in charge of an operation that rarely comes off the rails. *Lots of walks for dogs: miles of Brecon Beacons, mountains, canals and rivers.*

Hafod Y Garreg

A unique opportunity to stay in the oldest house in Wales – a fascinating, 1402 cruck-framed hall house, built for Henry IV as a hunting lodge. Informal Annie and John have filled it with a charming mix of Venetian mirrors, Indian rugs, pewter plates, gorgeous fabrics and oak furniture. Dine by candlelight in the fabulous dining room – maybe pheasant pie with chilli jam and hazelnut mash: delicious. Bedrooms are luxurious and comfortable with Egyptian cotton bed linen. Reach the Grade II*-listed house by a bumpy track across gated fields crowded with chickens, cats… a special, secluded and relaxed place. *Dogs have to be on a lead in garden, and around sheep in farmland. Mind chickens and the cat too!*

Meals	Lunch & dinner £5.95–£20.
Closed	3pm-6pm (7pm Sunday).

 Bowl of chicken on arrival – if owners are eating in!

Rooms	2 doubles: £86.
	Singles from £80.
	£6 per dog per night (if dog sleeps in bedroom). Max. 2.
Meals	Dinner, 3 courses, £25. BYOB.
	Pubs/restaurants 2.5 miles.
Closed	Christmas.

 Gorgeous country walks straight from the door

Judy Hindmarsh
Bear Hotel
High Street,
Crickhowell NP8 1BW
Tel   +44 (0)1873 810408
Email   bearhotel@aol.com
Web   www.bearhotel.co.uk

Annie & John McKay
Hafod Y Garreg
Erwood,
Builth Wells LD2 3TQ
Tel   +44 (0)1982 560400
Email   john-annie@hafod-y.wanadoo.co.uk
Web   www.hafodygarreg.co.uk

Entry 204 Map 2

Entry 205 Map 2

The Harp

Chris Ireland and Angela Lyne have taken over this ancient Welsh longhouse, tucked up a dead-end lane near the parish church, and there are no plans to change. The wonderful interior is spick-and-span timeless: 14th-century slate flooring in the bar, tongue-and-groove in a room that fits a dozen diners, crannies crammed with memorabilia, an ancient curved settle, an antique reader's chair, two fires and a happy crowd. Accompany a pint of Wye Valley or Three Tuns bitter with a Welsh Black rump steak with chips, or sea bass with salsa verde. Or take a ploughman's to a seat under the sycamore and gaze on the spectacular Radnor Valley. Life in this tiny village, like its glorious pub, remains delightfully unchanged. *Walks to Worsell Wood with a stream to play in. Good long walk to Hergest Ridge.*

Dougal loves West Wittering beach in West Sussex! When the tide is out, he can run for miles along the golden sands and soft sandy dunes.

Meals	Lunch from £5. Dinner from £10. Sunday lunch, 3 courses, from £17. Not Monday or Tuesday-Friday lunch.
Closed	Tues-Fri lunch. 3pm-6pm Sat & Sun & Mon all day.

 Grand walks from the door (keeping an eye out for cattle & sheep), and a black lab to play with

Chris Ireland & Angela Lyne
The Harp
Old Radnor,
Presteigne LD8 2RH
Tel   +44 (0)1544 350655
Email   mail@harpinnradnor.co.uk
Web   www.harpinnradnor.co.uk

Entry 206 Map 2

Five year old Coco loves playing fetch all around Regent's Park.

Fairyhill

This lovely country house on the Gower sits in 24 acres of beautiful silence with a sun-trapping terrace at the back for lunch in summer. Potter about and find a walled garden, a stream-fed lake, free-range ducks and an ancient orchard. Inside, country-house interiors come fully loaded: smart fabrics, warm colours, deep sofas, the daily papers. There's an open fire in the bar, a grand piano in the sitting room, then delicious food in the restaurant, most locally sourced. Stylish bedrooms hit the spot. Most are big and fancy, a couple are small, but sweet. Some have painted beams, others a sofa or a wall of golden paper. Sparkling bathrooms, some with separate showers, have deep baths, white robes and fancy oils; if that's not enough, there's a treatment room, too. Outside, the Gower waits – wild heathland, rugged coastline, some of the best beaches in the land – so explore by day, then return for a good meal, perhaps scallops with cauliflower and chorizo, Gower lamb with gratin potatoes, baked honey and amaretto cheesecake. The wine list is one of the best in Wales, so don't expect to go thirsty. *Children over eight welcome. River to jump in, beach walks.*

Rooms	3 doubles; 5 twin/doubles: £190–£290. Singles from £170. Dinner, B&B from £135 p.p. Dogs £10 per night.
Meals	Lunch from £20. Dinner £35–£45.
Closed	First 3 weeks in January, Monday & Tuesday, November–March.

24 acres of grounds to explore, & beautiful white-sand Gower beaches beyond

	Andrew Hetherington & Paul Davies
	Fairyhill
	Reynoldston, Gower Peninsula,
	Swansea SA3 1BS
Tel	+44 (0)1792 390139
Email	postbox@fairyhill.net
Web	www.fairyhill.net

Entry 207 Map 2

Scotland

Photo: The Old House,
entry 210

Darroch Learg Hotel

The country here is glorious – river, forest, mountain, sky – so walk by Loch Muick, climb Lochnagar, fish the Dee or drop down to Braemar for the Highland Games. Swing back to Darroch Learg and find nothing but good things. This is a smart family-run hotel firmly rooted in a graceful past: an old country house with roaring fires, polished brass, Zoffany wallpaper and ambrosial food in a much-admired restaurant. Ever-present Nigel and Fiona look after guests with great aplomb and many return year after year. Everything is just as it should be: tartan fabrics on the walls in the hall, Canadian pitch pine windows and doors, fabulous views sweeping south across Balmoral forest. Bedrooms upstairs come in different shapes and sizes; all have warmth and comfort in spades. Big grand rooms at the front thrill with padded window seats, wallpapered bathrooms, old oak furniture, perhaps a four-poster bed. Spotlessly cosy rooms in the eaves are equally lovely, just not quite as big. You get warm colours, pretty furniture, crisp white linen and bathrobes to pad about in. A perfect highland retreat. *River and four acres of private woodland from the back door.*

Rooms	10 twin/doubles;
	2 four-posters: £140–£250.
	Dinner, B&B (obligatory at weekends)
	£105–£160 p.p.
	Max. 2 dogs (by arrangement).
Meals	Sunday lunch £24. Dinner £45.
Closed	Christmas & last 3 weeks in January.
	Towels, dog beds and bowls

Nigel & Fiona Franks
Darroch Learg Hotel
56 Braemar Road,
Ballater AB35 5UX
Tel   +44 (0)1339 755443
Email   enquiries@darrochlearg.co.uk
Web   www.darrochlearg.co.uk

Entry 208 Map 9

Isle of Shuna Cottages

Peace, beauty, seclusion... no roads, no cars, a turbine, solar panels – welcome to the island of Shuna. With your own boat you can stock up in Oban and visit nearby Craobh Haven (eat at the pub or take a cruise to Correvreckan Whirlpool, one of many local wonders). The island's cottages are owned and maintained by enthusiastic, charismatic Eddie: 'South End House', with spell-binding views south to Jura; 'Boat House', high on stilts, with a boat shed below to the jetty; and 'Garden House', bow-windowed, white and pretty, 200m up the track. Spot otters, seals, eagles, deer, picnic on unspoilt beaches, chop logs, catch fish... Then it's back home to books, games and pure spring water. Backing onto dense woodland, 'Garden House' is well-proportioned inside, with bedrooms up and down and a homely feel. Spacious, light-filled 'Boat House', newly encased in wood and cosily furnished in Scandi style, comes with a kitchen that's a pleasure to work in and a wood-burner that belts out the heat. Pleasures here are simple but rich, and walkers, dogs and kids will adore it. Linen & towels not included. *Dogs can have a whole island to themselves as long as they don't chase the sheep!*

Rooms	1 cottage for 6 (1 double en suite, 2 twins; 1 bathroom), 1 cottage for 8 (1 double, 1 twin, 1 bunk room for 4) & 1 cottage for 12 (2 doubles, 2 twins, 1 double bunk room): £550-£1,200.
Meals	Self-catering.
Closed	October-March.

The island with all its woods, rabbits, pheasants and ocean all around is an absolute dog's paradise!

Andrew Gully
Isle of Shuna Cottages
Dunmore,
Easdale, Oban PA34 4RF
Tel   +44 (0)1852 300434
Email   info@islandofshuna.co.uk
Web   www.islandofshuna.co.uk

The Old House

An extremely comfortable home for a family holiday, or a secret hideaway for two. You feel miles from anywhere (and the night skies are gloriously unpolluted), yet the train from London chugs into the local village. The former sporting lodge has been renovated from top to toe with sensitivity and along green lines with solar panels and a micro hydro powerhouse. On the ground floor is a golden yellow sitting room with a wood-burning stove and a railway-sleeper mantelpiece, and the four-poster bedroom is next door – along with a utility room and a Belfast sink for washing the day's catch; the 'wet room' is so large the whole family could scrub up at once. Upstairs are two light and pleasingly simple twin rooms with valley views. Leave the car behind – delightful Erica or John can pick you up from the village station – and hike to your heart's content. You are spoilt for choice – walk up the hill on the other side of the river for magical woodlands, or climb 2,500 feet up Ben Udlaidh for views to the islands. The pretty garden slopes towards the river, you can relax on the decking and help yourself to home-grown veg. *Secure garden, river to jump in and woodland walks.*

Rooms	1 house for 6 (1 four-poster, 2 twins each with separate bath/shower rooms): £550–£1,020. Prices are based on 2 people. Additional guests £75 per week each. Dogs £15 per week.
Meals	Self-catering.
Closed	Rarely.

 Biscuits, water & blankets. Expert advice on wild, carefree walks & a special welcome from terrier Boris the Arbuthnott

John & Erica Kerr
The Old House
Arichastlich,
Glen Orchy PA33 1BD
Tel   +44 (0)1838 200399
Email   theoldhouse@glen-orchy.co.uk
Web   www.glen-orchy.co.uk

Entry 210 Map 8

Tiroran House

The setting is magnificent – 17 acres of lush gardens rolling down to Loch Scridian with the Ross of Mull rising beyond. Otters and dolphins pass by, red deer visit the garden. As for this welcoming 1850 shooting lodge, you'll be hard pressed to find a more comfortable island base, so it's no surprise to discover it was recently voted 'Best Country House Hotel in Scotland'. There are fires in the drawing rooms, fresh flowers everywhere, games to be played, books to be read. Big airy bedrooms hit the spot: crisp linen on pretty beds, beautiful fabrics and the odd chaise longue, watery views and silence guaranteed. You eat in a smart dining room with views down to the water. The food is exceptional with much from the island or waters around it, perhaps hand-dived scallops, local venison, dark chocolate and salted caramel tart. You're bang in the middle of Mull with loads to do: Tobermory, the prettiest town in the Hebrides; Calgary and its magical beach; day trips to Iona with its famous monastery; boat trips to Fingal's Cave. Come back for afternoon tea – it's as good as the Ritz. *Wonderful walks.*

Rooms	5 doubles; 5 twin/doubles: £175–£220.
Meals	Dinner, 4 courses, £48.
Closed	Rarely.

Ideal dog walking territory & towels on supply from dog-loving hosts

Laurence & Katie Mackay
Tiroran House
Tiroran,
Isle of Mull PA69 6ES
Tel   +44 (0)1681 705232
Email   info@tiroran.com
Web   www.tiroran.com

Treshnish Farm

On Mull's wild northwest coast, your heart will soar. Let it be blown back to the Charringtons' award-winning farm, a 1,900-acre slice of nature where cattle and sheep roam happily amid birds, orchids and wildlife. Two bumpy miles and four gates from the road, in a cluster of four sea-facing crofters' cottages (a mile from the farm), 'West' melts into the landscape. Artworks and ethnic throws bring colour inside, open-plan but for a simple twin and, through this, the bathroom. There's a bright corner kitchen, a wood-burner, heating and electricity… but it's blissfully free of mod cons. Lovely to watch the fire fade from your raised handmade double bed, and wake to the sound and sight of the sea. Or lie in the shared garden watching for red deer by day, shooting stars at night. Back at the farmstead, the flexible (for two or four) 'Studio' is a converted dairy/byre whose high ceilings, skylights and primary colours make small seem big. The setting is dramatic and remote but the welcome is warm, eco principles impressive, and Calgary beach is three miles as the sea eagle flies. *Short breaks November–March. Walks and beaches to roam.*

Rooms	1 cottage for 4 (1 twin, 1 double in alcove in living room; 1 bathroom); 1 cottage for 4 (2 doubles, 1 in sleeping gallery, 2 additional single beds; 1 shower room, 1 bathroom): £270–£625. Dogs £15 per stay. Max. 2 (contact if more).
Meals	Self-catering.
Closed	Never.
	Advice on good walks

Carolyne Charrington
Treshnish Farm
Calgary, Dervaig,
Isle of Mull PA75 6QX

Tel	+44 (0)1688 400249
Email	enquiries@treshnish.co.uk
Web	www.treshnish.co.uk

Entry 212 Maps 8 & 10

Ballantrae Harbour Cottages

Come for windswept family walks along miles of pebble beach, or take the high road to Culzean Castle, high above the Firth of Clyde (or the ferry from Cairnryan for a day in Belfast!). Come home to toasty floors and wood-burners, memory-foam mattresses and kitchens that are a delight to work in. There are three cottages here, independent but close enough should you be one big party; there's a table for 12 in the largest. 'Fisherman's Cottage' is just that (and it's a lovely renovation); the other two are attractive eco builds. All three lie on the outskirts of untouristy Ballantrae (shop, post office, pub), a stroll from the old harbour, with safely fenced gardens from which you can sniff the sea. The interiors are new and spacious, fresh and fabulous, with themed furnishings (red for 'Beach', blue for 'Shore', dove-grey for 'Fisherman's') and great welcoming touches. Wooden shelves are home to iPod docks, games, guide books and shells, driftwood mirrors decorate restful walls, and entrance halls and porches display baskets of umbrellas, shrimping nets and cricket bats. The detail is second to none. *Short breaks available during off peak times. Each cottage has a secure garden; dog-friendly beach four miles (open to dogs all year), river walk too.*

Rooms	1 cottage for 2; 1 cottage for 4 (1 twin/double, 1 double); 1 cottage for 6 (1 twin/double, 1 double, 1 twin): £340–£900. Dogs £20 per stay. All cottages have porch and utility room for dogs.
Meals	Self-catering.
Closed	Never.

🐾 Dog biscuits

Hamish & Emma Dalrymple
Ballantrae Harbour Cottages
Harbour Green,
Ballantrae, Girvan KA26 0NS
Mobile   +44 (0)7974 008048
Email   info@ballantraeholidaycottages.com
Web   www.ballantraeholidaycottages.com

Alton Albany Farm

Discover Ayrshire… pine forests, hills and wild beauty. Alasdair and Andrea (sculptor and garden photographer) are generous hosts who love having you to stay – your visit starts with tea, coffee and cake. There's an arty vibe with their work on display; the dining room brims with garden books and games; large bedrooms have cosy lamps and more books. Big breakfasts by a log fire are a treat, perhaps with haggis, garden fruit, homemade bread. Rich in wildlife and orchids the garden has a rambling charm, the salmon-filled river Stinchar runs past and dogs are welcome – residents Clover and Daisy are friendly. Great fish restaurant nearby. *Special group rates for six friends or family. Large garden and riverside field for games and stick throwing. Woodland and hills. Beaches seven miles. Dogs also welcome in The Dog House (self-catering apartment for working dogs).*

Nancy jumps in the car as soon as her owners start packing for their holiday in the Wye Valley. She loves the long woodland walks and the tea rooms!

Rooms	2 doubles, sharing bath with twin; 1 twin, sharing bath with double: £67–£75. Rooms let to same party only. Singles £45. £5 per dog per night. Max. 2 per bedroom.
Meals	Pubs/restaurants 15-minute drive.
Closed	Rarely.

 A choice of walks, a basket of towels by the door and a selection of treats

Andrea & Alasdair Currie
Alton Albany Farm, Barr,
Girvan KA26 0TL

Tel	+44 (0)1465 861148
Mobile	+44 (0)7881 908764
Email	alasdair@gardenexposures.co.uk
Web	www.altonalbanyfarmbandb.wordpress.com

Entry 214 Map 8

Ashton Court in the snow is the perfect place for Coco the Chow Chow from Northern China.

West Holmhead Cottage, Craig Farm

This forgotten corner of Scotland is blissfully empty – red squirrels, buzzards, kites and otters are its reclusive residents. Among the hills and forests is a farm run by Richard and Mas; going one step further than organic, they practice bio-dynamic farming (homeopathy for the soil) in sympathy with the stunning surroundings. Their 450 acres are allowed to flourish naturally: orchids, mushrooms, ancient woodland provide pasture for their cattle and sheep. You stay in their spotless white-painted cottage (one of two on a quiet lane), where books are in abundance and local walks described in detail on handwritten cards. It is neither lavish nor showy, having a down-to-earth feel that echoes the owners' values. Furniture is simple but not cheap, the doors are old but the windows double-glazed, there's a wood-burner in the carpeted sitting room and a log fire in the single bedroom downstairs. Beds are pine, walls are creamy white and there are fresh flowers dotted about. It is almost eerily peaceful here – people come to write and read, or to bike and sail. Such raw beauty is a balm to anyone's tired soul. *Plenty of rabbits to chase. Loch Ken to swim in – if you dare risk the crayfish! Lots of walks in forests and hills and on long beaches.*

Rooms	1 cottage for 5 (1 double, 1 twin, 1 single; 1 bath/shower): £340–£510. Short breaks from £240 (min. 3 nights). Max. 1 dog (ask if more). If out leave dogs in kitchen/utility. We're a sheep and cattle farm – so no sheep chasing!
Meals	Self-catering.
Closed	Rarely.

 Advice on walks, sun-trap garden, log stove for winter, and interesting things lurking in the bottom of a dry-stone wall... hours of entertainment!

Mas Smyth & Richard Cunningham
West Holmhead Cottage,
Craig Farm, Balmaclellan,
Castle Douglas DG7 3QR
Tel   +44 (0)1644 420636
Email   mas@craigfarm.co.uk
Web   www.craigfarm.co.uk

Entry 215 Map 8

White Hill

Fresh air, huge gardens and stacks of Scottish charm. The aged paint exterior is forgotten once you're inside this treasure-trove of history and heritage. The Bell-Irvings are natural hosts; twenty generations of their family have lived here and worn the floorboards dancing. Throw logs on the fire, ramble round the azalea'd gardens or explore the woods, fish the river, and dine opulently under the gaze of portraits of their 'rellies'. Breakfast is a delightfully hearty affair. A very special chance to share a real ancestral home in the Scottish borders with a kind, funny, lovely couple (and their very friendly springer spaniel). *There is a large woodland garden (not fenced in), a river 400 yards away for dogs to jump into and swim. Plenty of walks on the farm.*

Elsie, one of the many dogs that used to frequent the Sawday offices!

Rooms	2 twins: £88.
	Singles £54.
	£5 per dog per night. Max. 2 dogs per room.
Meals	Dinner £30 (by prior arrangement).
	Pubs/restaurants 4 miles.
Closed	Rarely.

 Bonio for the dogs before they go to bed, dog bed if required, advice on walks

Robin & Janet Bell-Irving
White Hill,
Ecclefechan,
Lockerbie DG11 1AL
Tel   +44 (0)1576 510206
Email   johnbi@talktalk.net
Web   www.aboutscotland.com/south/whitehill.html

Entry 216 Map 9

Conrad the boxer on a breathtaking walk in Friston Forest in Sussex. Conrad loves diving into huge piles of leaves and jumping out!

Blue Hue

A sparkling example of modern style, Blue Hue is part of Scottish Canals' grand plan to help a new audience discover the magic of its traditional waterways, and what could give you a more thorough introduction to canal life than sleeping on the water itself? It's a remarkably comfy experience – all the furniture is custom-built and everything is cleverly designed to feel light and spacious. It's all open-plan, with a clean, blue colour scheme both inside and out (giving the boat its name), and it's got a fully equipped kitchen with gas oven, bespoke bathroom with power shower, and even a wood-burner for the chillier evenings. Best of all, the tailor-made, raised double bed means you can just lie back and watch canal life pass by your window. A great canal-side pub is conveniently close. Just ten miles from Edinburgh, Blue Hue is handily placed for a city break, whilst being a calm spot to retreat to after a day wandering the old town, visiting the castle or discovering the plethora of attractions the city has to offer. *Minimum stay three nights. Book through Sawday's Canopy & Stars online or by phone.*

Rooms	Boat for 4 (1 double, 1 sofabed): from £75 per night. Max. 1 dog (small). Dogs may be left in the boat but any damage must be paid for.
Meals	Self-catering.
Closed	Never.

Plenty of towels and a hair dryer for when your dog decides to take a swim!

Sawday's Canopy & Stars
Blue Hue
Ratho EH28 8RA

Tel	+44 (0)117 204 7830
Email	enquiries@canopyandstars.co.uk
Web	www.canopyandstars.co.uk/bluehue

Entry 217 Map 9

21 Shoregate

Welcome to an immaculate fisherman's cottage just above exquisite Crail's harbour. Views from the garden stretch over rooftops to the Firth of Forth; bliss to eat out here on a summer's day. Inside is small and perfect: cool colours and pretty objets run throughout, while plump armchairs and sofa front the wood-burner; roll out the Scrabble, choose a DVD. The ground floor is open-plan with a Shaker-style kitchen that holds all you need, plus a dining table for four. Upstairs are two bedrooms, not huge but stylish, with thick mattresses, crisp linen, smart carpets, lovely quilts – and a super little bathroom between them. Small but beautifully formed, No 21 would suit close friends or a family, or a couple of romancers. Stroll down to the Lobster Store, a wooden hut on the harbour wall that sells just-caught lobster and crab – Crail once supplied London with 20,000 lobsters a year! There are several fish restaurants here, and the best fish and chips in Scotland at Anstruther. Head off for golf along the coast (St Andrew's is close) and handsome Edinburgh – under an hour. *Minimum stay four nights. Children over five welcome. Small fenced garden behind. Walk heaven: Fife coastal path just by front door.*

Rooms	1 cottage for 4 (1 double, 1 twin; 1 bath/shower room): £440–£750. £20 per dog per stay. Max. 1 per guest.
Meals	Self-catering.
Closed	Rarely.
	Dog bowls, 2 dog towels, welcome to use and lose any dog toys. Local know-how of dog-friendly beaches, pubs and restaurants all in a useful guide

Susan Irvine
21 Shoregate
Crail KY10 3SU
Mobile   +44 (0)7879 480529
Email   tattie@dircon.co.uk
Web   www.21shoregate.com

Entry 218 Map 9

CANOPY&STARS

Highland

Inshriach House

Inshriach House was built in 1906 as a shooting lodge, and the estate has been collecting interesting pieces of historic flotsam ever since: the steading is 18th century, the dairy's Victorian, and the squash court dates from the 1930s. The owners tell us they are "a bit like The Wombles," and one look at their three off-grid sleeping spaces tells you why. The Beermoth, a 1956 Commer Q4 Fire Service truck, now features an over-the-top Victorian cast-iron bedstead, a salvaged oak parquet floor, and a wood-burner with a hearth of ex-snooker table slate. Inshriach Yurt sits majestically on recycled fence post decking, looking down to the river Spey; outside is your repurposed truck wheel barbecue. The Bothy Project up in the woods with mezzanine double and outdoor shower is part of a Scotland-wide network of artists' residency spaces, while down by the river is an ingenious new 'horsebox sauna'. Whichever you choose, loos and showers are quite a walk away over rough ground, but this means you'll always be in wonderful isolation. *Minimum stay two nights. Book through Sawday's Canopy & Stars online or by phone.*

Rooms	Yurt for 2 (1 double); 1 bothy for 2 (1 double); 1 truck for 2 (1 double): from £60 per night. Max. 2 dogs per space. Must be kept on a lead near the farm; there is a £20 fine if any of them kills a chicken.
Meals	Self-catering.
Closed	Rarely.

 Fantastic walks through the National Park in all directions

Sawday's Canopy & Stars
Inshriach House
Aviemore PH22 1QP

Tel	+44 (0)117 204 7830
Email	enquiries@canopyandstars.co.uk
Web	www.canopyandstars.co.uk/inshriach

Entry 219 Map 8

Kilcamb Lodge Hotel & Restaurant

A stupendous setting, with Loch Sunart at the end of the garden and Glas Bheinn rising beyond. Kilcamb has all the ingredients of the perfect country house: a drawing room with a roaring fire; an elegant dining room for excellent food; super-comfy bedrooms that don't shy from colour; views that feed the soul. The feel here is shipwreck-chic; the 12-acre garden has half a mile of shore. Stroll to the water's edge and look for dolphins, otters and seals. Ducks and geese fly by, and if you're lucky you'll see eagles. Back inside, you'll find stained-glass windows on the landing, flowers in the bedrooms, and a laid-back lounge bar and brasserie. Or dress up for a five-course dinner and feast on king scallops with pea purée and Stornoway black pudding, roasted loin of Argyll lamb with apricot mousse, goats' cheese mash with caper and mint butter, and banana crème brûlée. Bedrooms, some new, come in two styles: contemporary or traditional. Expect big beds, smart white towels and shiny bathrooms. Kind staff go the extra mile. *Min. stay two nights at weekends in May. Secure, safe grounds of 22 acres with a loch to jump into. Wonderful walks too.*

Rooms	7 doubles: £190–£295.
	3 suites for 2: £290–£375.
	Price includes dinner for 2.
	£10 per dog per night. Max. 2 per
	bedroom. May be left alone in bedrooms
	by arrangement if well behaved.
	4 dog-friendly bedrooms.
Meals	Lunch from £8.50.
	Dinner included; non-residents £49.50.
Closed	Jan. Limited opening Nov & Feb.
	Bonio biscuits, doggie bags, blanket and food mat; dog-sitting service too

David & Sally Ruthven-Fox
Kilcamb Lodge Hotel & Restaurant
Strontian,
Acharacle PH36 4HY
Tel   +44 (0)1967 402257
Email enquiries@kilcamblodge.co.uk
Web   www.kilcamblodge.co.uk

Entry 220 Maps 8 & 10

Croft 103

A breathtaking combination: cutting-edge design and uninterrupted views across water and mountain. These two highly individual, luxurious boltholes, one on the shore, one built into the heather-clad hillside, are labours of love for the owners and carbon negative too, with sheep's wool insulation, local Douglas fir, solar collectors, a wind turbine. Step in to find beautifully upholstered furniture, wood-burning stoves, sleek kitchens, state-of-the-art sound systems, baths big enough for two. 'The Hill' has sliding glass doors, a bed of leather and lacquered steel, an outdoors bath on a patio overlooking the sea. 'The Shore' brings outdoors in with an open-plan kitchen/dining area off a view-filled terrace, a big feather-topped bed, custom-made rugs, ceramics by Lotte Glob. Tempting to stay put, but do venture forth: to Britain's largest accessible limestone cave, Smoo, and its naturally lit waterfall. In high summer you may play a round of midnight golf, with porpoises in the bay for company. The beaches are stunning and unspoiled, the walking is sublime... for romantics who want to be alone, it doesn't get better than this. *Hill walking from the door, shore walking, sandy beaches three miles away.*

Rooms	2 houses for 2 (1 double; 1 bathroom): £1,000–£1,600. Short breaks from £220 per night (min. 3 nights). £30 per dog per week.
Meals	Self-catering.
Closed	Rarely.

Advice on walks and a surprise dog treat

Fiona Mackay
Croft 103
Port-Na-Con, Laid,
Loch Eriboll, Lairg IV27 4UN

Tel	+44 (0)1971 511202
Email	fiona@visitmackays.com
Web	www.croft103.com

Entry 221 Map 11

Thrumster House

A Victorian laird's house in an 8,500 acre estate. Drive south a mile to the 5,000-year-old neolithic remains of the Yarrow Archeological Trail for brochs, round houses and long cairns, then back to the big old house, 'steamboat gothic' in the words of an American guest. The vaulted hall gives an ecclesiastical feel, with fires burning at both ends and a grand piano on the landing (it gets played wonderfully). Big bedrooms have mahogany dressers, brass beds, floral wallpapers, lots of books. Islay and Catherine look after guests well and conversation flows. There's woodland to walk through and free trout fishing in the lochs too. *Woodland walks. "Doggie Days" sometimes held, with talks and classes in aid of the local Labrador rescue charity.*

Arisaig House

Imposing Arisaig sits in a walkers' paradise; the views to Skye are to die for. It was once a hotel; now Sarah, who has known Arisaig all her life, revels in returning house and gardens to their former glory. The sitting room is bright with Sanderson sofas, portraits and paintings and a huge open fire, and bedrooms are spacious and charming. Lovely Sarah serves breakfasts, high teas and dinners at the long oak table: don't miss the Stornoway black pudding! Wander through 20 acres of well-established and beautifully cared for gardens with terraces, rose gardens, walled gardens and woodlands. Make a start at the elegant main terrace with its beds of roses, herbs and lavender, and exceptional views. Old steps, walls and paths link the various parts, fecund veg beds, an orchard and soft fruit cages provide much for the table. The peace is palpable, birds and wildlife abound and you can stay all day. *Gardens, fields, hills, beaches: perfect setting for a happy dog!*

Rooms	1 double; 1 twin: £95. Singles £50. Max. 2 dogs.
Meals	Dinner, 3 courses with wine, £30.
Closed	Rarely.

 Towels for drying and a dog cage if needed

Rooms	4 twin/doubles: £145–£165. 6 suites for 2: £145–£165. Singles £85. 9 dog-friendly bedrooms.
Meals	Dinner, 3 courses, from £25. Pub/restaurant 3 miles.
Closed	Rarely.

 Dog treats by the front door, water bowls provided

Islay & Catherine MacLeod
Thrumster House
Thrumster, Wick KW1 5TX
Tel   +44 (0)1955 651387
Mobile   +44 (0)7840 750407
Email   cat.macleod@btinternet.com
Web   www.thrumster.co.uk

Entry 222 Map 12

Sarah Winnington-Ingram
Arisaig House
Arisaig PH39 4NR
Tel   +44 (0)1687 450730
Email   sarahwi@arisaighouse.co.uk
Web   www.arisaighouse.co.uk

Entry 223 Maps 8 & 10

Dalmunzie House

Dalmunzie is quite some sight, an ancient hunting lodge lost to the world in one of Scotland's most dramatic landscapes. You're cradled by mountains in a vast valley; it's as good a spot as any to escape the world. Surprisingly, you're not that remote – Perth is a mere 30 miles south – but the sense of solitude is magnificent, as is the view. As for the hotel, you potter up a one-mile drive to find a small enclave of friendly souls. Interiors are just the ticket: warm, cosy and quietly grand. You find sofas in front of open fires, a smart restaurant for delicious Scottish food, a snug bar for a good malt, a breakfast room with a big view. Country-house bedrooms have colour and style. Some are grand, others simpler, several have ancient claw-foot baths. There's loads to do: fantastic walking, mountain bike trails, royal Deeside, the Highland games at Braemar, even skiing up the road in winter. As for the tricky golf course, it was almost certainly laid out by Alister MacKenzie, who later designed Augusta National; the famous par three at Amen Corner is all but identical to the 7th here. *Stunning walks, mountains.*

Rooms	10 doubles; 5 four-posters; 1 twin; 1 family room for 4: £140-£240. Dinner, B&B from £85 p.p. Dogs £5 per night.
Meals	Lunch from £4.50. Packed lunch £10. Dinner, 4 courses, £45.
Closed	Occasionally in winter.
	Doggie treats and poop bags

Nick Jefford & Jen Gleeson
Dalmunzie House
Spittal O'Glenshee,
Blairgowrie PH10 7QG
Tel   +44 (0)1250 885224
Email   reservations@dalmunzie.com
Web   www.dalmunzie.com

Entry 224 Map 9

Oldhamstocks Cottage

At one end of a charming, rural Scottish village is this immaculately restored, one-storey cottage – the sturdy pinkstone stable block has become a warm cosy hideaway for four. The cottage faces south so you get a bright sunny sitting room, a well-equipped little kitchen in duck-egg blue, with a wooden dining table, two comfy bedrooms with top-of-the-range beds, duvets and White Company linen, and a spotless white bathroom. There's also a large secure garage with room for storing bikes, fishing tackle, golf clubs and muddy boots. Thanks to the unspoilt sandy beaches, the rolling Lammermuir Hills and 19 fabulous golf courses, walkers and golfers will relish the position – and the Southern Upland Way starts and finishes in the next village. Edinburgh is close, a 35-minute drive (though most people take the train from Dunbar). For winter there's a lovely coal fire for cosy nights in with games and DVDs, generously provided; for summer, a delightful enclosed garden with table and chairs, its door leading to the village and a small play park for children. All this, and the friendly helpful owners living next door. *Min. stay four nights on weekdays, three nights at weekend, seven nights in high season. Garden, coastline and hills.*

Rooms	1 cottage for 4
	(1 double, 1 twin; 1 bath/shower room):
	£320–£620.
	Short breaks (Fri-Mon/Mon-Fri) from £200.
	Dogs £20 per week. Max. 1 per person.
Meals	Self-catering.
Closed	Never.

 A walled garden for safe doggie fun, walks from the back door to the beach, chews & a basket on their return (remember to bring bedding)

Olivia Reynolds
Oldhamstocks Cottage
Oldhamstocks,
Dunbar TD13 5XN
Tel   +44 (0)1368 830233
Email   olivia@oldhamstockscottage.com
Web   www.oldhamstockscottage.com

Entry 225 Map 9

The Bowtop & Cottage

In the woodland garden in front of Horseshoe Cottage stands a rare and authentic 1930s Gypsy caravan. Rented as one space, cottage and caravan together sleep a party of four – and up to two well-behaved dogs. How dreamy to sleep outdoors, separated from the night skies by a lovingly restored bowtop caravan, a stunning original from master painter Jim Berry (a distant relative of the owner). On chillier nights an original Queenie stove keeps you and the kettle warm. The rosy interior is beautifully decorated, while the bed, not quite a full double, is the type that's so cosy and comfy you won't want to get up in the morning! The pretty colours and style match those of Horseshoe Cottage a few yards away, converted from the old stables, and together they make a stylish pair. Inside there's a bright sitting room, galley kitchen (no oven), bathroom with a shower, and two bedrooms. There's oil-fired central heating, a wood-burning stove, and a view of the legendary Eildon Hills. *Bookings begin on Monday, Wednesday or Friday. Book through Sawday's Canopy & Stars online or by phone.*

Rooms	Cottage for 4 (1 double, 1 twin). Bowtop: 1 double. From £90 per night. Dogs £5 per night. Max. 2. Dogs welcome in cottage only. Keep dogs on leads and away from free-range chickens!
Meals	Self-catering.
Closed	Never.

🐾 Dog biscuits on arrival, and towels for drying wet fur. Recommendations for dog-friendly pubs and places to visit

Sawday's Canopy & Stars
The Bowtop & Cottage
Roulotte Retreat, Bowden Mill House,
Melrose TD6 0SU

Tel   +44 (0)117 204 7830
Email   enquiries@canopyandstars.co.uk
Web   www.canopyandstars.co.uk/bowtopcottage

The Potting Shed

Once this housed the heating for the garden glasshouses; now the richly-coloured stonework has been exposed and a floor-to-ceiling glass window allows light to flood in to a crisp, contemporary interior. It's the perfect bolthole and very private, a mile down a bumpy track, with a wildflower meadow between you and the owners. You have your own garden with a table and chairs, and a delightful deck area overlooking the river Leader. Inside find pale oak floors with rugs, a wood-burning stove in the sitting room, reclaimed tables, a state-of-the-art heat storage range cooker and quirky touches such as old wooden wine boxes instead of tiles behind the sink. The bedroom is simply furnished and cosy with a well-dressed bed; red blinds splash colour onto white walls, as does local artwork; the bathroom is modern and functional with fluffy towels and Sedbergh Soap Company goodies. A generous basket is yours: home-baked bread, jam, eggs from the hens, logs – what a lovely gift to arrive to. Walks, and fishing, abound but you may find it hard to leave the sylvan setting and the peace. *Dog heaven: woods full of smells and on the doorstep of the Earlston footpath network which includes riverside, woodland and hill walks.*

Rooms	1 cottage for 2 (1 double; 1 shower room): £300–£450. Short breaks available. Max. 2 dogs.
Meals	Self-catering.
Closed	Rarely.

Discount on a locally made British leather dog collar, with your pooch's name; leaflets and advice on local walks and a river to jump in

Kate Comins
The Potting Shed
Cowdenknowes,
Earlston TD4 6AA
Tel   +44 (0)1896 848124
Email   kate.comins@yahoo.co.uk
Web   www.pottingshedholidays.com

Entry 227 Map 8

Trossachs Yurts

A fusion of Kyrgyz design and local materials, these three yurts have a homely, earthy feel, with thick rugs, rough tapestries and wood-burning stoves adding comfort. 'Ben Ledi' and 'Ben Lomond' yurts share the woodland just a little way on from 'Stuc a'Chroin' yurt. In each is a double bed, a double futon, and space for an extra child. From the boardwalk leading to the communal kitchen are impressive views across Flanders Moss National Nature Reserve. Arts and crafts courses may be taking place too, from willow crafting to Japanese block printing and yoga. There's an abundance of local produce, including veg from the kitchen garden, steaks for the barbecue, local eggs and homemade bread. With peaceful walks, lochs for swimming and the beauty of the Trossachs National Park to explore, you won't be short of ways to create a memorable stay. *Bookings begin on Monday or Friday. Book through Sawday's Canopy & Stars online or by phone.*

Rooms	3 yurts for 4 (1 double, 1 double futon, 1 single futon for child): from £75 per night. Max. 2 dogs. Dogs allowed in Ben Lomond only.
Meals	Self-catering.
Closed	Never.

Great walks by Loch Lomond & in the Trossachs, then a cosy basket & food bowls for dogs with clean paws

Sawday's Canopy & Stars
Trossachs Yurts
West Moss-side Organic Farm and Centre
FK8 3QJ

Tel	+44 (0)117 204 7830
Email	enquiries@canopyandstars.co.uk
Web	www.canopyandstars.co.uk/trossachs

Entry 228 Map 8

Alastair
Sawday's

'More than a bed
for the night…'

Britain
France
Ireland
Italy
Portugal
Spain

www.sawdays.co.uk

Self-Catering | B&B | Hotel | Pub | Treehouses, Cabins, Yurts & More

England

Bath & N.E. Somerset

1   Dog biscuits

2   Dog biscuits and bowls

Bristol

3   Treats, towels and water bowls

4   'Ring O Bones' dog treats on the bar, towels, dog cushion/basket for room if required, and advice on dog-friendly walks

Buckinghamshire

5   Doggie treats on the bar

6   Homemade dog biscuits with proceeds to Search Dogs Buckinghamshire, & freshly topped up water bowls

7   Plenty of fresh water & dog biscuits on the bar

8   Dog biscuits always kept on the bar

Cambridgeshire

9   Walking maps, and three King Charles Cavaliers to act as guides

Cheshire

10   Dog biscuits & water bowls; dog beds

in the dog-friendly rooms. Dog beer (made from meat stock) for sale!

11   Dog towels, recommendations for walks, dog-sitting – and a Bonio before bed!

12   Dogs welcome in the Brandy Snug. Dog biscuits on the bar and water bowls outside. Dog Beer (made from meat stock) is for sale here!

13   Dogs welcome in the Whisky Snug. Dog biscuits on the bar and water bowls at the entrance. Dog Beer (made from meat stock) is for sale!

Cornwall

15   Bag of chews on arrival, towels for drying off, outside hot/cold shower. Dog-sitting available. Dog walking itinerary on request (and doggie bags)

16   A perfect place for mutts to stay, often frequented by 'Dodger', star of TV programme *Doc Martin*; water bowls in bar

17   A dog walker's paradise! Dog bowls provided

18   A fleecy blanket to snuggle in – perfect after a run to the lighthouse

19 For dog walking there's the refreshing pooch-tastic coastal path, plus local pub & restaurant maps

20 Bowls, blankets and beds

21 Homemade dog biscuits on arrival; bowl, blankets and towels. Resident Jasper can be walked at any time when he is 'at work'!

22 Bacon fat biscuits, half-baked pigs' ears and gravy biscuits

23 Advice on walks, provision of a dog basket on request, and heated floorboards in winter

24 Welcome biscuits, dog towels & bowls

25 Bed, blanket, towels & bowls

26 Booklet with dog-friendly pubs, places to visit and walks. A bag of dog treats and bowls

27 Blankets, bowls and towels, and a designated area especially for dogs in the entrance

28 Advice on walks

29 Blankets, towels, dog bags and a tasty treat. Advice on walks and beaches

30 Toy cupboard filled with squeakies, balls & tug toys to take to the beach

31 One field always kept empty for dogs to run free

32 A box of doggy treats, and towels for wet dogs

33 Resident dogs Brook and Peggy always leave a tin of treats for guest dogs along with towels and a blanket

34 A tasty morning sausage in the kitchen, a big welcome from the resident pugs, and a dog-sitting service

35 Loan of Ordnance Survey maps and walk books of the area; lots of advice on dog-friendly beaches & pubs

Cumbria

36 Iced water in the bar for visiting dogs, bowls & towels in the bedrooms

37 Advice on walks with local OS maps to borrow and dog-friendly pub suggestions (three in village)

38 Local OS maps to borrow for walks and a list of dog-friendly pubs

39 Towels, drying facilities, walks; on-site shop sells dog food

40 A welcome doggie treat for all hounds

41 Suggestions for dog-friendly walks; water, food bowl & dog bed all provided for your return

42 Pigs' ears from the farm when available

43 Water bowl and advice on walks

44 Dogs outnumber humans 3 to 1 in the Scales Farm workforce so there would probably be mutiny if canine guests were not welcomed!

45 A vast garden for dogs to explore full of exciting whiffs, & ten acres of private woodland

46 A whole woodland of new smells to discover

Derbyshire

47 Water bowls, towels, poop scooper and bags

48 Towels on offer for muddy paws, tasty leftovers & bones at bedtime

49 Dog bowls and beds

50 Dog bowls and baskets

Devon

51 Tin of dog treats on arrival, doggie towels & tips for dog-friendly walks and pubs

52 Dog bed, towel and bowls

53 Dog walk guide

54 Lots of advice on dog-friendly walks, beaches and places to eat out. Towels can be provided for drying soggy dogs & plenty of doggy accessories – just ask!

55 Towels, blankets, bowls, leads and dog treats

56 Dog treats, poop bags and lots of information on local dog walks, dog-friendly pubs and the best beaches all year round

57 Biscuits and blanket

58 Twenty acres of woodland for wonderful walks

59 Bonio biscuit to keep tails wagging

60 Drying towels, carpet runner for the entrance when wet

61 Bed, towels and bowls

62 Blankets, towels, biscuits, water bowl

63 Pigs' ears & assorted treats

64 A Bonio in your room, dog biscuits at reception; towels, hose, spare leads – and emergency dog food & water bowls just in case

65 Down path to river – swimming

from jetty for you and your dog.
Hose for washing off (for both of
you!). Basket, water and food bowls

66 Your hosts love dogs, beaches are
right outside & lovely countryside is
all around

67 Advice on walks

68 Miles and miles of coastal walks

69 Welcome biscuit for all dogs, poop
bins, bowls, and dog survival kit
(anything and everything for a dog
on holiday!)

70 Bowls, baskets and poop bags

71 Dog's dinner of meat and rice (£5);
dog bed and bowl with treats as a
welcome to the room

72 A plethora of good country walks
(and dog-friendly pubs); hose and
indoor drying-off space with towels
galore. Multi-coloured bribery
biscuits; evening pooch-sitting too!

73 Dog biscuits, and afternoon tea for
guests comes with a Bonio for the dogs

Dorset

74 Dog bed and bowls

75 Dog bowls

76 Advice on walks, towel for drying
and poop scoop. Plenty of space in
roomy kitchen & living room

77 A 'doggie breakfast': local sausage
and bacon cooked to perfection with
a splash of milk to wash it down

78 Tweed bag with dog treats, poop
bags and VIP dog beds

79 Advice on walks and the river Stour
is nearby for a splash

80 Large information pack with maps
for walks from the Hut together
with towels for drying dogs

81 Dog-friendly guide to the village and
surrounding area, and all doggie
arrivals are given a treat

82 Advice on walks, blankets, doggie
towels and Bonio

83 Dog treats – and beds and bowls if
needed

84 Pigs' ears, advice on walks, towels
and a hose outside the kitchen
window for washing muddy paws

Essex

85 Dog bowl; wonderful walking on the
doorstep with field & woodland smells

86 A doggie bag filled with homemade biscuits, towels for muddy paws and a scrumptious sausage for breakfast

Gloucestershire

87 Dog bowls & a mystery treat provided

88 Dog beds and treats as well as details of dog-friendly walks. 10% of the overnight charge is donated to Teckels Animal Sanctuaries

89 Dog biscuits and bowls

90 Dog bed, towel for drying off and a cold sausage or two from the kitchen. Free maps on favourite local walks too

91 Advice on walks

92 Advice on walks, outside tap for washing muddy paws

93 A warm welcome for dogs & a sausage for the well-behaved ones

94 Advice on walks

95 Walks with our dogs in the day & friendly dog-sitting at night

96 Dog biscuits, towels

97 The Court doggie breakfast: a small plate of biscuits; good walks locally – just keep an eye out for sheep!

Hampshire

98 Lily dog treats, breakfast and dinner treats too! Chews and butcher's bone; real sheepskin rug to flop onto

99 Endless sticks in the woods and a river to splash through

100 Packet of sausages in brown paper for the dog

101 Bow-wow heaven in the woods! Maps & advice on walks. Enclosed porches, dust sheets, dog cage, Aga in kitchen for sleeping against & dog gates between rooms

102 Bedding, bowls & towels. Laminated maps of local walks & dog-friendly pubs. Medium-sized dog cage on request

103 Bed time biscuits, a hose for muddy paws, towels for drying and advice on walks

Herefordshire

104 Dog towels, blankets and poop-scoop bags; advice on walks

105 Dog bowl on request

106 Fresh water by the door

107 Fresh water by the door

108 Walking opportunities galore

109 Roast beef tidbits & other doggie treats; dogs welcome throughout. Secure garden, walks through the orchards and into woods beyond; Malvern Hills 10-minute drive

Hertfordshire

110 Fresh water & dog biscuits in the bar & the garden. Edge of National Park beech woods: lots of wonderful forest walking.

Isle of Wight

111 Advice on walks

Kent

112 Doggie 'overnight bag' – basket, towels and a pig's ear

113 Dog biscuits

Lancashire

114 Lovely dog beds to borrow, water bowls in the bars & river to swim in at the end of the garden

Leicestershire

115 Advice on walks, towels available and a treat provided on arrival

116 Advice on walks. a 'drying' room for wet dogs and Bullet, our friendly spaniel, never minds sharing his home!

Lincolnshire

117 Hose for washing muddy paws, towels provided on request, folders of walks, maps and spare lead; owners on site for advice

118 Much advice on local walks, maps loaned when required

London

119 Dog treats, and advice on walks, dog-friendly pubs and places to eat

Norfolk

120 Dog bowls

121 Walks, water bowls, towels for a rub down & wellies for guests who forgot theirs

122 Generous garden & big rooms with paw-friendly flooring

123 Local organic dog biscuits; towels on request

124 Advice on walks

Northamptonshire

125 Advice about walks, maps available

Northumberland

126 Towels, bowls, biscuits on arrival and beds on request

127 Dog treats at the bar, bed in room, bowl, dog mat and toy

128 Doggie 'welcome pack' with a Bonio biscuit, towel, blanket and poop bags. Dogs may dine with their owners

129 Heavenly forest & lakeside walks

Oxfordshire

130 Local walking guides, tennis balls for the garden & a chew for every visiting dog!

131 Advice about walks

132 Scrumptious pigs' ears at the ready

Rutland

133 Alfie the springer shares treats & walks. His top tip: sit by the youngest family member at meals (they may drop something!)

Shropshire

134 A private patio for pooches, the perfect spot for their sundowner after a hard day's walk. Guide to circular walks

135 Dog biscuits, water bowls, leads, poop bags, towels, lots of information on walks, attractions and dog-friendly pubs

136 The run of extensive grounds, and a splash in the lake

137 A comfy dog bed large enough for 2! Welcome jar of homemade dog biscuits (whilst owners enjoy homemade Victoria sponge) Book of dog-friendly local walks, and advice

138 Dog bed and a doggie treat, plus advice on beautiful walks over Shropshire Hills – all from the door!

139 A juicy bone direct from the village butcher's shop

140 A tour of the grounds from resident lab Copper, & a bone from the village butcher's shop

141 A jar of biscuits for every dog & details of local dog-friendly pubs & places to visit

Somerset

142 Garden for dogs to roam, and direct access to a public walkway through fields

143 Miles & miles of river, woodland and moorland to roam right from the door

Suffolk

144 Dog biscuits. detailed dog walks on OS maps, towels and local vet information

145 Good advice about more than 15 local dog-friendly walks, dog bowls and towels

146 Dog biscuits provided for hungry dogs

147 Biscuits, bowls, blankets & brilliant walks on the doorstep

148 Fabulous walks on beaches, heaths & forest

149 Homemade biscuits, towels, tap, poop bags & bin; secured long leash outside each room. Special doggie table: bring your dog while you eat

150 Always the odd treat for doggie visitors; drying towels and blankets available. Advice on walks, dog-friendly pubs and other places

151 Towels for drying, advice on walks

Surrey

152 Biscuits on arrival, towels for wet muddy dogs, a hose, shampoo and doggie blankets

Sussex

153 Treats are plentiful as are old towels for cleaning down

154 Towels for drying, and advice on walks

155 Dog treats on arrival

156 Advice and maps for walks, bowls, pigs' ears and a tasty sausage for breakfast

157 Woodland with lots of interesting sights and smells: dog heaven! Towel available after a wet walk

Warwickshire

158 Delicious home-cooked pigs' ears for sale behind the bar

159 Pigs' ears, dog biscuits and blankets

160 Dog chews, water & plenty of fuss provided

161 Edible treats and lots of spoiling

Wiltshire

162 A pub is man's best friend – & man's best friend is always welcome here. Dog bowl and dog treats at the bar

Worcestershire

163 Towels, dog bowl & doggie treats

164 Towels, water bowls & doggie treats

Yorkshire

165 Dog washing facilities and towels

166 Recommendations for dog-friendly walks. 10% of the overnight charge is donated to Teckels Animal Sanctuaries

167 Recommendations for dog-friendly walks. 10% of the overnight charge is donated to Teckels Animal Sanctuaries

168 Bowl, doggie treats, and the best local info on where to walk – and where to enjoy a friendly pub or two!

169 Every dog receives a guide to local dog-friendly pubs & beaches

170 Leaf through the dog-walk guide and pick a route, then step out of your carriage into the country

171 A swim in the lake from the jetty

172 Every pooch gets a Lucky Dog Surprise Bag, and a folder filled with local trails – owners bring your walking boots!

173 Every pooch gets a Lucky Dog Surprise Bag and a folder filled with local trails – owners bring your walking boots!

174 Advice on walks; towels, water and three resident whippets

175 River walks & snoozes in front of an open fire

176 Bronte and owner lead a guided walk from the house – 14 to choose from!

Wales

Anglesey

177 Dog biscuits, towels for drying, advice on walks and dog-friendly beaches and venues

Carmarthenshire

178 Details of dog-friendly walks, poop bags and towels for drying

Ceredigion

179 Dog bowls. Mick will tell you the best walks

180 Dog treat included in welcome pack

181 Lots of advice on walks; no dog fee for Sawday's guests; Edward & William, the resident spaniels, are ultra-friendly

Denbighshire

182 Gravy bones in the bar, dog towels, & their own book for the very best walks

183 Treats, towels and snug blankets

Flintshire

184 Cosy dog blankets, dog biscuits and a roaring open fire for evening naps

Gwynedd

185 Advice on walks & maps in Welcome Pack, special towel, biscuits in Welcome Hamper; Facebook page for uploading your dog photos & anecdotes too!

186 Advice on walks & maps in Welcome Pack, special towel, biscuits in Welcome Hamper. Facebook page for uploading your dog photos & anecdotes too!

187 2 dog bowls, 2 doggie blankets, hide chews, biscuits, dog ball-launcher, towels, spare lead & advice on the best dog walks in the area

188 The four resident dogs are very welcoming to visitors!

Monmouthshire

189 Advice on local dog-friendly places, drinking bowls and dog blankets

190 Dog bowl and hose for muddy paws; lowdown on good walks from two to six miles

191 A bespoke dog kennel, made by The Hobbit, who has made all the outdoor furniture at Upper Meend Farm

192 Advice on walks

193 Advice for walks, dog towels available

Pembrokeshire

194 Newport Sands is dog-friendly all year with dunes & miles of sand – & cafés for exhausted owners

195 A jar of dog biscuits will greet your dog on arrival. Water bowls are dotted about the camp, extra towels available for wet dogs; advice on walks, OS maps & guide books too

Powys

196 A river for heaps of fun, an outside tap with hose for washing muddy

paws, and an open fire or Esse range to snooze by. It's a dog's paradise!

197 Bowls and blankets and beds on request

198 A whole cabinet dedicated to dogs, various size dog treats for various size dogs, gravy bones, marrow bones, dog towels, sheets, bowls and poop bags

199 Spare collars, leads and dog bowls. and two toasty log-burners to lounge by

200 Advice on walks

201 Towels for drying wet dogs

202 Free dog-sitting for owners who fancy a night out on the town – or a supper down the pub

203 A banger for brekkie! Dogs can snooze on the heated floor & enjoy a marshmallow in front of the fire

204 Bowl of chicken on arrival – if owners are eating in!

205 Gorgeous country walks straight from the door

206 Grand walks from the door (keeping an eye out for cattle & sheep), and a black lab to play with

Swansea

207 24 acres of grounds to explore, & beautiful white-sand Gower beaches beyond

Scotland

Aberdeenshire

208 Towels, dog beds and bowls

Argyll & Bute

209 The island with all its woods, rabbits, pheasants and ocean all around is an absolute dog's paradise!

210 Biscuits, water & blankets. Expert advice on wild, carefree walks & a special welcome from terrier Boris the Arbuthnott

211 Ideal dog walking territory & towels on supply from dog-loving hosts

212 Advice on good walks

Ayrshire

213 Dog biscuits

214 A choice of walks, a basket of towels by the door and a selection of treats

Dumfries & Galloway

215 Advice on walks, sun-trap garden, log stove for winter, and interesting things lurking in the bottom of a dry-stone wall… hours of entertainment!

216 Bonio for the dogs before they go to bed, dog bed if required, advice on walks

Edinburgh

217 Plenty of towels and a hair dryer for when your dog decides to take a swim!

Fife

218 Dog bowls, two dog towels, welcome to use and lose any dog toys. Local know-how of dog-friendly beaches, pubs and restaurants all in a useful guide

Highland

219 Fantastic walks through the National Park in all directions

220 Bonio biscuits, doggie bags, blanket and food mat; dog-sitting service too

221 Advice on walks and a surprise dog treat

222 Towels for drying and a dog cage if needed

223 Dog treats by the front door, water bowls provided

Perth & Kinross

224 Doggie treats and poop bags

Scottish Borders

225 A walled garden for safe doggie fun, walks from the back door to the beach, chews & a basket on their return (remember to bring bedding)

226 Dog biscuits on arrival, and towels for drying wet fur. Recommendations for dog-friendly pubs and places to visit

227 Discount on a locally made British leather dog collar, with your pooch's name; leaflets and advice on local walks and a river to jump in

Stirling

228 Great walks by Loch Lomond & in the Trossachs, then a cosy basket & food bowls for dogs with clean paws

Quick reference indices

Wheelchair-accessible
At least one bedroom and bathroom accessible for wheelchair users. Phone for details.

England
Buckinghamshire 8
Cambridgeshire 9
Cheshire 12 • 13
Cornwall 18 • 19 • 20 • 21 • 27 • 29
Cumbria 39
Devon 60 • 62 • 68
Dorset 74 • 76 • 78 •
Gloucestershire 91 • 92 • 95
Herefordshire 109
Leicestershire 115
Lincolnshire 117
Norfolk 122
Northumberland 128 • 129
Oxfordshire 130
Rutland 133
Shropshire 138 • 141
Suffolk 144 • 145 • 147 • 148 • 151
Yorkshire 165 • 170 • 175

Wales
Ceredigion 179 • 180
Denbighshire 182 • 183
Gwynedd 185 • 188
Powys 201 • 204

Scotland
Argyll & Bute 210 • 211 • 212
Ayrshire 213
Highland 221

Pets live here
Owners' pets live at the property.

England
Bath & N.E. Somerset 1
Bristol 3
Cambridgeshire 9
Cheshire 11
Cornwall 15 • 19 • 29 • 32 • 33 • 34 • 35 •
Cumbria 37 • 44 • 45
Derbyshire 49 • 50
Devon 55 • 56 • 59 • 61 • 62 • 63 • 64 • 65 • 67 • 68 • 69 • 73
Dorset 77 • 82 • 83 • 84
Gloucestershire 91 • 95 • 96 • 97
Hampshire 98 • 102 • 103
Herefordshire 104 • 107
Kent 113
Lancashire 114
Leicestershire 116
Lincolnshire 117 • 118
London 119
Norfolk 124
Northamptonshire 125
Northumberland 128
Shropshire 135 • 140 • 141
Somerset 142
Suffolk 150 • 151
Surrey 152
Sussex 155 • 157
Warwickshire 158
Yorkshire 167 • 174 • 176

Wales
Carmarthenshire 178
Ceredigion 180 • 181
Denbighshire 182 • 183
Flintshire 184 •

Gwynedd 188
Monmouthshire 191 • 192 • 193
Pembrokeshire 195
Powys 198 • 199 • 202 • 203 • 205

Scotland

Aberdeenshire 208
Argyll & Bute 211 • 212
Ayrshire 214
Dumfries & Galloway 216
Highland 219 • 220 • 222 • 223
Scottish Borders 226 • 227

Licensed

These places are licensed to sell alcohol.

England

Cornwall 16 • 18 • 19 • 20 • 21 • 24 • 27 • 34
Cumbria 36 • 37 • 39
Derbyshire 48
Devon 55 • 59 • 61 • 62 • 64 • 66 • 68 • 69 • 70 • 71
Dorset 74 • 75 • 78 • 83
Essex 85 • 86
Gloucestershire 88 • 91
Herefordshire 104
Lancashire 114
Norfolk 121
Northumberland 126 • 127 • 128 • 129
Oxfordshire 130 • 132
Rutland 133
Shropshire 134 • 135 • 140
Suffolk 145 • 147 • 149
Sussex 155
Yorkshire 165

Wales

Carmarthenshire 178
Ceredigion 181
Denbighshire 182 • 183
Monmouthshire 190
Pembrokeshire 194
Powys 198
Swansea 207

Scotland

Aberdeenshire 208
Argyll & Bute 211
Highland 220 • 223
Perth & Kinross 224

Bikes

Bikes on the premises to hire or borrow.

England

Cheshire 11
Cornwall 18 • 22 • 28 • 29 • 35
Cumbria 37 • 39 • 43
Devon 65
Hampshire 102
Herefordshire 105
Leicestershire 116
Shropshire 134 • 140
Suffolk 144 • 145 • 150
Sussex 156 • 157
Warwickshire 161
Yorkshire 165

Wales

Powys 202 • 203

Scotland

Argyll & Bute 211
Dumfries & Galloway 215
Highland 220 • 221 • 222 • 223 •

Quick reference indices

Today's pet goes online. Why? So that its cuteness can go global. Tweeting, posting, instagramming, blogging – it's no big deal. The 'Social Savvy Critters' infographic has revealed that 14% of dog owners maintain a Facebook page for their pet, 6% tweet for their dogs, and 27% have their own YouTube page – or PetTube. Read on...

PetTube.com

The 'funniest pet videos' in the world: cats, hamsters, dogs and all. You can upload videos of your own beloved's antics, give it a title like 'Zeke has March Madness' and make it into the Hall of Fame. Or take a turn at captioning the Photo of the Week. You could waste a whole lifetime on here.

Globally Famous Dogs

The best connected dog in the world is Beast. A white fluffy Hungarian Puli, his owners are Mark (Facebook) Zuckerberg and wife Cilla. At the last count he had 1,669,038 fans. Each new posting of photogenic Beast gets trillions of likes.

Khloe Kardashian called Boo, a Pomeranian, from California, "the world's cutest dog". *Boo: The Adventures of the Cutest Dog in the World*, written under the pen name J H Lee, has been published in ten languages. Boo has been appointed 'spokesdog' for Virgin America airlines. Boo is small enough to fit in a bucket, twice.

Tuna, a Chiweenie (a Chihuahua Dachshund cross) is the world's cutest dog with an overbite. Abandoned, he was brought to a farmer's market in search of adoption. Courtney Dasher fell for him and decided to share her love through Instagram. In spite of his looks, Tuna is globally adored.

Ming's Blog

Ming resides, and rules the roost, at a country manor in Wiltshire. Great Chalfield's gardens open to the public through the National Trust.

For a privileged dog, Ming's life is unusually demanding. "Oh dear yet again I am late with my blog. Trying to pin Patsy down to help me is quite difficult as now we are closed the house seems busier than ever. We have been having lots of good walks and sometimes at the weekend Robert and Patsy take us to buy the papers and they stop off at the glove factory (coffee) shop where they allow us to amble around. They have delicious flapjacks that we enjoy very much."

It is a charmed life but tragedy occasionally steps in. "On our many walks across the fields to collect the daily newspaper we meet up with the horses having breakfast with Gangus the guinea fowl joining in. Sadly all Gangus's friends and family were killed by the fox so now he joins in on breakfast with Harvey..."

At the annual plant fair in May, 900 visitors tip up, most of them to see Ming. Ming loves her time "pottering around after Patsy in the garden and managing the odd snooze with the sun on my back", but her busiest month is September. "At this time of year there are so many different animals to check out. Of course being on squirrel duty takes up a huge amount of my time."

Find Ming at www.greatchalfield.co.uk

PetMed.com

Super-sensible, vet-approved site, with a blog for new pet parents. You can't find fault with their philosophy, that you don't have to dominate your dog to get it to respect you. 'Surviving the First Night with your Puppy' explains separation anxiety beautifully. Don't abandon it to the kitchen! Security versus coddling – note the difference.

PetYourDog.com

Pure breeds and hybrids: they're all here. Airedoodles: "intelligent, friendly and loveable, require large space, love exercise and get along well with other pets in the family… They are trainable but can be stubborn during training sessions." Bichon Frises: "clowns that want to entertain and please their masters… The Bichon was owned by royalty in the 16th century for the traits that people of today continue to pursue."

Dogster.com

Articles and forums on all things dog. 'Do your dogs like to have their photo taken?' 'How Rupee the dog went from a garbage dump to Mount Everest.' 'Five reasons why I love my retractable leash.'

Photo: Rosie Davies (Millie)

Informative in American style, serious but not too serious.

Drivingwithdogs.co.uk

Browse by Motorway: how brilliant is that. Follow Jem the Border Collie's exploration of the British motorways to find walks, beaches, pubs and services to suit you and your dog's needs.

DateMyPet.com

The leading online dating website for pet lovers. "We emailed a couple of times through datemypet.com, met up at a dog park and the rest is history! We've been married a month and have a very busy household with two dogs and my cat." Guardian Soulmates, watch this space.

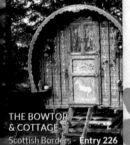

Membership

BECOME A MEMBER OF SAWDAY'S

ACCREDITATION

Guests trust our choices. Our stamp of approval works brilliantly in your own marketing, too.

WEBSITE

We'll show off your photos alongside a well-written, sparkling description of your Special Place.

BOOKS AND APPS

We've sold over 1.4 million guidebooks, and recently launched our Pubs iPhone app. Our guides are much loved and set us apart.

OWNER EVENTS

From time to time we arrange informal regional gatherings. They are a great opportunity to meet us and fellow Sawday's members.

A MEMBER AREA

You can upload special offers to your page, add more photos and much more.

MEMBER NEWSLETTER

Full of interesting and useful snippets from your world and ours.

PR & MARKETING

Our database of guests and the British press regularly turn to us for inspiration. Public awareness of Sawday's is high – via our themed website collections, articles, monthly newsletters and competitions. The coverage we get is wonderful, and you reap the benefits.

DEDICATED MEMBERSHIP TEAM

We speak your language and know your market, and are always on hand to help.

Our Membership Team

"Sawday's has never once let us down – invaluable."

theguardian

"A great resource to find that extra special place to stay."

THE TIMES

Join us

BECOME A MEMBER OF SAWDAY'S

Delighting in individuality

THINGS WE LOVE

Character, charm and authenticity

Good conversation, humour and a sense of fun

All sorts of buildings, from the crumbling but dignified
to the modern and stylish

Open-minded, friendly owners who love welcoming guests

Free-range pets and children

Hardly any rules and regulations

Get in touch with our friendly membership team

+44 (0)117 204 7810

specialplaces@sawdays.co.uk

or apply online

www.sawdays.co.uk/joinus

"The only membership I want. They are the best!"

SUE BATHURST, THE GUEST HOUSE

Alastair Sawday has been publishing books for over 20 years, finding Special Places to Stay in Britain and abroad. All our properties are inspected by us and are chosen for their charm and individuality, and now with 17 titles to choose from there are plenty of places to explore. You can buy any of our books at a reader discount of 25%* on the RRP.

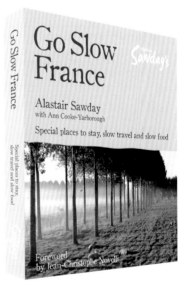

www.sawdays.co.uk/bookshop

Special Places to Stay series

List of titles:	RRP	Discount price
British Bed & Breakfast	£15.99	£11.99
Special Places to Stay in Britain for Garden Lovers	£19.99	£14.99
British Hotels and Inns	£15.99	£11.99
Pubs & Inns of England & Wales	£15.99	£11.99
Venues	£11.99	£8.99
Cotswolds	£9.99	£7.49
Wales	£9.99	£7.49
Dog-friendly Breaks in Britain	£14.99	£11.24
French Bed & Breakfast	£15.99	£11.99
French Self-Catering	£14.99	£9.74
French Châteaux & Hotels	£15.99	£11.99
Italy	£15.99	£11.99
Portugal	£12.99	£9.74
Spain	£15.99	£11.99
India	£11.99	£8.99
Go Slow England & Wales	£19.99	£14.99
Go Slow France	£19.99	£14.99

*postage and packaging is added to each order

How to order:
You can order online at: www.sawdays.co.uk/bookshop/
or call: +44 (0)117 204 7810

Abergavenny	189, 190	Dartmouth	68, 72
Acharacle	220	Denbigh	183
Adhurst	99	Derby	116
Arisaig	223	Dolgellau	185
Aviemore	219	Dorchester	81, 82
Bakewell	49, 50	Dunbar	225
Ballater	208	Earlston	227
Banwell	142	East Grinstead	153
Bath	1, 2	Edinburgh	217
Baughurst	98	Fairford	87
Bembridge	111	Faringdon	130
Bishop's Castle	135, 136	Faversham	113
Blairgowrie	224	Fordingbridge	102
Braunton	54	Girvan	213, 214
Brechfa	178	Glen Orchy	210
Brecon	198-202	Godalming	152
Bridport	80	Halifax	176
Bristol	3, 4	Hambledon	100
Bude	15	Hay-on-Wye	105
Builth Wells	197, 205	Helston	28, 34-35
Cardigan	180	Hereford	106, 107
Carlisle	42, 43	Hexham	128, 129
Carnforth	36	High Peak	47
Castle Acre	120	Holyhead	177
Castle Douglas	215	Honiton	69
Cheltenham	90, 96	Horncastle	118
Child Okeford	79	Horsham	154
Chipping Campden	91, 97	Huntingdon	9
Chipping Norton	132	Ilfracombe	53
Christchurch	74	Ipswich	145, 146
Chulmleigh	58	Isle of Mull	211, 212
Cirencester	88, 89, 95	Kenardington	112
Cleobury Mortimer	138	King's Lynn	122
Clitheroe	114	Kingsbridge	66
Colyton	73	Kirkby Stephen	37-39
Combe Martin	52	Lairg	221
Crail	218	Launceston	33
Craven Arms	141	Lavenham	144
Crediton	59	Leintwardine	139, 140
Crickhowell	204	Liskeard	31, 32

Llandysul	181	Redruth	29
Llanfairwaterdine	137	Richmond	171-174
Llangollen	182	Robertsbridge	157
Lockerbie	216	Ross-on-Wye	104
London	119	Rye	155, 156
Louth	117	Salisbury	78
Lynton	51	Sampford Courtenay	60
Machynlleth	196	Saxmundham	147, 148
Malpas	10, 11	Seaton	70
Manningtree	86	Settle	165, 166
Matlock	48	Sherborne	83
Melrose	226	Shipston-on-Stour	158
Melton Mowbray	115	Shipton-Under-Wychwood	131
Milford Haven	195	Skipton	167
Mold	184	South Molton	55
Monmouth	191, 192	Southam	161
Morpeth	126	St Ives	24
New Forest	101	Stanford-le-Hope	85
Newmarket	151	Stirling	228
Newnham	92	Stratford-upon-Avon	159
Newport	194	Stroud	94
Newquay	20-23	Sturminster Newton	84
Newton Abbot	61	Swansea	207
Newton-by-the-Sea	127	Tal y Llyn	186
North Duffield	170	Tavistock	63
Norwich	121, 124	Tenbury Wells	163, 164
Oakham	133	Tintagel	16
Oban	209	Torquay	71
Okehampton	62	Torrington	57
Oswestry	134	Totnes	67
Padstow	18, 19	Tregaron	179
Pateley Bridge	168	Truro	30
Penrith	40-41, 44-45	Umberleigh	56
Penzance	25-27	Usk	193
Peterborough	125	Walsingham	123
Petersfield	103	Wareham	75
Pickering	169	Wick	222
Port Isaac	17	Wimborne	76, 77
Portmeirion	187	Woodbridge	149, 150
Pwllheli	188	Yelverton	64, 65

Beaconsfield	6	Ledbury	109
Coleford	93	Marlow	8
Crickhowell	204	Presteigne	206
Dulverton	143	Salisbury	162
Hemel Hempstead	110	Stratford-upon-Avon	160
High Wycombe	7	Ulverston	46
Kington	108	Uxbridge	5
Knutsford	12, 13	Whitby	175

Photo: Jake Eastman

(1) Hotel

Pembrokeshire (2)

(3)
(4) **Llys Meddyg**

This fabulous restaurant with rooms has a bit of everything: cool rooms that pack a designer punch, super food in a sparkling restaurant, a cellar bar for drinks before dinner, a fabulous garden for summer treats. It's a very friendly place with charming staff on hand to help, and it draws in a local crowd who come for the seriously good food, perhaps mussel and saffron soup, rib of Welsh beef with hand-cut chips, cherry soufflé with pistachio ice cream. You eat in style with a fire burning at one end of the restaurant and good art hanging on the walls. Excellent bedrooms are split between the main house (decidedly funky) and the mews behind (away from the road). All have the same fresh style: Farrow & Ball colours, good art, oak beds, fancy bathrooms with fluffy robes. Best of all is the back garden with a mountain-fed stream pouring past. In summer, a café/bistro opens up out here – coffee and cake or steak and chips – with doors that open onto the garden. Don't miss Pembrokeshire's fabulous coastal path for its windswept cliffs, sandy beaches and secluded coves. *Estuary path from the doorstep: doggie heaven.*

(5) Rooms	4 doubles; 4 twin/doubles; 1 suite for 2: £100–£180. Singles from £85. No charge but dogs must be clean and well behaved! Max. 2 per bedroom. 3 dog-friendly bedrooms.	
(6) Meals	Lunch from £7. Dinner from £14.	
(7) Closed	Rarely.	
(8)	Newport Sands is dog-friendly all year with dunes & miles of sand – & cafés for exhausted owners	

Louise & Edward Sykes
Llys Meddyg
East Street,
Newport SA42 0SY
Tel   +44 (0)1239 820008
Email   info@llysmeddyg.com
Web   www.llysmeddyg.com

(9)   Entry 194 Map 1   (10)